Donated by
Ian Thomson

Not for loan

The National Parliaments in the European Union

EUROPEAN MONOGRAPHS

Editor-in-Chief Professor David O'Keeffe

In this series *European Monographs* this book
The National Parliaments in the European Union: A Critical View on EU Constitution-Building is the fiftieth title.

The titles published in this series are listed at the end of this volume.

EUROPEAN MONOGRAPHS

The National Parliaments in the European Union: A Critical View on EU Constitution-Building

Philipp Kiiver

KLUWER LAW
INTERNATIONAL

A C.I.P Catalogue record for this book is available from the Library of Congress.

ISBN 9041124527

Published by Kluwer Law International,
P.O. Box 85889, 2508 CN The Hague, The Netherlands
sales@kluwerlaw.com
http://www.kluwerlaw.com

Sold and distributed in North, Central and South America
by Aspen Publishers, Inc.
7201 McKinney Circle, Frederick, MD 21704, USA

Sold and distributed in all other countries by
Turpin Distribution Services Ltd.,
Stratton Business Park,
Pegasus Drive, Biggleswade, Bedfordshire,
SG18 8TQ, United Kingdom

Printed on acid-free paper

Printed in The Netherlands

Маме посвящается

Contents

Preface

When the EU Constitutional Treaty was put to a popular vote in France and the Netherlands, the result was a rejection so shattering that it called into question the very fundamentals of European integration. Arguably, the 'no' was not so much directed against that particular treaty, or even against European integration as such, but, among other things, at the dissatisfactory way in which the EU is functioning today. If the referendum on a new treaty meant an opportunity for the citizens to let off steam, they clearly used it. And obviously they had a point: what kind of Europe is it, where the only means of democratic input is the occasional treaty rejection? Where are the representative bodies that engage in day-to-day scrutiny of EU policies, and that are themselves subjected to recurring expressions of the popular will? Enter the national parliaments, who are increasingly addressed, courted and encouraged to play a bigger part in the European Union: either next to the European Parliament, or in its stead; either with new formal powers and privileges as included in the Constitutional Treaty, or with competences that would go far beyond that. This book seeks to shed light on the balance between national parliamentarism and European integration, and on the political and constitutional implications of demands to give the national parliaments a greater role in the EU. It raises the question whether the national parliaments truly deserve our unequivocal support. It is a question to which everybody seems to know the answer, but also one that is rarely seriously asked.

I am grateful to all those who have directly or indirectly contributed to my work and to the completion of this book, in particular Monica Claes, Deirdre Curtin, Adam Cygan, Bruno de Witte, Elvier Geurink, Aalt Willem Heringa, Ron Holzhacker, Jit Peters, Tapio Raunio, Joop van den Berg, Luc Verhey, as well as David O'Keeffe, who provided valuable comments as he reviewed the manuscript for publication. Thanks to Ewa Szkatula, Karel van der Linde and Vincent Verschoor at Kluwer, and to Julie Box for the language review.

Special thanks go to my wife Hannah, and her family, for their love and support throughout.

Philipp Kiiver

Maastricht, September 2005

Summary

This book addresses the question whether national parliaments deserve a greater role in the European Union. It is set against the trend in the current debate – before and after the EU Constitutional Treaty project – towards emphasizing a primary or complementary role for the national parliaments in EU democracy and parliamentarism. The book distils and exposes the different perspectives from which stronger national parliaments might appear desirable in the first place, and thereby creates a reference framework from which to assess the feasibility and desirability of stronger national parliaments as against the possible objectives as identified under the different perspectives. The book thereby questions the shallow academic and political consensus that currently supports an enhanced role for national parliaments in the EU and shows that, depending on the point of view, it is not necessarily the most desirable cause to subscribe to. Without providing any final answers as to the appropriate role of national parliaments, it contributes to the analytical sobriety that is essential to any discussion on whether the national parliaments truly deserve our encouragement and support.

The book combines political reasoning with concepts from European and comparative constitutional law; furthermore, findings of empirical and analytical political science research on the effect of European integration on national parliaments are incorporated in the analysis. The book tackles the questions of what role national parliaments play in the EU already; what is the constitutionally and methodologically most sensible manner to address the national parliaments at treaty level; how the national parliaments of the EU-25 have organized their domestic scrutiny mechanisms; what makes a national parliament 'strong', what factors contribute to its 'weakness'. It then goes on to assess as to how far is it feasible and desirable, in the light of the different perspectives on the issue, to sharpen national parliamentary scrutiny of EU affairs, to enhance inter-parliamentary co-operation, to set up a new EU institution comprising national MPs, to have the national parliaments elect the European Commission, to turn the parliaments collectively into guardians of the principle of subsidiarity; finally, and more fundamentally, the book addresses the question in how far support for the national parliaments can be reconciled with ever closer union?

A national parliament's attitude towards oversight on EU affairs is to a large extent determined by its pre-existing institutional role and its relation to its government, as well as the degree to which European integration is salient among political parties and the electorate itself. The roles, competences and self-perception of parliaments differ from one Member State to another, and self-constraint in EU affairs can have valid reasons and even be a conscious choice; consequently the conclusion that one particular parliament is too permissive as regards EU affairs does not mean that *all* national parliaments can, should, or even want to develop greater activity in that field.

Generally, the addressing of 'the' national parliaments as a category of institutions turns out to be highly problematic. In the light of the heterogeneity and constitutional autonomy of the Member States, national parliaments can neither be easily defined, nor, at least in the case of lower chambers, singled out as actors independent from their governments, or presumed to act as a collective in sustainable solidarity as against their own governments. The term 'national parliaments' itself at present covers several assemblies that are either not elected, or not parliamentary in character, that do not control the government, or that in the presence of regional assemblies do not always have legislative competence; the term is, for the purpose of the allocation of concrete powers and privileges by virtue of EU treaty provisions, too vague. Unlike the European Union, the European Convention on Human Rights, where it addresses the right to vote, refers to the national 'legislature', and not 'national parliaments', and thereby features a workable term for its particular needs. For EU purposes, where parliaments are addressed in a broader capacity than just law-makers, and where actual powers and privileges are to be allocated, an authoritative and exhaustive list of addressed institutions, annexed to the relevant EU instrument, would not only be methodologically sound, it would also make the underlying policy choices visible and trigger reflection about the purpose of the entire exercise.

The exercise of strengthening national parliaments at the EU level is a measure that is neither impossible nor prohibited, but artificial as it requires a conscious effort. The exercise can be easily fitted into an agenda favouring national sovereignty, statehood and intergovernmentalism. It might seem desirable for the purpose of strengthening democracy at the national level, enhancing control over delegated competences and, pragmatically, for the purpose of consolidating national policy or co-opting (or implicating) MPs, including the opposition, into government bargaining. Embracing both the European Parliament and the national parliaments as fulfilling complementary functions in the EU as a constitutionally pluralist multi-level polity is meanwhile highly reconciliatory, but deceptive: national parliamentary activity is carried out in accordance with the parliaments' national constitutional representative mandate and election-based incentives. The accountability process revolves around the question as to how far the government has stuck to, and fought for, the pre-determined national standpoint in EU bargaining, and whether it succeeded in preventing policies that are detrimental to the national interest. National interest is of course always present, but it needs to be reconciled with the preferences of other Member States; routinely sharpened domestic parliamentary polarization in the run-up to negotiations emphasizes the national stakes, and generally the intergovernmental element in EU decision-making, while decreasing EU decision-making efficiency and eclipsing left-right discourse on EU level with domestic we-they debates. Genuine European parliamentarism does not emerge from particularized debates, if such debates emerge at all, and the EU will not become more parliamentary either if national MPs leave their deliberative forum behind, convene in Brussels, and merely duplicate the tasks of existing EU institutions. Duplication could apply to the functions of the Council (if an inter-parliamentary conference is divided into national delegations), the European Parliament (if such conference is divided by political colour, also for the purpose of electing the Commission) or the Intergovernmental Conferences (via the hardly less detached Convention method).

Subsidiarity enforcement via the national parliaments may be subtly drafted, and remind the Commission of its duty to justify its proposals under that heading, but awarding the national parliaments binding 'red-card' vetoes and direct access to the ECJ, beyond a more informal setup, in that context triggers the same concern about over-emphasizing national stakes, disrupting the EU decision-making process, eclipsing left-right cleavages in the European Parliament, distorting national constitutional government-parliament and centre-regions relations with clumsy intrusions and rights-conferrals from EU level, as well as carrying domestic political battles between government, opposition or a hostile upper chamber to the EU level and, once there, to court. It is recalled instead that the normative priority in EU constitution-building can very much remain the consolidation of the weight of the European Parliament, and of left-right cleavages as appropriately expressed at the EU level. Proponents of that integrationist cause, who might otherwise embrace the alleged capacity of national parliaments to 'bring Europe closer to the citizens' or to enhance the stability of the EU via transparency and subsidiarity, should be careful about expressing their support for stronger national parliaments in the European Union too hastily.

Introduction

The role of the national parliaments in the European Union has become a salient political and constitutional question, a question that represents a top item on the agenda of European integration. Attracting growing political and scholarly attention throughout the 1990s, addressed in the Nice Declaration on the future of the Union,[1] and featuring prominently before, during and after the first ratification attempt for the EU Constitutional Treaty, the national parliaments find themselves in the middle of an intriguing debate as to what their role should be in the EU. Calls for stronger or more active national parliaments abound, and their advocates emerge from the most unlikely quarters: Eurosceptics and Europhiles, scholars as well as pragmatics, in both Brussels and the national capitals, seem for various reasons to have acquired a taste for greater national parliamentary involvement in the European Union. All the more reason for us to take a closer look at the national parliaments, at their character and their qualities, and also at those who call for an enhancement of their role in the EU. What exactly do all these advocates expect of the national parliaments? Can the national parliaments really be all things to all men? There is a strong tendency in the ongoing debate to embrace the national parliaments for vaguely defined purposes, such as 'more democracy' or 'more transparency', without clarifying what effects and what side-effects might be triggered; a tendency to support the cause without asking whether, and for what purpose, stronger national parliaments would be desirable to have in the first place; a tendency, in short, to take the second step and skip the first. The purpose of this volume is to finally make that very first step. It will develop a theoretical reference framework to analyze the actual desirability of stronger national parliaments in the EU, from different distinguishable perspectives, so that from there on we can take the next steps with the necessary analytical sobriety. This work will not definitely answer the question whether the national parliaments deserve a greater role in the European Union's constitutional architecture, but it will raise that question in the first place, and thereby do what is all too often omitted. And it will finally show that supporting stronger national parliaments in the EU is not such self-evident a cause as it might seem, that it is not a cause that everyone can or should hastily subscribe to. At a time when the European Union engages in ambitious and perhaps over-ambitious constitution-building exercises, it is all the more important, with respect to the national parliaments, to ask the right questions – and to think twice before answering them.

Of course, those who are attached to national sovereignty and statehood will not think twice, and will keep putting forward the national parliaments as the

1 Nice Final Act, Declaration No. 23 (5).

only true source of democratic legitimacy in the European Union. For too long now, or so their argument goes, national parliaments have been giving away powers to Brussels, allowing their governments to pass binding EU legislation in the Council while escaping all public scrutiny and democratic accountability. Only if national parliaments retain legislative competences of their own and otherwise strictly call their governments to account for what they decide in Brussels, perhaps even participate directly in EU decision-making, or so the argument would continue, can democracy in the European Union be preserved. Europhiles, on the other hand, who traditionally emphasize the importance of strengthening the European Parliament, rather than the Member States' parliaments, also increasingly understand that more national parliamentary involvement, and more lively domestic debates about European integration, may perhaps bring Europe closer to the citizens. It might make the decision-making process more transparent and thereby stabilize the system as a whole. At the same time it might be useful to court the national parliaments in order to prevent them, or their electorate, from turning hostile to European integration – for instance when it comes to treaty ratification. Scholarly advocates of multi-level governance, multi-level constitutionalism or constitutional pluralism should rejoice if the national level of parliamentarism would effectively complement the European Parliament and the other loci of EU decision-making. Even to the national governments, a greater involvement of their parliaments might for pragmatic reasons appear attractive. With such broad support, it seems that the national parliaments are bound to get a bigger part in the play or, if not a bigger part, at least more attention, a more visible place on the stage.

And indeed, various proposals are on the market to strengthen the national parliaments in EU context. Most of them do not even require treaty amendments. Proposals range from greater awareness of the European dimension in national parliamentary debates, to stricter parliamentary oversight on individual governments at EU policy; from more interest in the EU policy process, to a more efficient organization of parliamentary committee systems; from more intensive inter-parliamentary co-operation and networking, to forms of direct and collective input of the national parliaments in the EU decision-making process. In line with the trend, the EU Constitutional Treaty project[2] represents a major effort to explicitly address the national parliaments on treaty level. The Convention that drafted the Constitutional Treaty already comprised national parliamentarians,[3] and the document it came up with turned out to be the first treaty to explicitly recognize the national parliaments' contribution to the democratic legitimacy of the EU, next to the European Parliament;[4] in fact, this was the first treaty in fifty

2 Treaty establishing a Constitution for Europe (hereinafter TCE), text as of 29 October 2004, CIG 87/2/04 REV 2. All references to the TCE are based on this version.

3 See also Article IV-443 (2) TCE.

4 Article I-46 (2) TCE.

years to mention the term 'national parliaments' in its text proper in the first place. The text as adopted by the Convention and the subsequent intergovernmental conference expanded existing notification mechanisms to keep national parliaments in the loop of EU affairs.[5] Going a step further, the text included two immediate veto mechanisms for the national parliaments in EU decision-making: an early warning system against alleged breaches of the principle of subsidiarity in EU legislative proposals, with the possibility to force the initiator – typically the Commission – to reconsider a proposal if enough national parliaments have filed complaints,[6] as well as the possibility for any national parliament to veto the application of the passerelle clause, and thereby to block a unanimous vote in the European Council to move towards qualified majority voting or towards co-decision with the European Parliament in a given policy area.[7]

Not all of the Constitutional Treaty features were that innovative when the Convention and the IGC adopted them, not all of them are even terribly significant by themselves, and not all of them would strictly require a new treaty in order to work. Experiments with collective subsidiarity control in the national parliaments have, for instance, already started before the ratification process for the Treaty was even fully unfolded.[8] We should note, however, that even a formally modest or mere symbolic involvement of the national parliaments in the EU may stimulate political desire on the part of the parliaments to become more active in other areas, and to become more conscious of the powers they already have as regards EU affairs. New treaty provisions addressing the national parliaments are thus merely evidence of a larger phenomenon, namely that national parliaments seem to have become indispensable in the European Union's present and future constitution-building ambitions.

What is all too often omitted in this constitution-building enterprise, before and after the Constitutional Treaty, however, is the question whether the assumed benefits from greater national parliamentary involvement can be gained in the

---

5 Articles 1 and 2 of the TCE Protocol on the role of national parliaments in the European Union (distribution of all EU consultation papers and legislative proposals among the national parliaments), Article I-18 (2) (notification prior to the application of the flexibility clause), Articles I-42 (2), III-260, III-261, III-273 and III-276 (national parliamentary monitoring of the activities of Europol and Eurojust), Article I-58 (2) (notification about incoming EU membership applications), Article IV-443 (1) (notification of Treaty revision initiatives) and Article IV-444 (3) (notification prior to the intended application of the passerelle clause) TCE.

6 Articles I-11 (3) and III-259 TCE, as well as TCE Protocol on the role of national parliaments in the European Union and TCE Protocol on the application of the principles of subsidiarity and proportionality.

7 Article IV-444 (3) TCE.

8 See 7.4 *infra*.

first place, and at what price they would come. As noted at the outset, where endorsement of national parliaments has entered the mainstream, and where such ideas are woven into EU treaty drafting, a critical reflection about the underlying thoughts and the consequences of such an endorsement is very much in order. This is exactly the purpose of this book. It will explore from various perspectives what addressing the national parliaments in the EU means in theory, what it means in practice, where the deficiencies of concrete suggestions to that effect lie, and, more fundamentally, in how far stimulation of national parliamentarism is compatible with European parliamentarism and progressive European integration.

We shall start our analysis by clarifying the theoretical background, and the constitutional-law implications, of addressing national parliaments at EU level (chapter 1). Who exactly are 'the national parliaments' to begin with? The term is typically, for the sake of convenience, used as a self-explanatory catch-all denomination, but it actually points to a quite heterogeneous group, if we can speak of a group at all. How can these national parliaments then be sensibly addressed at EU level, such as by virtue of treaty provisions? These are questions that are not only relevant to treaty drafters, but to anyone who seeks to make an analytically credible argument on the role of national parliaments in the EU, whether as a proponent or detractor of the cause to enhance their role.

Once we have set out the theoretical fundamentals, we shall then turn to the practical side of the story (chapter 2), which is again something that is too often overlooked, especially in legal scholarship which could profit much more than it does from the empirical work of political scientists. In what will be a comparative overview, we shall examine the ways in which different national parliaments in the EU-25 are dealing with European integration today. At what stage do parliaments become active at scrutinizing their governments and their EU policies? How do parliamentary committee systems function in practice? On what national legal bases is European scrutiny in the parliaments conducted? What is it that makes a parliament eventually a strong and critical scrutinizer, what makes it a permissive rubber-stamp? How do we measure that, and can we speak of 'weakness' and 'strength' in the present context at all? That factual overview, which will draw *inter alia* on findings from, indeed, political science, will help us identify existing similarities and variations and, crucially, the underlying reasons for the particular shape of scrutiny mechanisms, and for the particular behaviour of national parliamentarians. This will allow us to draw broader conclusions as to the capacities of national parliaments to deliver what is increasingly demanded of them in EU context. For there are not only theoretical obstacles concerning the stimulation of the national parliaments in EU affairs, there are also practical ones: not all parliaments are alike, not all of them have the same agenda, there are reasons why they behave like they do, and these reasons are worth considering for both supporters and sceptics.

Bearing in mind the theoretical and practical caveats that will have been distilled at that point, we shall then ask what exactly can be demanded of the national parliaments. For that purpose we shall critically assess a set of prominent proposals on how to give the national parliaments a greater role in the EU: the proposal that national parliaments should sharpen their domestic scrutiny of EU affairs (chapter 3), the proposal to step up inter-parliamentary co-operation, between national parliaments themselves and with the European Parliament (chapter 4), the occasionally floated proposal to create a 'Third Chamber' at EU level comprising national parliamentarians, next to the European Parliament and the Council, as well as the idea to resort more often to the Convention method of treaty revision (chapter 5), the proposal to promote accountability of the European Commission to the national parliaments (chapter 6) and the proposal, as it had been incorporated in the EU Constitutional Treaty but as it would also to a large extent work without a new treaty, to turn the national parliaments into guardians of the principle of subsidiarity, perhaps at some point to equip them with absolute veto powers and *locus standi* before the European Court of Justice (chapter 7).

It should be noted that nothing hinges on the strict separation of the above ideas from each other. In fact, they can very much overlap. Consider the following scenario: a group of national parliamentarians examines an incoming Commission proposal; they check it for compliance with the principle of subsidiarity; they go on and meet with their colleagues from other Member States in an inter-parliamentary conference to discuss it; they decide to write a complaint to the Commission on grounds of a perceived violation of subsidiarity; and they do that against the will of their own government, which intends to support the Commission proposal in the Council in its original form. Here we have in fact a blend of almost all of the above aspects: parliamentary scrutiny of EU documentation; subsidiarity control; inter-parliamentary co-operation; an inter-parliamentary gathering as a form of an EU-level body comprising national MPs; a confrontation between national parliaments and the Commission which may call into question the underlying hierarchies; and a tension in domestic government-parliament relations over the course of European integration. It is nonetheless helpful to consider the various elements one by one, not just for the sake of convenience and structure in *this* discussion, but in *any* discussion on the subject, because the elements' individual assessment allows to better evaluate what they eventually add up to.

Our assessment of the national parliaments' capacity to deliver what is expected of them under the various headings, the desirability of such delivery (which depends on the expectations), in short the sought reference framework for any future debate on the national parliaments, will essentially be based on two distinct perspectives on the matter. Assuming (1) a national constitutional point of view, we will consider what a stronger parliament (i.e. one that scrutinizes more sharply, networks more effectively, etc.) could mean for an individual Member State, for national players, and for an individual parliamentary system facing the challenge of European integration. From (2) a European perspective, we will then take a global view on the issue and consider what sharper scrutiny and stronger national parliaments could mean for the EU institutions and the EU architecture as a whole.

Under the individual heading, the main question will be in how far we can make any generalizations about 'the national parliaments' as a category of players, in the light of their heterogeneity. We must note that since not all parliaments are alike, it is not unproblematic to simply transfer experiences and preferences from one Member State to another, or to draw simple conclusions for the European parliamentary landscape as a whole.

Under the all-European heading, the main question will be whether the parliaments can live up to the expectations, or the rhetoric, of their respective advocates. Having identified and exposed the different purposes that national parliaments are to serve in the first place, we shall contrast the distinguished goals against their very own premises. We shall explore whether the proposals and scenarios are constitutionally sound, in the sense that they are methodologically well-crafted (not lofty and illusory) and fit into constitutional realities (without being overly distortive); whether a greater role for the national parliaments as proposed is feasible in the first place, in the light of existing inter-institutional relations in the EU and the Member States; whether there are any real benefits to reap as suggested, and whether the benefits of their involvement as assumed will outweigh the possible costs, which relates to increases or in fact decreases of transparency and legitimacy of EU action, efficiency of EU decision-making, as well as to the psychology and the constitution-building priorities in European integration.

Finally, we shall put the question whether the national parliaments deserve a greater role or not into the context of broader normative approaches towards European integration in general, and European parliamentarism in particular (chapter 8). For all the appeal of pragmatic solutions in EU constitution-building, the truth remains that national parliamentarism fits into some agendas better than others. As noted at the very beginning, those attached to national sovereignty and statehood will keep putting forward the national parliaments as the only true source of democratic legitimacy in the European Union. This implies that if legitimacy is to be derived from parliamentarism, priority should remain with the parliaments of the Member States. Meanwhile, as also noted at the very beginning, Europhiles would rather emphasize that the key to European parliamentarism lies primarily and appropriately with the European Parliament, not the national parliaments. In the end we are therefore presented with two extreme alternatives: full parliamentarization of the EU, modeled after a federal democratic nation-state, or a step back towards purely intergovernmental co-operation, together with a large-scale repatriation of competences from Brussels back to the Member States. Assuming that neither of these extremes is likely to materialize any time soon, we are left with the task of finding a middle way, and to define the proper place for national parliaments for the time being. Can the national parliaments play a European role? Can strong national parliamentarism be reconciled with ever-closer union? Will multi-level governance, multi-level constitutionalism and dual legitimacy theories accommodate both the European Parliament and the national parliaments on an equal footing? And if they will, should we accept that as a satisfactory solution?

It appears that advocating a greater role for the European Parliament, while at the same time assigning the national parliaments a European role, is an option that conveniently embraces both levels of parliamentarism without any clear normative constitutional priorities. However the progressive consolidation of European parliamentarism will require the definition of at least some priorities. Simply taking everything on board that calls itself a parliament may be the most reconciliatory, but not necessarily the best of choices. This outlook will not provide a final answer to what the appropriate role of national parliaments in the EU should be. But it will show that the national parliamentary avenue is not the only way to the future of Europe, and that even if it was, it is not going to be toll-free for everyone.

It is nowadays seductive to find that a particular national parliament is too ineffective or too permissive in European affairs, and that it should scrutinize EU matters more meticulously, network more actively and debate more passionately. It is similarly tempting to make sweeping statements to the effect that the national parliaments in general deserve a bigger role, and that they should take their due place in the European constitutional landscape. What this book will do is essentially try and reach a new balance of argument: those who demand a stronger national parliament on the basis of empirical observations are invited to consider the big picture, too; those who demand stronger national parliaments on the basis of observations of the big picture are invited to have a look at what their demands will mean on the ground, theoretically and practically; the rest of us are invited to keep a critical perspective in the debate around the national parliaments and the constitutional future of Europe. Ultimately the question is not *how* the national parliaments can be strengthened; the question is whether they should be. The purpose of the present volume is to identify the different perspectives on that question, and the internal consistency of the existing solutions.

1 National parliaments in a European constitutional perspective

1.1 Introduction

Before we throw ourselves into the discussion on how the involvement of the national parliaments in EU decision-making can be enhanced, and whether that is worthwhile in the first place, depending on the purpose, let us consider what the addressing of the national parliaments actually means to the European Union. Whenever we discuss the relationship between national parliaments and the EU, what we actually discuss is the relationship between, on the one hand, a set of institutions within the national constitutional orders of the Member States, and on the other hand an international organization of which these Member States form part. Of course there are more sophisticated approaches to the EU as a unique multi-level polity, a polity that has evolved to become more than just a free-trade area, a polity that features its very own brand of constitutionalism, and we will come to these points in due course. Yet in defining a theoretical starting point, we cannot escape the fact that formally the EU is still a treaty-based organization comprising Member States, and that national parliaments are organs within these Member States.[1] This point in turn raises a number of follow-up questions, which we shall consider hereafter: what role do national parliaments, as a set of Member State institutions, play in the EU setting already? How, then, do we find a means to single out these institutions in that setting, so that we can address them further, assuming that we want to? And how can we then address them most appropriately, once they are singled out, in the persisting setting of an international-law framework? These questions are not only relevant for the practical purpose of drafting treaty provisions; considering them also helps to identify the very purpose of the exercise, and to become aware of some structural impediments that come with the setting in which it would have to be carried out.

1.2 National parliaments and European integration

Usually discussions about the consequences of European integration on the parliaments of the Member States start out with a sobering statement: the national

1 See on the distinction between 'constitutionalising' and 'conservatory' elements in the EU order, whereby the latter tend to preserve the autonomy of the Member States: Dashwood (1998); see further 3.2 and 3.3 *infra*.

parliaments are the 'losers of integration'.[2] Indeed, the European integration process implies a shift of legislative and other sovereign decision-making competences from the Member State level to the European institutions in a growing number of areas. Parliaments, where and in as far as they are domestic law-makers, lose regulatory powers to, in particular, the Council of Ministers which, notwithstanding the co-decision procedure with the European Parliament, is the decisive legislative body of the EU. Still, the national parliaments do retain certain 'European functions'. The three original and most fundamental such functions can be brought under the headings of the ratification of European treaties, the implementation of EU framework legislation into national law, and the continued enforcement of accountability of the governments when they act at EU level. However, the meaningful and effective fulfilment of these functions should be assessed with due regard to both the legal and practical constraints.

1.2.1 Ratification functions

As to the first function, indeed the constituent European treaties were all subject to ratification by all the Member States.[3] In addition to the treaties proper, ratification is required for other fundamental acts bearing constitutional implications, most prominently treaty amendments,[4] enlargements,[5] as well as other acts meaning *de facto* treaty amendments.[6] However, while the national parliaments can enjoy considerable potential importance where and in as far as their assent is required for the ratification of treaties or decisions, it should be noted that this importance is purely a matter of national constitutional law.

Firstly, the parliaments are not mentioned anywhere in the relevant treaty provisions, as the respective ratification clauses merely provide that the High Contracting Parties or Member States are to complete ratification 'in accordance with their respective constitutional requirements'. Thus, depending on domestic law, ratification procedures vary from one Member State to another. Majority requirements for voting in parliament may for instance differ between the threshold for ordinary

---

2 Cf. Rometsch/Wessels (1996), p. 334; Maurer/Wessels (2001), p. 28; Swedish Riksdag (2001), p. 11; Raunio/Wiberg (2001), p. 62; Rizzuto (2003), p. 2.

3 Article 313 EC, Article 52 EU, see also Article IV-447 (1) TCE. All references to the EC Treaty and the EU Treaty are based on the Nice consolidated versions.

4 Article 48 EU, Article IV-443 (3) resp. IV-445 (2) TCE.

5 Article 49 EU, Article I-58 (2) TCE.

6 Ratification is required under the European Community regime *inter alia* for changes in the EC institutional structure, for the move to direct EC taxation and to a uniform election system for the European Parliament. Furthermore, conventions under the Third Pillar regime require ratification as well. For an overview see European Convention (2002b).

statutes, as is the case in the UK, to special thresholds of two-thirds or three-fifths majorities, where ratification necessitates a national constitutional amendment. In some Member States, ratification can be (made) subject to a referendum, which bypasses the parliament and its sole veto position altogether. In Belgium, the European treaties are subject to ratification by the sub-national assemblies as well.

Secondly, even where a parliament is competent to ratify treaties or decisions alone, realism would also command a more nuanced approach. The drafting and negotiating process within the Council, the European Council or the intergovernmental conferences is a classical example of international diplomacy and thus typically a *domaine réservé* of the executive. Parliamentary input to foreign policy, including the ratification stage, is traditionally at its weakest.[7] Even the Convention which drafted the Constitutional Treaty, and which included national parliamentarians, was followed by an IGC. Once the secretive horse-trading and hand-tying there is over, and the treaty ready to be ratified, national parliaments, or the voters in a referendum, are faced with a take-it-or-leave-it choice, without any possibility of amending some details of the package. An outright refusal by a national parliament to ratify a European treaty would provoke a crisis in the integration process, it would provoke a domestic crisis if the government parties in parliament refuse to support a treaty which their own government has already signed, and it might damage their own Member State's reputation and standing as a reliable partner in the long run. The parliaments of the new Member States which acceded in 2004 already had a taste of marginalization as they allowed their governments to conduct accession negotiations, while ratifying the Association Agreements and the Accession Treaty and implementing the *acquis communautaire*, all under constraints on parliamentary supervision such as speed, confidentiality of negotiations and the paramount national objective of joining the EU at initially almost any cost.[8] A parliamentary 'no' in a ratification vote – even if there has been a change of government in the meantime – is even more hazardous than a 'no' in a referendum, by the way, since it implies that not even the political elite is firm in its international commitment. Ratification functions should, for these reasons, not always be attributed to national parliaments alone, and not without making the necessary qualifications, such as the ones mentioned above.

1.2.2 Implementation functions

The second original European function of the national parliaments derives from their capacity as domestic legislators, where and in as far as the national parliaments are competent to implement secondary European law, in particular

7 See Ameller (1966), p. 315 *et seq*.
8 Albi (2005), p. 61 *et seq*.

directives (European Framework Laws), into national law. Again, the national parliaments are not explicitly mentioned in Article 249 (3) EC or the corresponding Article I-33 (1) of the Constitutional Treaty. The choice of forms and methods to transpose European framework legislation is left to 'the national authorities', which may or may not be the Member States parliaments. That again, just like the details of the ratification procedures for treaties, depends on national constitutional rules. The competent authority may for instance be the government itself when regulating by decree or ordinance, or an independent agency or a sub-national law-maker, such as an autonomous province or federal state. Meanwhile, even if it is the national parliament which is competent to implement framework legislation, failure to do so in a timely and correct manner constitutes a breach of European law, unlike it is the case with the ratification of treaties. Under certain conditions, even non-implemented or wrongly implemented framework legislation can take direct effect. Regulations (European Laws) take direct binding effect in the Member States anyway.[9]

The margin of discretion that directives leave to national legislators at the implementation stage should not be overestimated either. Even where the parliament is competent to legislate itself, in fact little room for creativity is left since typical framework legislation is highly elaborate. This is not even a recent phenomenon. Already in the 1970s, the great detail of directives and the narrow margin of discretion of parliaments has been noted.[10] Where implementation discretion is narrowed down or even excluded completely, framework legislation becomes a *fait accompli*, and the implementation process similar to the take-it-or-leave-it choice that comes with treaties, again with no realistic option to 'leave it'.

The technical complexity and sheer amount of legislation also puts parliaments under strain, as it for instance materialized during the flood of single-market directives in the late 1980s which all had to be transposed in a short time. The Italian parliament famously resorted to blank delegation of implementation powers to the government under the La Pergola Law, and the model of transposition by government ordinance is quite common in other Member States as well.[11] Finally, even where a parliament itself adopts the required legislation, MPs are not necessarily aware of the European origin of the bills which are drafted and introduced, just like the majority of domestic bills are, by the government.[12] Thus, implementation functions as regards secondary EU law should not be solely attributed to the national parliaments either, and again not without the necessary qualifications.

---

9 Article 249 (2) EC, Article I-33 TCE.

10 Niblock (1971), p. 23; Sasse (1975), p. 76.

11 Pappas (1995); Mancini (2000), p. 244 *et seq*. welcomes this option as a more reliable means of implementation.

12 Hoetjes (2001), p. 346.

1.2.3 Accountability functions

The third European function of national parliaments derives from their role as representative institutions, where and in as far as they control and legitimize the actions of the government, and act as a link between the government and the citizens. All of the EU Member States are parliamentary or semi-parliamentary democracies where the national government relies on the confidence, or the absence of non-confidence, by a majority in parliament, its chambers or only its lower chamber, to stay in office. Parliaments or chambers in turn, especially where the government relies on their confidence, are able to submit the government to scrutiny, ask questions, insert amendments to government policies, and ultimately threaten the government with a motion of censure or a refusal to affirm confidence. Parliamentary scrutiny and ministerial responsibility are theoretically not limited to purely domestic policies, but they also cover a government's conduct of external relations with foreign states or international organizations. The latter complex makes the formulation and conduct of EU-related policies by the government subject to domestic parliamentary oversight. This is what forms the basis for the indirect popular representation in the activities of the Council of Ministers and the European Council.[13] Article I-46 (2) of the Constitutional Treaty may have made this role of the national parliaments explicit, but, just like the first two European functions, it derives from purely domestic constitutional rules, it had been applicable all along in those cases where it is applicable, and it should again not escape the necessary qualifications. For the inherent impediments to the effective enforcement of government accountability in EU context are notorious, and they lie at the very heart of the perceived parliamentary gap in the European Union.

In the early days, national parliamentarians had a more immediate access to the decision-making of the EEC via the dual mandate, which awarded some MPs a seat in the European Parliamentary Assembly, the consultative body that was to become the European Parliament. Yet this was an opportunity for a number of *parliamentarians*, not the national parliaments as such, and it was lost in 1979 with the first direct elections to the European Parliament and the abolition of the automatic dual mandate. The national parliaments found themselves to be outsiders in the European decision-making process. In order to have a substantive impact there, they were essentially left with the option of trying to influence their own government domestically, before decisions were being adopted in Brussels.

---

13 Another 'European function' of the national parliaments, which is sometimes identified under a separate heading, is their indirect involvement in the nomination or appointment by the governments of functionaries to the Commission, the European Court of Justice and the Court of First Instance, the Court of Auditors or the European Central Bank. This indirect involvement however derives from the same rules of ministerial responsibility and parliamentary scrutiny of government action.

Still the parliaments' remoteness from those who were the insiders placed constraints on their participation. To begin with, while the Council consists of ministers, and national ministers are familiar and relatively available figures, by far most Council decisions are pre-cooked in Coreper by specialist civil servants from the national ministerial bureaucracies.[14] In theory, ministerial responsibility to parliament extends not only to ministers' personal actions or omissions, but also the persons or institutions for which they are responsible. In the practice of Brussels decision-making, however, the activities of Coreper remain highly intransparent. The area of delegated regulation by the similarly intransparent comitology orbiting the Commission is even further removed from the Council's immediate domain. In the Council itself, closed-doors diplomacy further impedes national parliamentary oversight – something the Convention actually sought to tackle by imposing an open-doors policy.[15] Calling ministers to account for their negotiating and voting behaviour in the Council is hardly possible if the minutes are treated as confidential.[16] Usually the Council does not even hold a formal voting, but decides by consensus.

The facets of the national parliaments' outsider position in the EU are not limited to the above points. The transnational character of EU decision-making forces outside scrutinizers to take into account the interests of other Member States, which are often expressed spontaneously and informally. Domestic criticism of a minister's conduct of Council negotiations can thus be rebutted with a reference to the need to reach compromises. Ministers will again be better informed than their parliament about what else might have been achievable in the Council.[17] Co-decision by the Council with the European Parliament further means that a legislative draft and a common position can change considerably in a series of readings, Commission interventions and conciliation rounds. Keeping track of the process thereby becomes even more difficult to outsiders. At that, since the agenda is dictated externally, national parliaments are under constant time pressure,[18] and once an item is put on the Council agenda, the decisive deals may have already long been struck. The introduction of qualified majority voting in the Council by the Single European Act meant yet another blow to the potential controlling opportunities for the national parliaments. In essence the argument goes that no matter how strict parliamentary supervision of a minister is, the latter can still be outvoted,

14 Maurer (2002), p. 10 with references.

15 See 3.5.1 *infra*.

16 Miller/Ware (1996), although Niblock (1971), p. 48 noted that secrecy in the Council is, due to the great number of involved officials, compromised by considerable leakage of information.

17 Niblock (1971), p. 48.

18 Weber-Panariello (1995), p. 307.

and while ministers' lack of bargaining skills can still be criticized afterwards, it is futile to call them to account for the policy outcome itself.[19]

Thus, the removal of the decision-making locus from a Member State's capital to Brussels and Strasbourg (and Luxembourg), the amount and complexity of the processed legislation, the intransparent, transnational and via QMV supranational character of the decision-making process, as well as its pace during the decisive stages, are all easily capable of marginalizing a national parliament. What is typical is a widening information lag of the parliaments behind the executive apparatus.[20] Paradoxically, one might add, the setting up of the European layer of government is based on treaties which have been ratified by the national parliaments themselves. The marginalization of national parliaments therefore appears like a 'self-mutilation'.[21] However, even if we wished to stick to that unflattering assessment, we have already placed certain qualifications with respect to parliamentary discretion in ratification procedures.

If we accept the European integration process as a given, then optimizing a parliament's access to, and processing of, EU-related information requires additional organizational efforts. But not only the ability, also the willingness to exercise scrutiny of the individual government's EU policy in fact depends on the respective parliament itself. Conventionally, neither is perceived to be adequate for ensuring effective national parliamentary oversight over the Council's activities, as we shall further discuss later on. This brings us to the larger problem of the often-criticized parliamentary deficit of the European Union. The Council, which has received law-making powers, is not a parliament itself. It is neither elected like one, nor is it behaving like one. It is not accountable to the European Parliament either, nor to any other single representative institution. Only the individual ministers who make up the Council each remain formally accountable to their own national parliaments at home, each under their own rules and subject to their own qualifications. Due to the mentioned constraints to national parliamentary scrutiny of EU policy, including the reluctance of many MPs to take interest, however, the Member States' governments seem to have escaped parliamentary influence, openness and accountability, on both national and European level.[22] At the same time, however, the deficient parliamentary oversight on the national level is no longer understood as a purely domestic subject-matter. The issue has been addressed at EU level and in treaty drafting context throughout the 1990s. In that sense the Convention, and the Constitutional Treaty it produced, represents merely the latest effort in what

---

19 Holding a minister to account domestically is not only problematic when he is outvoted under QMV, but also when he abstains under unanimity voting, see Smismans (1998), p. 56.

20 Miller/Ware (1996); Raunio (1999).

21 Raunio (1999), p. 181; Maurer/Wessels (2001), p. 28.

22 Lodge (1991); Ronge (1998), p. 68; Swedish Riksdag (2001), p. 1; Harlow (2002), p. 45.

is a series of measures and gestures to draw the national parliaments from the periphery of the Union into the limelight.

1.2.4 National parliaments addressed: the state of affairs in EU law

It was at the Maastricht intergovernmental conference that the role of national parliaments first became the subject of prominent discussion in treaty-drafting context at the European level. The European Parliament had already conducted a gathering, the *Assizes* of 1990, together with the national parliaments in the run-up to the IGC, to discuss the future of Europe.[23] The IGC itself then included two declarations in the Final Act that addressed the national parliaments specifically and explicitly. The approach then taken may be qualified as three-fold. First, the timely availability of EU documentation, in particular legislative proposals, was recognized as a prerequisite for *ex ante* scrutiny by the national parliaments. Second, inter-parliamentary co-operation and exchanges of information with the European Parliament was encouraged. Third, an institutionalized collective involvement of the national parliaments in the EU was suggested through the *Assizes*. Declaration 14 called for a repetition of the *Assizes*, while declaration 13 addressed the issue of timely information and inter-parliamentary co-operation:

> The [Maastricht Intergovernmental] Conference considers that it is important to encourage greater involvement of national parliaments in the activities of the European Union.
>
> To this end, the exchange of information between national parliaments and the European Parliament should be stepped up. In this context, the governments of the Member States will ensure, inter alia, that national parliaments receive Commission proposals for legislation in good time for information or possible examination.
>
> Similarly, the Conference considers that it is important for contacts between the national parliaments and the European Parliament to be stepped up, in particular through the granting of appropriate reciprocal facilities and regular meetings between members of parliament interested in the same issues.

The declarations were no legally binding documents, but they, in particular declaration 13, paved the way for the Protocol on the role of the national parliaments in the EU that was annexed to the 1997 Treaty of Amsterdam. The Protocol was legally binding, and it took the addressing of the national parliaments a step further along the earlier lines. Thus, part I further formalized information flows to the national parliaments by obliging the national governments to forward legislative

23 See 4.6 *infra* on possible frictions between MEPs and national MPs, as well as 5 *infra* for a further discussion of the idea to make the *Assizes* a quasi-permanent EU institution.

proposals to their parliaments; in addition, it provided for a six-weeks time window for national parliamentary scrutiny of proposals:

> I. Information for national Parliaments of Member States
>
> 1. All Commission consultation documents (green and white papers and communications) shall be promptly forwarded to national parliaments of the Member States.
> 2. Commission proposals for legislation as defined by the Council in accordance with Article 151.3 of the Treaty establishing the European Community, shall be made available in good time so that the Government of each Member State may ensure that its own national parliament receives them as appropriate.
> 3. A six-week period shall elapse between a legislative proposal or a proposal for a measure to be adopted under Title VI of the Treaty on European Union being made available in all languages to the European Parliament and the Council by the Commission and the date when it is placed on a Council agenda for decision either for the adoption of an act or for adoption of a common position pursuant to article 189b or 189c, subject to exceptions on grounds of urgency, the reasons for which shall be stated in the act or common position.

The idea of repeating the *Assizes* of 1990 was abandoned; however, part II of the Protocol went on to recognize the role of COSAC, the conference of the European Affairs Committees of the national parliaments plus a delegation from the European Parliament.[24] COSAC had already been meeting twice yearly since 1989 for the purpose of informally exchanging information; now it was given the right to make contributions on draft EU legislation in general, on matters concerning the area of freedom, security and justice in particular, as well as on the principle of subsidiarity and fundamental rights. Still, contributions made by COSAC were not to bind national parliaments or prejudge their position.

The Convention affirmed the provisions from the Amsterdam Protocol when it adopted the Protocol on the role of the national parliaments to be annexed to the EU Constitutional Treaty. Going further, it insisted on improving information flows by having the Commission *send* its proposals to the national parliaments, rather than having the governments *forward* them; in addition, it emphasized the governments' obligation to respect the six-weeks time window for scrutiny.[25] As we have previously noted, the Convention also included in the text specific instances where the national parliaments should be kept informed about EU developments, such as *inter alia* about plans for treaty revision, including a veto for any national parliament to block the application of the passerelle clause, about incoming EU membership applications or, more broadly, about the performance of Europol and

24 COSAC is a French acronym for *C*onférence des *o*rganes *s*pécialisés dans les *a*ffaires *c*ommunautaires et européennes des parlements de l'Union européenne.

25 See further on information facilities 3.5.1 *infra*.

Eurojust.[26] The role of COSAC was affirmed; so was the Convention method of treaty revision which had been applied to draft the Constitutional Treaty in the first place, as well as, before that, the EU Charter of Fundamental Rights. Since MEPs and national MPs together formed a majority of Convention members, these fora can themselves be considered as largely inter-parliamentary in nature, and as a new form of involvement of national parliamentarians in treaty drafting.[27] Finally, and most prominently, the Convention officially declared the national parliaments to be part of the Union's construction of representative democracy, and at the same time it accorded the national parliaments the role of guardians of the principle of subsidiarity in EU legislative proposals, by means of an early warning system of collective intervention in cases of perceived breaches.[28]

Neither of these EU-level instruments prescribes or petrifies the role of the national parliaments. As seen, national parliaments already fulfil certain European functions as a matter of domestic constitutional law, by ratifying treaties, implementing directives and holding to account the governments, where applicable; to do that, they do not require any EU declarations or protocols. The facilities that the mentioned instruments in turn provide do not necessarily mean an improvement to all parliaments either: in those national parliaments which insist on timely information already, they bring about no practical changes for the better. In fact, increased flows of paper may yet prove detrimental to parliamentary oversight.[29] As we shall see later on, even for the apparent novelty of subsidiarity monitoring the parliaments would not strictly need a new treaty provision: nothing precludes them from paying attention to that principle in their regular scrutiny work. What all this brings us to is the fact that defining the role of the national parliaments in the EU, by way of treaties or other EU-level efforts, is not as simple an objective as it may seem. The national parliaments are after all not EU institutions, which can be set up, re-shaped and abolished. They are pre-existing domestic bodies that are rooted in their very own constitutional setting, and which should be approached with great prudence, if at all. And before we embark on the discussion whether and how to do that, as well as to illustrate the need for caution in both drafting the measures and defining the intended addressees, let us clarify a number of fundamental notions which shall be used throughout. Who exactly are the national parliaments to start with, and what are the limits to exercises of courting them, or even assigning them new roles, from an EU perspective? Such a discussion should not only help us evaluate future attempts to that effect more soberly, but also see the existing EU-level declarations and protocols on the national parliaments in an entirely new light.

---

26 See for references n. 5 *et seq. supra*.

27 See for a discussion 5.6 *infra*.

28 See for a discussion 7 *infra*.

29 See 3.5.1 *infra*.

1.3 Who are the 'national parliaments?'

'The national parliaments should be more effective at scrutinizing their governments' EU policy'. This sentence summarizes a demand which we will, along with other demands for greater involvement of national parliaments in EU affairs, shortly test for validity and internal consistency from different possible perspectives. But what are this claim's underlying implications? Who are the addressees of this claim?

A global comparative and historical analysis will reveal considerable variations as to the meaning of the word 'parliament'.[30] Within the European Union, the term seems far more straightforward – in any event, when 'the national parliaments' are referred to, it is usually clear which institutions are meant. However, when we explore the definitions of what characterizes a national parliament, the obviousness of the concept instantly diminishes. And we should by all means explore the underlying definitions when the activity of national parliaments is invoked for a particular purpose, and justified with reference to particular competences or qualities which they allegedly possess.

The European functions of national parliaments that we have outlined are highly interconnected. They are all intended to show, where they are linked to the national parliaments as a roughly defined set of actors, different sides of what appear to be the same coins. Thus, a reference to national parliaments as bodies competent to ratify treaties, which is done by way of statute, bears a connection to the parliamentary law-making capacity. This law-making capacity is also the basis for national parliaments' role at implementing European framework legislation. Where treaties are ratified, and framework legislation implemented in a rubber-stamping fashion, it may reveal the origins of the passive or ineffective position of a parliament at controlling the government before the adoption of the texts in Brussels, or at holding it to account afterwards. This passivity or ineffectiveness in turn fuels demands for greater efforts at scrutinizing the individual governments, for more inter-parliamentary co-operation with other national parliaments or with the European Parliament, and for a formal, direct and collective input to EU policy. These proposed collective European roles again lead back to the individual domestic roles of national parliaments. Thus, the early warning system for the principle of subsidiarity as it was inserted in the Constitutional Treaty again addresses national parliaments as law-makers, who presumably have an interest in retaining, or even 'repatriating', regulatory competences from the EU. Apart from that, since they are assumedly the ones who ratified the treaties in the first place, they may be also the ones who should police the boundaries of the powers they have conferred upon the EU institutions. The Convention method of treaty drafting, which involves

30 See Laundy (1989).

national parliamentarians, sets in there as well. It takes into account that it will mostly be national parliamentarians who will have to ratify the treaties thus drafted. Where treaties have to be ratified by referendum, the Convention method equally draws on national parliaments' capacity to give an impression of legitimacy to the draft text, and to act as fora for public debate. And public debate as a core element of democracy, and the connection of elected MPs to their citizens, in the end lies at the heart of the demands to stimulate national parliamentary activity to address the much-lamented democratic deficit of the European Union. Yet these functions are not all necessarily linked to what is understood to be a national parliament.

We may start out with defining a national parliament as the law-making branch of government, according to the classical Montesqueuvian separation of powers doctrine. This would however ignore the fact that, for instance, the French government enjoys autonomous regulatory powers which are not derived from statute, but from the French Constitution.[31] Apart from that, and not only in France but in any modern Western parliamentary democracy, the government is closely involved in the law-making agenda, and much of the initiation and drafting of legislation is carried out by the government.[32] The Dutch Constitution even insists that the legislator consists of the Government (including the King) and the States-General *together*.[33] Furthermore, defining a national parliament for the purposes of EU involvement via its legislative competences often, and with the trend towards devolution increasingly so, collides with the status of sub-national legislators. In those Member States which have a federal, decentralized or devolved constitutional structure, there simply might not be a supreme law-maker for the entire country in certain policy areas, only regional bodies.[34] Earlier on we noted the possible inclusion of a referendum in treaty ratification procedures, which bypasses parliament in its law-making or ratifying capacity. Combined with the role of sub-national assemblies, this also puts into a relative perspective the idea that national parliaments are the pre-destined guardians of the principle of subsidiarity, other than the fact that they are external actors who have little to gain from competence creeps to the EU and are perhaps at least more likely to take subsidiarity more seriously than the Commission and the Council do. The national parliaments may have neither ratified the conferral of powers to the EU in the first place, at least not alone, and they may not be the recipients, at least not the only recipients, of powers which flow back to the

---

31 Article 37 French Constitution.

32 Harlow (2002), p. 85; Weber-Panariello (1995), p. 311.

33 Article 81 Dutch Constitution.

34 Arguably, sub-state assemblies may also be called 'national parliaments', so the term 'State parliaments' as denoting the central national-level assemblies might seem more accurate. 'National parliaments' is however a more widely used term, and we shall use it here as well, see Bengtson (2003), endnote 1.

Member States under subsidiarity or repatriation of competences. We will discuss the relation between subsidiarity and national parliamentarism in greater detail later on.[35]

Alternatively to the above approach, and we may also derive that from the introductory paragraphs, we could define a national parliament broadly as a Member State's central representative assembly which elects or at least dismisses the national government, and which holds it to account. This seems to be a robust definition comprising the unicameral parliaments, the lower chambers of the bicameral parliaments and the senates with censure powers in the EU Member States. One problem here arises with respect to directly elected presidents in semi-presidential systems, for example Finland and France. There the presidents (as part of the government in the broad sense) are not accountable to parliament at all, in the sense that they do not depend on parliamentary confidence like a Prime Minister does. Interestingly, the original draft of Article I-46 (2) of the Constitutional Treaty, which spelt out the dual legitimacy of the EU via the European Parliament and the national parliaments, indeed omitted the position of directly elected presidents who may sit on the European Council. It merely mentioned the accountability of the governments to their national parliaments, not the direct accountability of heads of state to their citizens.[36] Only in a later version was a reference to presidents and their own democratic legitimacy inserted. This initial omission is very telling as regards the nature of the exercise of addressing the national parliaments at EU level, as we shall see shortly: it is easy to overlook national idiosyncrasies if one simply assumes that European democracies are all more or less the same.

Turning back to our main point concerning the national parliaments as a link in the Council's accountability chain, another, and in constitutional terms more serious problem arises with respect to the upper chambers in some bicameral national parliaments. The *raison d'être* of a senate, where it does exist, varies from one Member State to another. So does its mode of election, its powers and, most importantly, its relation to the national government.[37] A senate to which the national government is not accountable, because the senate neither elects nor dismisses it, can hardly be a link in the chain of democratic accountability leading up to the Council. The German government is for instance not accountable to the *Bundesrat*, the representation of the *Länder* governments on federal level.

---

35 See 7.2 *infra*.

36 Article 45 (2) draft TCE as of 18 July 2003, CONV 850/03: 'Citizens are directly represented at Union level in the European Parliament. Member States are represented in the European Council and in the Council of Ministers by their governments, themselves accountable to national parliaments, elected by their citizens'.

37 See Knippenberg (2002).

What is more, the *Bundesrat* is not even a parliament in terms of composition in the first place, for it comprises sixteen sub-national executives. It is staffed with ministers or otherwise with civil servants.[38] For exactly these reasons, members of the *Bundesrat* were not part of the German parliamentary delegation which was sent with a dual mandate to the European Parliament until 1979. Only members of the directly elected Federal Diet qualified for a dual parliamentary mandate. Today, however, the *Bundesrat* is almost naturally included in the list of addressees as being a 'national parliament', or at least part of it.

The standards by which we assess the parliamentary character of a national institution should be observed even more strictly as regards the House of Lords of the United Kingdom. While scoring very well in comparative research in terms of efficiency and excellent quality of its thorough EU-related reports,[39] the Lords still remains an unelected institution. Some other senates in Europe show at least a partly dubious democratic and representative foundation, such as the one in the Netherlands, which is but indirectly elected, the one in Ireland, which is partly appointed by the Prime Minister, or the one in Belgium, which includes the King's children as senators for life.[40] Turning back to the Lords, it should further be noted that the UK government is not accountable to the Lords in the strict sense of an inverse parliamentary confidence rule: the government need not enjoy support in the Lords, and the Lords cannot defeat a sitting government in a vote, and force it to step down, like the Commons can. In the end this means that neither is the government accountable to the Lords, nor is the Lords accountable to the people. Surely, when national parliaments are invoked as fora for public debate, which may be a third criterion to infer from the introduction, even an indirectly elected, partly elected or totally unelected senate can play an important role as a recognizable locus for deliberations, as a check on extreme positions, and as an enforcer of public, perhaps moral rather than formal government accountability. Yet even then, a misleading impression of homogeneity should be avoided. The self-perception and deliberative capacity as a forum varies from one chamber to another, also between the two chambers of the same parliament. In a word, rooted in their own countries' history and culture, the differences between the bodies conventionally covered by the term 'the national parliaments' are considerable. Their heterogeneity as regards powers and functions should serve as a first caveat in our discussion, and any discussion on the national parliaments in the EU, for that matter.

---

38 Agostini (2001), p. 33 notes that the German *Bundesrat* therefore can 'hardly be taken as a model for "parliamentarisation" of European decision-making processes'.

39 Cf. Duff (1994), p. 163; Norton (1995a), p. 13 *et seq*.; Weber-Panariello (1995), p. 311.

40 See Article 55 Dutch Constitution, Article 18 Irish Constitution, Article 72 Belgian Constitution, respectively.

1.4 Parliaments as unitary institutions?

The term 'the national parliaments' bears not only a misleading implication that the addressed institutions are an easily identifiable group of bodies. In the present context it further implies that parliaments can be singled out as independent actors, and contrasted with the national governments. This implication should be reviewed even more critically than the first one. When speaking of national parliaments as democratic institutions which can for instance legitimize laws, or the actions of others, through their consent, then it is not parliament as such which is decisive. What is decisive is its composition. A primary reason why a parliament is central to a democratic society is the fact that the citizens can bring about a shift of majorities at recurring elections, and can thus replace one set of policies with another. The majority which has thus become a minority can still articulate its alternative policy proposals there, it can polarize with its competing simplified agenda, challenge the government and the majority on which it relies, and hope to become a parliamentary majority again after the next elections. Otherwise opposition parties may hope to take office or join a coalition in mid-term. In fact, one of the primary reasons why national parliaments may be attractive as democratic building blocks in the European Union is that they are the primary locus where the opposition can make its voice heard.[41] Such possibilities are severely restricted where the Member State is externally represented through, say, the ministry of foreign affairs.

National parliaments or their lower chambers are assemblies of competing political parties which are either in government or in opposition. To depict parliaments as unitary institutions with an adversarial position *vis-à-vis* the government would be to ignore the reason why they are democratic, and thus potentially attractive to the EU, in the first place. Simplified government-versus-parliament juxtapositions usually do not reflect the theoretical or practical model of national constitutions.[42] A parliament, or rather its majority, is elected to support a functioning government for the period of its term, after which the electorate can decide on the redistribution of seats. The vital supervising and debating tasks, the control and communication, then mainly derive from the activity of opposition parties, intra-government challengers or intra-coalition defectors. This does not mean that at times a parliament cannot be more or less united as against a government. Still, the *a priori* non-unitary nature of parliaments, and the typically non-adversarial nature of the majority's relation with the government, should be our second fundamental caveat which is to remind us not to resort to simplicisms when talking about 'the national parliaments' in the EU.

41 Holzhacker (2002), p. 461.

42 See Niblock (1971), p. 50; Döring (1995); Pahre (1997); Maurer/Wessels (2001), p. 451.

1.5 Scrutiny, oversight or control?

One last remark on terminology is in order. In the context of national parliamentary activity, both in policy documents and in the literature, it often appears that the terms 'scrutiny', 'debate', 'sifting' or 'examination' of documents, 'participation', 'involvement', 'oversight' or 'control' with respect to European affairs are used somewhat interchangeably. At the same time, a national parliament's entering into public deliberation about an EU proposal is arguably not quite the same thing as a national parliament's tying a minister to a negotiating mandate or issuing a formal veto against the adoption of a decision in the European Council. We shall indeed use the different terms in the present discussion as appears most appropriate in a given context, for the distinction can be understood as both a matter of principle, as well as a matter of degree. The matter is rather one of principle when we turn to the empirical aspect of our discussion: in the different stages of national parliamentary participation in EU affairs, different terms denote different types of activities. Thus, a parliament or a committee thereof may 'sift' incoming documentation for the purpose of information gathering and prioritization, but it need not 'control' ministers in the sense of instructing them in the run-up to Council meetings afterwards; a parliament may engage in 'oversight' as regards the government, which can be ensured by insisting on timely information and updates, but the parliament need not necessarily hold a genuine 'debate' for that, neither in the committee nor in the plenary. Oversight does not imply control, participation does not imply debate.[43]

At the same time, the choice of wording may reveal an author's particular normative approach to the issue, in which case the distinctions between 'scrutiny', 'control', etc., become a matter of degree, rather than principle. Thus, the terms may be understood as points on a scale of preferred activism or restraint. On the 'weaker' end of that scale, we would find 'involvement' of the national parliaments as probably the most open-ended notion, which furthermore implies an external stimulation, as opposed to parliamentary 'participation' which at least contains an element of activity and self-consciousness; further towards the middle of the scale we would find 'debate' which necessarily implies activity but not much else; 'sifting' of documentation and 'scrutiny' of government policies can be considered a toothier approach to oversight; and parliamentary 'control', at the other end of the scale, is a notion that is very much concrete and covers *inter alia* the imposition of binding mandates. We shall see that different scholars and ideologues, as well as institutional actors, both national and European, all have their own motives for addressing the national parliaments in a manner that suits their own agenda. The choice of terminology as a choice of degree of involvement then gives clues as to these motives. Does a government really wish to tie its hands by subjecting its policies to systematic

43 See on the different scrutiny stages in practice 2 *infra*.

domestic parliamentary 'control', or does it merely wish to cater to a certain constituency by airing rhetoric about national parliamentary 'involvement'?[44] Does an IGC wish to submit future Commission proposals to tough 'scrutiny' in the national parliaments, or is it merely hinting at 'information or possible examination'?[45] Does the European Commission favour national parliamentary 'oversight' in EU affairs, or does it want the national parliaments to 'stimulate public debate' about European integration, which is not quite the same thing?[46]

In most cases the above terms, especially 'scrutiny' and 'oversight', will indeed be used more or less synonymously, as many of the terms are highly interrelated. We should however bear in mind the terminological fine-tuning, which becomes important not only for the empirical analysis of what exactly a parliament does, but also for the normative discussion on what exactly an author, or an institution, *wants* the national parliaments to do.

1.6 Addressing national parliaments and the issue of constitutional autonomy

Whether one prefers 'scrutiny', 'oversight' or 'control' as regards actual activity, a cautious use of terminology is also recommended when speaking of 'the national parliaments' in the European Union. The term 'the national parliaments' neither covers a homogenous group of institutions, nor does it denote monolithical bodies acting independently of, or in opposition to, their national governments, notwithstanding certain gradations in parliamentary autonomy depending on the country and subject-matter at hand. Instead, the term refers to a number of national institutions which sometimes roughly correspond with each other, and which are sometimes hardly comparable, but which, at least in most cases, consist of competing political parties, government or opposition. Of course, at the end of the day, the addressees of invitations for 'the national parliaments' to become more active in European affairs will seem clear. It is the thirteen unicameral parliaments of the EU-25, and the twelve bicameral parliaments including both their chambers, which adds up to thirty-seven individual assemblies.[47] Their democratic, communicative, controlling and law-making capacities, in spite of our above considerations, will

---

44 See on the governments' stake in parliamentary control 3.2 *infra*.

45 See on the Maastricht Declarations 1.2.4 *supra*.

46 See on the Commission's stance 3.3 *infra*.

47 Finland, Sweden, Denmark, Estonia, Latvia, Lithuania, Luxembourg, Portugal, Slovakia, Hungary, Greece, Malta and Cyprus have unicameral legislatures; Ireland, the UK, France, Spain, the Netherlands, Belgium, Germany, Austria, Poland, Italy, Slovenia and the Czech Republic have a bicameral system. As for candidate countries, Romania has a bicameral, Bulgaria and Croatia a unicameral parliament. Turkey's parliament is unicameral as well.

be taken more or less for granted, if such a qualification of their capacities and a definition of their purpose is carried out at all. And while 'addressing' the national parliaments in such a manner may very well be a political gesture, again for one purpose or another, the exercise, in the light of our above considerations, is bound to have lighter or heavier implications with respect to constitutional law. That is not to say that such an exercise is legally forbidden, or practically impossible to carry out. Our caveats however do tell us something about the dogmatic validity and conceptual solidity of the exercise, and in the end also about its normative value, as well as, indeed, its inherent practical constraints.

1.6.1 The international law background of the European Union

Earlier on, we identified the three original European functions of the national parliaments under the headings of treaty ratification, framework law implementation and holding the governments to account. While making the necessary qualifications, we also noted that the treaties themselves are, or have long remained silent on these functions. The national parliaments, where and in as far as they are affected, are hiding behind formulations such as 'respective constitutional requirements' for treaty ratification, and 'national authorities' for the implementation of secondary law. The parliaments' task of holding to account their governments, where and in as far as that applies to a chamber, has been a given since the 1950s, but it has only been recognized in a treaty project half a century later. It is the silence of the treaties which makes addressing the national parliaments a conscious exercise in the first place. And the reason for this silence as regards the national parliaments lies in the character of the foundations of the European Union itself.

The primary sources of EU law are all instruments of international law. They are formally concluded and ratified by sovereign *States*, while for the EU as such it is largely irrelevant which national authority is competent to commit the State externally and then to ratify these instruments domestically. Similarly, once directives are adopted, they are implemented into national law by the *States*. Again, as long as the desired result is achieved, it is largely irrelevant who the competent domestic authorities for this purpose are, whether they be parliaments, governments, agencies, sub-national legislators or other bodies. The European Union remains a treaty-based organization whose core decision-making bodies, the IGCs, the European Council and the Council of Ministers, are 'intergovernmental' in composition and purpose, in the sense that there, irrespective of the applicable decision-making procedures, Member States and their representatives are intended to act and bargain in the name of their own national interest.[48] Therefore, the conceptual starting point

48 In this sense, an 'integovernmental' element exists even in the Community Pillar, namely in the Council as opposed to the Commission and the European Parliament, which do not

should be, and historically the starting point actually was, uniform external representation of the Member States by the governments, and autonomy as regards the Member States' internal constitutional arrangements. Where the government holds the monopoly for acting on behalf of the Member State, the national parliament should be of no *a priori* concern in international relations.

Now obviously the European Union is not the United Nations, where inquiries into a Member State's level of democracy and parliamentarism can be rebuffed as a rude interference with internal affairs. The EU legal system already penetrates internal constitutional arrangements of the Member States to an extent which is unmatched among the existing treaty-based organizations. Monolithic external representation of sovereign Member States through their ministry of foreign affairs is no longer a reality, and even as a sovereignist fiction it is no longer convincing.

One example of how the sovereignist fiction is disrupted are the principles of direct effect and supremacy of Community law, and the requirement of its effective and uniform application throughout the Community territory. While formally the EU is not concerned with the relationship between a Member State's legislature and judiciary, the *Simmenthal* doctrine in fact confers tasks of judicial review of statutory law which many national judges have not known before.[49] As European integration moves beyond the classical scope of an international organization, the European Union, to borrow a term from corporate law, is 'piercing the veil' of Member States' external sovereignty, and reaches out to internal constitutional bodies very much beyond the ministry of foreign affairs.

A second example of such 'piercing the veil' may be found in the involvement of the regions at EU level. Indeed it seems, although we will come back to that, that by the setting up of the Committee of the Regions, the regions succeeded in 'breaking open the traditional duopoly of member states and European institutions'.[50] Again, while the EU is formally not concerned with the constitutional structure of Member States, and while it does not prescribe the existence of sub-national entities, let alone the powers that these entities should have, it clearly reaches into the very heart of the Member States' territorial sovereignty or integrity. In line with that development is the amended wording of Article 203 EC, which stipulates that Member States are to be represented in the Council by officials 'at ministerial level'. This is to accommodate ministers of regional governments, not just those of the national government, to act on behalf of a Member State.[51]

---

receive instructions from the national capitals. The term shall also be used on later occasions with this particular meaning.

49 *Simmenthal SpA* v. *Ministero delle Finanze*, ECJ 35/76, [1976] ECR 1871, see also Claes (2005).

50 Jeffery (2004), p. 3; the reason for our qualification is that the regional representatives are still nominated by the Member States and appointed by the Council, see Article 263 EC, see also 1.7.1 *infra*.

51 See further Dashwood (2004), p. 373.

A third example of piercing the veil, which is perhaps not as prominent but nevertheless relevant, it the granting of voting rights to EU citizens for European and municipal elections in the Member State of residence. While the realization of voting rights for the European Parliament was relatively easy to achieve methodologically, the issue of municipal elections raised some peculiar questions.[52] Not only do Member States often link voting rights to nationality by virtue of constitutional provisions,[53] different Member States also have different approaches to local government, and award different powers and status to their municipalities. The aim was to avoid as much as possible any frictions while addressing at a European level a matter which is rooted in national constitutional diversity.

At this point we should insert an important qualification. It is not suggested that it is somehow *prohibited* under international law for states to reach into each other's constitutions. An exaggerated polarization between an over-intrusive European Union, on the one hand, and victimized Member States, on the other hand, would miss the fact that, in a way, the Member States *are* the European Union. None of the mentioned piercings have been imposed unilaterally. They have all been voluntarily and unanimously agreed upon by the Member States. In ratifying treaties, the Member States are binding themselves, and certainly treaty-based arrangements may stipulate deeper constitutional integration. They may and they do. Still these arrangements continue to have the background of an international organization, and the starting point is therefore not constitutional homogeneity, but national external sovereignty and internal diversity. Even if we define the EU as a *sui generis* polity, its legal and constitutional basis remains unaltered. This implies a number of inherent constraints for the justification and effect of arrangements of constitutional integration, especially as regards the role of political bodies like parliaments.

1.6.2 National legislatures in the ECHR

To illustrate the consequences of the EU's international-law basis for the exercise of addressing national parliaments, we can draw a parallel to another European multilateral international instrument where national parliaments are addressed. Article 3 of the First Protocol to the European Convention on Human Rights (ECHR) guarantees the right to freely elect the legislature within the contracting states. Just like the EU, the Council of Europe is based on an international treaty. Just like the EU constituent treaties, the ECHR and its protocols are treaties as well. Not unlike the treaties of the EU and its predecessors, although not in an identical manner, the ECHR as interpreted by the Strasbourg Court is capable

52 Reich (1999), p. 434 *et seq*.

53 See for an overview of old and new Member States in that respect: Albi (2005).

of having an impact on national constitutional arrangements within the contracting states. For example, the Court's case-law concerning the right to a fair trial and an independent tribunal under Article 6 ECHR has affected the domestic relations between law-maker and judge,[54] and government and judge,[55] by holding respective interference or overlapping functions to be incompatible with the ECHR. The right to vote for the legislature, however, although it directly addresses a central institution in a national constitutional order, is applied very leniently in practice.

Article 3 of the First ECHR Protocol entails an explicit positive obligation for the high contracting parties to hold 'free elections at reasonable intervals by secret ballot, under conditions which will ensure the free expression of the opinion of the people in the choice of the legislature'. According to Strasbourg case-law, the term 'legislature' is not limited to the national parliaments, but may, in cases of federalism or devolution in a state, cover regional parliaments with autonomous legislative powers as well.[56] Regional parliaments are then considered to be component parts of the national legislature. From the states' obligation to hold free elections, the individual right to vote and to stand as a candidate is derived. However the states enjoy a broad margin of appreciation in giving substance to that right. There is for instance no preference for a particular election system. Electoral laws may allow for 'wasted votes' resulting from district systems or minimum thresholds, they may contain a bias towards over-representation of rural areas, they may subsidize political parties, restrict candidature possibilities for categories of persons like civil servants or persons below a minimum age, and they may disenfranchise convicted prisoners or persons under preventive police surveillance.[57] Findings of violations of Article 3 of the First ECHR Protocol are extremely rare. Essentially a violation is found when a restriction of voting rights has been unlawful under national law

---

54 See e.g. *Procola* v. *Luxembourg*, ECtHR 28 September 1995, no. 14570/89 on bodies with both legislative and judicial functions; *Gorraiz Lizarraga et al.* v. *Spain*, ECtHR 27 April 2004, no. 62534/00 on legislative intervention into pending judicial proceedings.

55 See e.g. the case-law concerning military judges in Turkish state security courts, prominently in *Öcalan* v. *Turkey*, ECtHR 12 March 2003, no. 46221/99.

56 See *Mathieu-Mohin and Clerfayt* v. *Belgium*, ECtHR 2 March 1987, no. 9267/81 on the regional and language community assemblies in Belgium; *X* v. *Austria*, European Commission for Human Rights 12 July 1976, no. 7008/75 on the *Länder* parliaments in Austria; *Santoro* v. *Italy*, ECtHR 1 July 2004, no. 36681/97 on the regional Councils in Italy; *Py* v. *France*, ECtHR 11 January 2005, no. 66289/01 on the Congress of (French) New Caledonia, which also in EU context raises interesting questions as regards regional legislatures in overseas territories, see Kiiver (2005a).

57 See for references: Frowein/Peukert (1996); van Dijk/van Hoof (1998); Lawson/Schermers (1999); Heringa (2002).

itself,[58] where the entire population of a territory is disenfranchised,[59] or where a military junta dissolves parliament and abolishes democracy altogether.[60]

What are the parallels that we can draw to the EU here? Article 3 of the First ECHR Protocol, read in conjunction with the reference to the principle of democracy in the preamble to the ECHR, requires the existence of a representative legislature as a basis for a democratic society.[61] However the identification of who exactly *is* a legislature for that purpose is already less straightforward, since the role of sub-national assemblies has to be taken into account, and contrasted with instances where the provision does not apply, such as municipal elections, elections in provinces with less-than-autonomous regulatory powers, as well as referendums. Interestingly, heads of state may qualify as legislatures as well, provided that they have sufficient autonomous powers to issue decrees or are sufficiently involved in the law-making process via the right to veto legislation or to dissolve parliament.[62] When it finally comes to the details of election rules, the margin of appreciation leaves plenty of room for constitutional diversity. The exact delimitation of a parliament's competences, and its relation with the government, are even further removed from the ambit of the relevant ECHR provisions, and the Strasbourg Court is not likely to develop any judicial activism in that respect. Of course the Council of Europe serves a different purpose than the European Union does, yet both are treaty-based organizations, and therefore start out with an inherent respect for their Member States' constitutional autonomy, including their parliamentarism.

The lessons that the EU can learn from the ECHR is, firstly, that it helps to identify which criteria are applied to identify national parliaments as addressees in the first place. The ECHR speaks of the 'choice of the legislature', which points to law-making competences and duly allows for an extension of the concept to sub-national law-makers and presidents. The EU, by contrast, has so far not produced any clear and coherent model setting out which national institutions are addressed, in which capacity, and for which purpose. The Commission in its White Paper on European Governance,[63] the Constitutional Convention in its various reports

58 *Santoro* v. *Italy* cited above, where the disenfranchisement had been unlawfully prolonged, see Kiiver (2004).

59 *Matthews* v. *UK*, ECtHR 18 February 1999, no. 24833/94 on Gibraltar voters at elections to the European Parliament.

60 '*The Greek Case*', European Commission for Human Rights 5 November 1969, Yearbook XII (1969).

61 '*The Greek Case*', cited above.

62 *Guliyev* v. *Azerbaijan* (admissibility), ECtHR 27 May 2004, no. 35584/02; *Boskoski* v. *Macedonia* (admissibility), ECtHR 2 September 2004, no. 11676/04. The Court did not yet qualify a head of state as part of the legislature, but it no longer categorically rules out such a possibility and examines presidential powers case by case.

63 European Commission (2001).

and treaty drafts, and COSAC, the half-yearly conference of European Affairs Committees of the national parliaments plus a European Parliament delegation, all employ the term 'the national parliaments' without any further elaboration. Yet as we have seen, treaty ratification, secondary law implementation, law-making under subsidiarity, popular representation, holding the government to account and communication with the citizenry are all functions or capacities which are unevenly distributed among a range of national and sub-national institutions. Where the EU does not make clear what exactly it wants, and from whom, and in what capacity, the involvement of national bodies is set on a dubious footing at the very outset: it is not prohibited as a political gesture, but it remains unconvincing as a measure with constitution-building implications.

The second lesson to learn from the ECHR is that even where national parliaments are addressed in a particular well-defined capacity, such as 'legislature', the national margin of appreciation tends to be wide. The width of the margin is, apart from the political questions of parliamentarism which do not lend themselves for judicial review, inherent to an exercise of addressing national parliaments that is conducted on an international-law basis.[64] The margin is secured to avoid unwelcome constitutional tensions between the Member States, which are all globally democratic but not homogenous, on the one hand, and the organizations of which they form part, on the other hand.

1.6.3 The constitutional autonomy of EU Member States

Indeed, when we turn to the existing instances of EU-level addressing of the national parliaments, evidence of the persisting constitutional autonomy of the Member States is clearly visible. From the EU's point of view, the governing principle would be constitutional neutrality as regards the Member States. The Amsterdam Protocol on the role of national parliaments was for instance the first legally binding EU treaty-level instrument to directly address the national parliaments of the Member States. It provided, *inter alia*, for improved access to information, and it introduced a six-weeks time delay between the tabling of an EU legislative proposal and the proposal's placement on the Council agenda. This was meant to enable national parliaments to scrutinize the proposal, to make their voice heard, and possibly to instruct their governments *ex ante*. Nevertheless, the Amsterdam Protocol started out, in the first recital of the preamble, as follows:

> Recalling that scrutiny by individual national parliaments of their own government in relation to the activities of the Union is a matter for the particular constitutional organisation and practice of each Member State,

---

64 See Kiiver (2004).

The Protocol on the role of national parliaments in the European Union that had been annexed to the Constitutional Treaty started out with an almost identical recital. Such a qualification is also contained in Article 9 of the final report of working group IV of the Constitutional Convention.[65] In 2003 COSAC adopted non-binding guidelines stipulating desirable minimum procedural requirements for national parliamentary scrutiny in European affairs,[66] yet these guidelines also start out by reciting the above statement from the Amsterdam Protocol. National parliamentarians held, nota bene, a plurality of seats in the Convention, and they retain a majority in COSAC. Apparently, national MPs themselves do not wish to be tied in their domestic activity to binding guidelines that are adopted at the European level.[67] Certainly where treaty provisions are agreed upon by the governments, and not MPs, it would mean a radical departure from the status quo if the EU would dictate how national parliaments should organize their scrutiny mechanisms.[68] Weatherill (2003a: 63) actually links the principle of constitutional autonomy in that respect to the principle of subsidiarity. Regulation at the lowest sensible level could equally apply to a matter of constitutional law: 'Curing the relatively poor participation of national and sub-national parliaments in discussions about EC legislative proposals, both at the level of substance and of available competence, is accordingly not a job sensibly addressed "top-down" – at least, not exclusively or even predominantly so'.

Again, the EU has long gone beyond the classical shape of an international organization. Accordingly, questions regarding the democratic legitimacy of the Member States' governments who act in legislative capacity at EU level may well be justified. The discussion of such questions may indeed result in internal constitutional adaptations.[69] After all, not only by way of the singular events of treaty ratification, but also by way of day-to-day scrutiny of the governments' stance in the Council do national parliaments confer democratic legitimacy to EU activities, or so the German Federal Constitutional Court famously held in its *Maastricht decision*.[70] However, in the light of the character of the EU, whether as Member States coming together, as an agent of the Member States or as an autonomous international organization interacting with its Member States, the notions of

65 European Convention (2002d).

66 COSAC (2003) Guidelines for relations between governments and parliaments on Community issues (instructive minimum standards) or 'Copenhagen parliamentary Guidelines', 2003/C 154/01. For a more detailed discussion of COSAC under the heading of inter-parliamentary co-operation see 4 *infra*.

67 Bengtson (2003), p. 5.

68 Raunio (2004), p. 6.

69 Rizzuto (2003), p. 10.

70 *Brunner* v. *The EU Treaty*, BVerfG 12 October 1993, English translation in [1994] 1 CMLR 57; see also Cullen (1995), p. 68.

constitutional neutrality, national autonomy and even subsidiarity should be consistently borne in mind. They help understand the shape of existing arrangements, and may provide guidelines in how to address national parliaments in EU context, if that is desired, in the most sensible manner.

1.7 Pragmatism versus constitutionalism

In the above paragraphs, we have addressed some fundamental concepts to serve as a basis for our present discussion. Firstly, 'the national parliaments' are not an easily identifiable, let alone a homogenous group of institutions. In fact, we may even question whether one can speak of a group at all. Parliaments, legislators, democratically elected assemblies, in whichever capacity they are addressed, are all as unique as are the countries and systems that they represent. Secondly, these institutions are indeed, as said, assemblies. They serve as focal points for public debate by polarization of political discourse, whether they in the end feature majoritarian or consensual tendencies. For these purposes, parliament or the lower chamber thereof is primarily a forum for government and opposition to compete in, and the government relies on its own parliamentary majority, whether alone, or in coalition with other political parties, or in *de facto* coalitions supporting a minority cabinet. Adversarial government-versus-parliament models, or depictions of parliaments as unitary bodies, do therefore hardly reflect political or constitutional reality. Thirdly, the addressing of national parliaments from within a treaty-based organization with an intergovernmental core, i.e. with prominent bargaining fora for national governments, is bound to provoke tensions between progressive integration, on the one hand, and notions of constitutional neutrality, on the other hand. Since the EU-level perspective taken is rather global, the employed standards are inevitably crude. Whenever 'the national parliaments' are called upon to become active at the European level, whether the exact purpose of the exercise is defined or not, false impressions of homogeneity and unitary independence of the addressees are easily conveyed. This is inherent to the piercing of the national constitutional veil of the Member States.

1.7.1 National organs in treaty provisions

Of course, one might respond, this would not be the first time the European Union would pierce the veil of national constitutional autonomy. In fact, we have already identified a number of instances where national institutions are assigned a European function, a European mandate so to speak, in spite of their heterogeneity. Take the regions that are represented in the Committee of the Regions: there is no uniform definition of what a regional entity should be like in order to qualify for representation in this EU body, and there are considerable differences between them, but it seems to work nonetheless; take the 'national authorities' that have the task of implementing EU framework legislation or substantive policies, such as competition policy, in the Member States: the term covers virtually anything, executive and regulatory bodies, and it works; or take the national judges – 'court or tribunal' in the broad wording of Article 234 EC – that are assigned the European task of enforcing EU law, and if necessary to refer preliminary questions to the European Court of Justice: there is considerable heterogeneity in the judicial systems of the Member States, some of the affected bodies are even outside the ordinary judicial hierarchy, and yet national courts are addressed on treaty level for a European purpose, and it works extraordinarily well. So why should a similar exercise with respect to the national parliaments be more problematic than these other cases, where national constitutional organs, heterogeneous and ill-defined as they may be, already successfully fulfil European functions by virtue of primary EU law? Why would 'the national parliaments' be any less valid a notion than 'the regions', 'the national authorities' or 'court or tribunal'?

The reason is, quite simply, that we are dealing here with fundamentally different types of exercises. To start with, 'national authorities' are addressed in treaty provisions as agents which are assigned the duty to reach a previously defined objective. They are to implement decisions or carry out policies that have been agreed upon at EU level. It is not decisive who they are, what matters is that they complete their task – for example the task of transposing a directive correctly and in time. National authorities are, in other words, addressed in an objective-oriented way. Since the task is of higher relevance than the identity of the executor, EU law can afford, or is even compelled, to keep an all-embracing approach to the national organs that are competent to fulfil that task. The same can be said as regards national courts. They too are addressed in an objective-oriented manner, namely with the task of uniform application of EU law in the Member States. The task of referring preliminary questions to the ECJ has to be seen in the light of that objective. Again, it is not so much important what exactly is a court or tribunal – that is easily resolved on a case-to-case basis – as long as EU law gets enforced. And again, EU law can afford to, or is compelled to, remain open to the diversity of the Member States' internal arrangements, in that case the organization of the judicial system.

The national parliaments, on the other hand, would in our context not enter the scene as agents with a European objective-oriented mandate like the ones of 'national authorities' or 'courts'. Certainly, when they implement directives, then parliaments do execute decisions in as far as they constitute a competent 'national authority'. Yet when they are addressed as political bodies, they do not execute. They are not intended to be passive. They are intended to act. There is no substantive task or policy target that they are given beforehand. What is given are *powers and privileges* to use at discretion for political purposes, which distinguishes parliaments from 'courts' and 'authorities' as a matter of principle, not degree. And at that point it truly is important who exactly is the recipient of such powers and privileges. The more significant the privilege, for example binding or non-binding veto powers like the ones included in the EU Constitutional Treaty, the greater the importance of clarity.

So what about the regions then? The Committee of the Regions is not equipped with an executive mandate either, it is also intended to be a political and policy-making actor, and there really are quite some differences between, say, a Dutch Province and a German *Land.* True. Yet here we have to carefully distinguish between the Committee of the Regions, on the one hand, and the regions themselves, on the other hand. The regions themselves are not addressed in EU context, they are not given powers or privileges. They remain where they are. Powers are given instead to the Committee of the Regions, which is an EU institution. It is not the regions that are involved in the EU legislative process, but the Committee. Yet the Committee does consist of regional representatives? True again. They are, however, not directly recruited by treaty provisions either. The regional representatives are, according to Article 263 EC, nominated by the national governments. In other words, it is left to the discretion of the governments to decide, subject to a Council vote, what in their own country would qualify as a region, and to staff what are essentially national delegations with a fixed number of seats to another EU body.

There are ideas to create a 'Third Chamber' at EU level comprising national MPs, to act next to the European Parliament and the Council, and we will discuss that proposal later on.[71] Such a new chamber might indeed resemble the Committee of the Regions in the form of its recruitment: the governments get the task of filling a number of seats with what they consider to be national parliamentarians, according to their own constitutional arrangements. The same has essentially happened at the staffing of the European Convention, where the Member States (and candidate countries) each were to envoy two representatives of their national parliament. As long as the addressing of national parliaments does not take place in such a manner, however, the parliaments would have to be addressed directly.

To be sure, ill-crafted treaty provisions that clumsily intrude into national constitutional arrangements would certainly not bring about a collapse of the internal orders of the Member States. Yet the pragmatic solutions that they necessitate can have bizarre effects, and sometimes not even pragmatism is of any help. Suffice to point out three examples from the time when the Member States were still anticipating a swift entry into force of the Constitutional Treaty.

1.7.2 The Constitutional Treaty precedent

The Constitutional Treaty project has shown that the EU is capable of addressing national parliaments explicitly, and to furnish them with rights and privileges.

71 See 5 *infra*.

The project has also shown what kind of implementation measures we may expect when national parliaments are addressed in a vague and open-ended manner.

As a first example, we may recall that the early warning system against breaches of subsidiarity under the EU Constitutional Treaty was based on the counting of incoming complaints from the national parliaments, and the verification whether the number of complaints reached one-third or one-quarter, depending on the policy area, of the votes distributed. Two votes are distributed to each national parliament, which would have to be shared out in the case of bicameral parliaments.[72] The Belgian government inserted a Declaration in the Final Act to the effect that it considered the autonomous regional and language community assemblies in Belgium to form part of a composite national legislature, together with the two chambers of the federal parliament.[73] That is perfectly in line with the Belgian understanding of constitutional balance between the federal level and the autonomous entities, and it is also in line with the case-law of the European Court of Human Rights which, as we have noted earlier, equally treats the Belgian regional and communal assemblies as component parts of the national legislature.[74] This approach is however not quite in line with what the Convention apparently had had in mind, namely that each Member State have one national parliament which in turn should have either one or two chambers, not more. Regional assemblies were not intended to get a vote of their own, which we can deduce *a contrario* from the fact that regional assemblies are explicitly mentioned not as bodies that should wield a veto power, but as bodies that should be consulted by the national parliaments as the latter would deem fit.[75] What now if the Flemish Council files a complaint, considering itself a chamber of the national parliament, but the Belgian federal parliament, the national parliament proper, does not? How to distribute two votes among two chambers of the federal parliament, plus three regions, plus three language communities? The Belgian Council of State, prompted to give advice, was not quite sure either.[76]

Our second example also concerns the subsidiarity enforcement system, namely the envisaged jurisdiction of the European Court of Justice to rule in annulment actions on the basis of breaches of subsidiarity. Such annulment actions could be 'brought in accordance with the rules laid down in Article III-365 of the Constitution [the successor of Article 230 EC] by Member States, or notified by them in accordance with their legal order on behalf of their national Parliament or a

---

72 TCE on the application of the principles of subsidiarity and proportionality, see 7.3 *infra*.
73 TCE Declaration No. 49 by the Kingdom of Belgium on national parliaments.
74 See 1.5.2 *supra*.
75 Article 6 TCE Protocol on the application of the principles of subsidiarity and proportionality.
76 Belgian Council of State, Advice 37.954/AV, 37.970/AV, 37.977/AV, 37.978 AV of 2005.

chamber of it'.[77] In other words, Member States would still be privileged applicants for annulment actions, and they, that is their governments, may initiate proceedings either on their own initiative or on behalf of their national parliament. National parliaments themselves are not awarded *locus standi*, so they would have to request their governments to bring, in the name of the Member State, an action on their behalf. Since no further details are provided, it would be left to the Member States to regulate how exactly a national parliament could do that. In May 2005, the German government and the opposition parties struck a deal about statutes accompanying the ratification by Germany of the Constitutional Treaty, and they also duly agreed on the implementation of the above judicial enforcement mechanism: the right for the *Bundestag* to bring annulment actions against EU legislation before the ECJ on grounds of subsidiarity would be treated in analogy to the right of one-third of the *Bundestag* to subject domestic statutes to judicial review by the German Constitutional Court.[78] The government would thus bring an ECJ action on behalf of one-third of the *Bundestag*. Judicial review would be turned into a minority right. Of course the German government is free to start court proceedings on behalf of whomever it likes, as long as it represents the Member State as a whole. Still we are left to wonder whether 'on behalf of their national Parliament or a chamber of it' is the same thing as 'on behalf of a parliamentary minority'. By the way, the confusion works both ways: while the German opposition can apparently count on the government's goodwill, the UK House of Lords was initially very sceptical whether the British government could be persuaded to bring ECJ actions on its behalf.[79] That means that an institution which otherwise enjoys a status as a 'national parliament', for instance being represented in COSAC, would be precluded from exercising rights of indirect actions for judicial review.

Our third example concerns the veto right under the passerelle clause: under the Constitutional Treaty as adopted by the Convention and the IGC, all national parliaments would have to be informed beforehand if the European Council intended to move from unanimity to qualified majority voting, or to move to co-decision with the European Parliament, in a given policy area, and the move could be prevented if any one national parliament filed an objection: 'If a national Parliament makes known its opposition within six months of the date of such notification, the European decision referred to in paragraphs 1 or 2 [authorization of a change of procedure] shall not be adopted'.[80] Government and opposition in Germany

---

77 Article 8 TCE Protocol on the application of the principles of subsidiarity and proportionality, see further 5, *infra*.

78 Article 93 (1) 2 German Basic Law; the difference in the Constitutional Treaty compromise is that one-third of the Bundestag can only initiate an action if that is not overruled by the other two-thirds, see Heute im Bundestag release of 10 May 2005.

79 Statement of the Lords delegation during the 32nd COSAC, November 2004.

80 Article IV-444 (3) TCE.

agreed, in the same deal as mentioned above, to apply this veto in a way that would be essentially modelled after the domestic distribution of powers and the domestic legislative process: the *Bundesrat*, the representation of the *Länder* governments, could file a veto against the application of the passerelle clause at EU level if a matter concerns exclusive *Länder* competence; the *Bundestag* could do so in matters of exclusive federal competence; in all other matters a *Bundesrat* veto could be overruled by the *Bundestag* with a corresponding majority, with an absolute *Bundestag* majority overriding an absolute *Bundesrat* majority and a two-thirds majority in the *Bundestag* overriding a two-thirds majority in the *Bundesrat*. Again, since the Constitutional Treaty itself provided no details, a solution had to be found how to take account of the fact that two chambers of the same parliament are rarely co-equal. And again, we are left to wonder whether 'a national Parliament makes known its opposition', which is a formula that confers fairly unambiguous powers upon national institutions, is the same thing as 'a national Parliament makes known its opposition, provided that domestic law does not prevent it from doing so'.

1.7.3 National parliaments as a Community concept

All this brings us to two important remarks. First, it is one thing to invite national parliaments to show more interest in EU affairs; it is another thing to throw formal intervention powers at them without defining who exactly is addressed. Leaving it to the Member States, that is the governments, to decide what in their system is a national parliament may be appropriate for political gestures, but not for the distribution of votes or vetoes. We have seen that open-ended phrasing can lead to situations where Member States interpret 'national parliaments' as meaning 'regional parliaments', or 'national parliament' as meaning 'a parliamentary minority', or 'national parliaments using explicit treaty powers' as meaning 'national parliaments using explicit treaty powers only as deemed domestically appropriate'. There might of course be a fundamental objection to the raising of all these concerns: no matter what academics say about them, or so one might contend, in practice these arrangements could work nonetheless. Member States will find appropriate solutions, and time will tell about the real viability of the adopted designs. At this point it becomes important to emphasize again the target of our critique. First of all it would be useful to specify what defenders of pragmatic approaches exactly mean by 'work', as opposed to 'work as planned'. This is more than just a matter of legal aesthetics. A polity that adopts or reorganizes a decision-making process and codifies it in a binding and hard-to-amend document like a treaty would miss the entire point of codification if it left the actual rules open. The helpful thing about a written 'Constitution' is after all that it becomes clear beyond doubt which actors play what role in a legislative process. As EU constitution-building presently develops, however, Europeans will not even be able to say for sure how many national parliamentary veto points there are in their polity: depending on the Member States it might be any number between two dozen and about forty. Still, our discussion is not even so much to refute the 'workability' of arrangements in the first place, but primarily to contribute to analytical sobriety and intellectual preparation that will allow us to explain why something 'works' if it does, and if not, why not, and why a system got adopted if its way of application was unpredictable from the very beginning.

In the end, the only sensible solution would be to make the term 'national parliaments' a Community concept. That would limit the constitutional autonomy of the Member States, since the definition of what qualifies as a national parliament would be fixed at EU level, but it would prevent the Member States from opening the floodgates and spreading rights among, for instance, regional assemblies or opposition parties, and also from closing the gates to, say, upper chambers for domestic constitutional or political reasons. Instead, Member States would have to conform to an autonomous EU standard, namely that there be one parliament per country, each with probably up to two chambers. In fact, the most welcome option would be for the EU to produce an exhaustive list, an appendix to the relevant rights-conferring instrument, calling the intended recipients of rights and privileges by name: Sweden – *Riksdag*; Denmark – *Folketing*. Such an authoritative list does not exist as of yet. It would serve two important purposes. First, it would make visible the choices that the EU would have to make in taking some bodies on board although they do not necessarily deserve it, such as the non-parliamentary German *Bundesrat* or the unelected Lords in the UK, while at the same time keeping other bodies out while they actually have the better credentials as legislatures, such as indeed regional assemblies. Second, and that would be a most positive effect, it would require some serious thinking on the part of the authors of the relevant list. It would even open a precious opportunity to 'back out' of the exercise if the discovered problems turn out to be prohibitive and its effects undesirable. True, can-do pragmatism and compromise-finding characterizes large parts of the European integration process; yet when it comes to constructing and re-designing constitutional arrangements by virtue of treaty provisions, a minimum of conceptual preparation is surely not too much to ask.

As a second remark – and we are still talking about theoretical, not so much practical considerations which will follow shortly – we should note that even political invitations for the national parliaments to become more active in EU affairs bear a character of artificiality. Addressing and strengthening national parliaments, certainly by inserting respective treaty provisions, but also by way of non-binding EU-level rhetoric, is an artificial exercise in EU context in the sense that it requires a conscious choice. Parliaments do not represent the Member States externally themselves, and they therefore initially play no formal role in the EU of their own. To demand a greater role for the national parliaments of the EU Member States is then, essentially, to demand of the parliaments a greater activity than what a standard international-law framework would require, and more than what most of them seem ready to develop when left on their own.

These demands can result in practical measures taken in a top-down manner at EU level. Thus, the national parliaments can be effectively courted by explicitly mentioning them in European treaties, which at least symbolically upgrades their status from implicitly affected institutions to parts of a larger constitutional architecture. They can further be propped up with direct supplies of information. While the Amsterdam Protocol for instance merely obliged the national governments to forward Commission proposals to their parliaments, the Constitutional Treaty Protocol stipulated direct distribution of documents from the Commission to the national parliaments.[81] Whether an increased flow of paper from Brussels is really beneficial to parliamentary control is again another question.[82] The intention is however, on face value, to facilitate parliamentary scrutiny. The national parliaments can further be courted and stimulated by submitting to them reports in order to support political scrutiny of the activities of Europol and Eurojust, and by assigning them direct and collective formal powers in the EU decision-making process, next to their governments, such as the ones devised for the subsidiarity early warning system. By notifying and consulting them before important EU decisions are being adopted, such as the application of the passerelle clause, national parliaments are upgraded in their status as well. Each national parliament would be able to prevent the application of the passerelle under the relevant Constitutional Treaty provision, which in various ways is even more significant than the early warning system would be: as said, without any clear definition of what qualifies as a national parliament, national institutions would be given a binding veto with respect to decisions in the European Council. This veto would nota bene not coincide with the veto that a parliament would have anyway if it had to ratify a treaty amendment in the ordinary procedure.[83] In some Member States, European treaty amendments are subject to referendum, or subject to approval by special majority, or are in turn not subject to approval by senates. This would be a genuinely new power stipulated by a treaty.

The national parliaments could potentially be artificially propped up even more, for instance by making their intervention powers more binding or by awarding them independent standing as privileged applicants before the ECJ.[84] Their role can further be enhanced by involving them in new EU institutions comprising national MPs, or by letting them, instead of the European Parliament, elect or confirm the EU Commission.[85] Even when one measure or another proves only

---

81 See Article 2 of the Amsterdam Protocol respectively Articles 1 and 2 of the TCE Protocol on the role of national parliaments in the European Union.

82 Weatherill (2003a).

83 Apart from this being a negative veto power, as opposed to the positive affirmation required in ratification procedures, see De Witte (2004).

84 See 7.5.2 *infra*.

85 See 6 *infra*.

to have a marginal effect, or in fact to amount to little more than window-dressing, it remains a form of artificial intervention which must have an ultimate objective, namely the reaching of a desired situation to replace the current situation.

Let us be clear about this: artificiality is not *a priori* a particularly bad thing. A toy factory is for instance an artificial construction as well. It does not grow by itself, it has to be built, and it is by no means objectionable just because of that. But before we build one, we have to be sure whether it makes sense to do so if we already have one; or whether it makes sense to build one with a defective design; or whether it makes sense to have one if it ruins the landscape and pollutes the environment. It is all a matter of planning, of identifying who would profit from it and who would lose out, and in particular of estimating whether the anticipated positive effects as put forward by different planners outweigh a measure's negative side-effects. This is what needs to be carried out with respect to national parliaments, too. Providing them with stimulus, facilities and intervention powers in the EU can produce effects that may appear desirable from different points of view. The question is whether the negative side-effects will outweigh the benefits, and whether any benefits can be reaped at all, again depending on the viewpoint.

1.8 Conclusion

To briefly conclude our theoretical considerations, next time the EU makes any constitution-building leaps forward, we would be wise to take into account that distribution of formal powers by way of treaty provisions requires sober preparation, not just untamed ambition. Otherwise provisions end up in treaties, which are after all the primary sources of EU law, that would in fact be better placed in a European Council resolution or a White Paper. Objections that the devised mechanisms might work nonetheless are acceptable if no attention is paid to methodological treaty-drafting quality; the present critique does not juxtapose 'will work' and 'will not work' anyway, it just raises the question whether designs will work *as planned*, whether there is a plan at all, and whether the absence of a clear plan fits with the idea of having codified rules in a written constitutional document. Assigning EU duties to broadly defined national organs remains absolutely feasible, as long as it just matters that the job is done, not who does it; but assigning EU powers and privileges to political bodies that are as heterogeneous, and as difficult to single out as 'the national parliaments' requires more than just the mentioning of a catch-all term in a treaty. To clarify who is the intended recipient of powers and privileges, up to veto rights, the soundest measure to take – if that were deemed desirable in the first place, if only to know with a minimum degree of certainty how many veto players there are – would be to draw up an exhaustive list of beneficiaries. Omitting that would mean to miss out on a good opportunity for reflection about who is addressed, in what capacity and for what purpose, as well as an opportunity to step back from the exercise altogether; apart from that, open-ended distribution of powers to ill-defined national institutions is just poor legal craftsmanship.

In any event, whether by way of treaty provision or otherwise, we need to be aware that addressing the national parliaments in an EU context is an artificial exercise, that it requires a conscious effort. It may be done and it can be done, but that does not necessarily mean that it should be. Cost and achievable benefits have to be weighed against each other, depending on what exactly is sought. If we bear this in mind, it will also be much easier to remain sober when it comes to treaty drafting.

2 European scrutiny in a comparative perspective

2.1 Introduction

The individual role of national parliaments of holding their own governments to account for their EU policy is, notwithstanding direct collective parliamentary contributions, the only way for national parliaments to have an impact, albeit an indirect one, on the substance of EU legislation. The basis for this form of involvement in the EU decision-making process is the link of ministerial accountability towards parliament, or at least its lower chamber. As in a parliamentary system the cabinet relies on parliamentary confidence, or tolerance, to stay in office, parliament is able to supervise the executive, to conduct inquiries, to question and to steer ministers. The ultimate threat remains a motion of no-confidence against a minister, the Prime Minister or the cabinet as a whole, with varying procedural requirements, depending on the applicable constitutional rules. In the context of domestic legislation, parliament is further able to have a direct impact on policies in its capacity as law-maker by drawing up, amending, passing or rejecting bills, again subject to domestic law and practice. Since this option is unavailable with regard to binding European legislation which is proposed by the Commission and eventually (co-)adopted by the Council, parliamentary devices to sift EU legislative proposals, to scrutinize and to instruct the government *ex ante,* prior to the adoption of such legislation, gain added importance. Once the act is adopted, it becomes binding upon the Member State, whether or not it requires national transposition measures. Still the conduct of the minister in the Council may become subject to parliamentary criticism *ex post*. While the policy outcome is definitive, ministers may be sanctioned for their having supported it, or for their not having prevented it. So far the theoretical picture which, if it actually coincided with reality, would make our whole discussion more or less obsolete. However, the outsider position and the information gap behind the government and its bureaucracy, but also the sheer lack of interest in European affairs among many national MPs, as we shall see, puts constraints on national parliamentary scrutiny in that field. Nevertheless, a gradual procedural and institutional adaptation to the realities of EU membership within the national parliaments is discernible.

How are national parliaments then dealing with European affairs? This study does not purport to provide any exhaustive comparative or empirical analysis of the behaviour of the parliaments of twenty-five EU Member States, even if that were adequately possible within the scope of our discussion. On the other hand, it is our stated objective to question the validity and internal consistency of demands to the effect that national parliaments should sharpen their scrutiny mechanisms and become more active in European affairs. For that purpose we must identify the existing national variations in European scrutiny, and the underlying causes for these variations. This is where a brief comparative overview will indeed be useful to provide a factual background. In line with our preliminary caveats, the overview is to show that scrutiny mechanisms indeed differ from one Member State parliament to another, and the reasons why they differ are to help us estimate the effects of stimulating measures in that respect. We shall hereafter discuss the existing scrutiny mechanisms in the national parliaments under the following overlapping thematic categorizations: the time at which scrutiny sets in (chapter 2.2), the relative centralization of scrutiny (chapter 2.3), the methods of government influencing (chapter 2.4), the legal basis for scrutiny (chapter 2.5), and finally the relative 'strength' of national parliaments at European scrutiny (chapter 2.6), followed by a discussion of what are the factors that shape scrutiny practice in one way or another.

2.2 European scrutiny: *ex ante* and *ex post*

The term 'European scrutiny' covers a broad range of national parliamentary activities. In the context of the EU legislative process, but also in other EU decision-making instances, to create a first thread of reference for our discussion, we may distinguish between scrutiny *ex ante* and scrutiny *ex post.* The former sets in before an EU act becomes adopted, while the latter implies scrutiny in retrospect. Scrutiny *ex ante* firstly includes the receipt and the sifting of EU-related documentation by a national parliament. The primary focus in comparative studies tends to lie on the consideration of the Commission's legislative proposals, because of the amount, regularity and legal impact of these documents. Yet EU-related documentation may not be limited to that. It may also include White and Green Papers and the Commission's annual legislative programme, the Council's common positions, draft Council resolutions, resolutions of the European Parliament and conciliation committee drafts, draft acts or strategies under the Common Foreign and Security Policy, draft decisions of the Ecofin Council of the members of the euro-zone, papers related to the Open Method of Co-ordination such as the Lisbon agenda, draft texts from the European Council or IGCs, draft treaty amendments, agreements with third countries and documents related to EU enlargement. Wherever the broad term 'European affairs' is used in the present discussion, it should in principle be taken to include all these aspects. The important criterion for a 'European affair' here, however, since the immediate context is parliamentary oversight over the governments, is that it should be a question of EU policy to be ultimately decided by the national governments in the Council or the European Council.[1]

1 Decisions of the European Court of Justice where they, for instance, have an impact on the interpretation of EU legislation and the corresponding national implementation measures, may of course be qualified as a 'European affair' as well.

In addition to documents which originate from the EU institutions themselves, explanatory memorandums provided by the individual government, and annexed to EU documents to help determine the national standpoint, may also fall under EU-related documents to be sifted by a national parliament.

Following this sifting of documents, an interaction process with the government may follow. This includes the invitation, or the summoning, of ministers before the parliament or its committees. Here the minister may be asked to disclose information. It is also at this stage that a national parliament has its chance to influence the government, and thus the national standpoint to be adopted and defended in the Council. Influencing can take the form of parliamentary resolutions or opinions, with a varying weight ranging from recommendations to binding instructions or mandates, depending on the matter and the parliament at hand. Parliamentarians may also make heard their opinion in a more informal manner, during or following or actually even preceding deliberations with a Brussels-bound minister, in or outside a committee.

European scrutiny *ex post* then covers the questioning of ministers, or the government as a whole, after their participation in the adoption of EU decisions. This may lead to criticism or even sanctions in case of dissatisfaction. The consideration of annual or half-yearly government reports on the state of affairs in EU politics would also fall under scrutiny *ex post*, since the substantive decisions will already have been taken. We may note that scrutiny *ex post* would fit the term 'accountability' more accurately, as it implies a calling to account for actions taken, yet such retrospective scrutiny is no longer treated as the only aspect of accountability in a broader sense.[2]

The various stages and aspects of scrutiny sketched above are connectable to various degrees. Theoretically, several combinations are possible in national parliamentary scrutiny practice. Thus, a parliament that systematically reviews EU legislative proposals, then deliberates with Brussels-bound ministers and enforces a reporting back after they return to hold them to account, engages in full *ex ante* scrutiny and *ex post* oversight. A parliament that sifts proposals but does not systematically engage in a dialogue with the minister, or does not otherwise make known its views, focuses on document scrutiny only. A parliament that focuses on oral deliberations with the minister but does not carry out prior in-depth sifting of documents only scrutinizes government policies in a narrowed sense, and is less informed. A parliament that leaves the pre-legislative phase of decision-making unattended, but demands explanations from the government afterwards, misses out on the *ex ante* aspect of parliamentary control. A parliament that does engage in *ex ante* scrutiny but does not demand any reporting back on the outcome of Council meetings misses the *ex post* part. Lack of activity during both stages

---

2 Harlow (2002), p. 10.

consequently leads to absent parliamentary oversight. It would be difficult to find cases where certain aspects of oversight would lack completely. The degree to which the different forms and stages of oversight are present in a system is nevertheless crucial for establishing the degree of parliamentary control, present in its strongest form where all scrutiny aspects are put into practice. The expression 'strong' in the context of parliamentary scrutiny has of course something of a bias already, as it bears an evaluative implication ultimately based on a government-versus-parliament dichotomy. Nevertheless, we cannot ignore that effective control under checks and balances would for instance not derive from mere *ex post* information of a parliament. Indeed, a 'non-informed, non ex ante participating national parliament would be unlikely to dismiss its minister for matters of which it is ignorant'.[3]

The difference between *ex ante* and *ex post* approach to European scrutiny became prominently visible after the 1973 enlargement of the EEC. The national parliaments of the original Six had adapted differently to European integration, as some of them had set up a special European Affairs Committee or insisted on the right to be informed about EEC developments, but they mostly confined their oversight to the consideration of annual government reports.[4] The mechanisms established in the UK House of Commons and the Danish *Folketing* however put an emphasis on *ex ante* oversight, and thereby went beyond what was available to the parliaments of the Six. Indeed, the newcomers entered the EEC with a more sceptical view of ever-closer union and with stronger parliamentary traditions.[5] In addition, while the Six had already gotten used to EEC membership, for the newcomers it may have come as a 'shock of sudden competence restriction'.[6]

In the event, the UK Commons set up a system of systematic document sifting based on a report by Sir John Foster and inspired by the established practice of the consideration of domestic bills.[7] A special European Scrutiny Committee would filter out the most important pieces of incoming legislative proposals from Brussels, and refer them for debate and the possible adoption of a resolution to the floor. The mechanism was upgraded in 1980, when the UK Commons passed a Scrutiny Reserve Resolution which barred ministers from giving consent to measures in the Council if Parliament had not yet completed its scrutiny. Meanwhile, it was the Danish *Folketing* that became the 'unique archetype of a parliament' in its EEC-related control system.[8] Immediately after Denmark's EEC accession, a system was established that forced ministers to orally submit their position for upcoming

3 Smismans (1998), p. 57.
4 Sasse (1975), p. 78 *et seq.*; Judge (1995), p. 82 *et seq.*
5 Judge (1995); see Niblock (1971), p. 98 on the expected adaptation of the Commons.
6 Sasse (1975), p. 101.
7 See on the UK: Norton (1995c); Rogers (1995); Miller/Ware (1996); Munro (1996); Cygan (1998); Carter (2001); Cygan (2001).
8 Maurer/Wessels (2001), p. 20.

Council meetings for *ex ante* approval to the parliament's Market Relations Committee. The instructions they would receive there were, and still are, binding upon them in the sense of a parliamentary mandate for negotiations.[9] The Danish model remains the most prominent, and most controversial oversight mechanism to date, although not necessarily the most inclusive one, as we will see hereafter.

2.3 The committee system

Our second thread in this overview concerns the procedural and institutional setting for EU-related national parliamentary oversight, namely the question which committees are involved in the scrutiny process. The European Affairs Committees usually attract most attention in this context, yet the picture cannot be complete without also including the sectoral committees, such as the ones for agriculture, legal affairs, environment and economic affairs. The rationale for setting up a European Affairs Committee is essentially the same as the rationale for setting up a committee system in the first place, namely sectoral specialization of MPs to address the information advantage of the government over policies which have become too complex for a plenary debate to handle.[10] Indeed, all of the national parliaments of the EU Member States have by now established a European Affairs Committee, or assigned a pre-existing committee such a function, to deal with the effects of European integration. However we should note that the role, status, competence and composition of these European Affairs Committees differs greatly from one national parliament to another,[11] which has to do with the procedures under which they operate.

The question arises which committees should play the predominant role in the treatment of European affairs, and what exactly is a 'European affair'. Typically, the bigger integration matters with a horizontal and cross-departmental scope fall within the immediate ambit of European Affairs Committees. Such matters may include European Councils and IGCs, institutional reform of the EU, the EU Charter of Fundamental Rights, or the enlargement process. To some extent these matters may overlap with what would otherwise be plain foreign affairs. The more intriguing question concerns the day-to-day EU legislative process. Thus, is a Commission proposal on safety standards in the agricultural sector a matter for the European Affairs Committee, due to its origin, or a matter for the committee for agriculture, due to its content?

---

9 Fitzmaurice (1979), see for further details and references on the Danish model 2.5 and 2.6 *infra*.

10 Norton (1995a), p. 7 *et seq*.

11 See Norton (1995), Maurer/Wessels (2001), Travers *et al*. (2003).

In a centralized system of scrutiny, all or most EU-related matters would fall within the competence of a European Affairs Committee, where EU-related expertise is accumulated. The already mentioned prototype for such a system is the Market Relations Committee, today called Europe Committee, of the parliament of Denmark.[12] The Committee, which receives extensive EU-related documentation and explanatory memorandums from the government, controls Brussels-bound ministers by tying them to negotiation mandates for subsequent Council meetings. Usually on the Friday before a Council meeting, the competent minister or state secretary appears before the Committee, and orally outlines a draft mandate on the basis of which the government is intending to negotiate. During the deliberations that follow, a minister might adapt his or her proposal so as to ensure that it is not disapproved of. The mandate is passed by tacit approval, and the absence of a majority against it is noted without formal voting by the Committee's chairman at the end of each round of discussion. The mandate is binding upon the minister politically, but is in practice so authoritative that it entails a quasi-legally binding instruction.[13] If in the Council a compromise would require deviations from a given mandate, the minister seeks to obtain a new mandate, and the European Affairs Committee may hold a special meeting for that purpose. After the Council meeting the minister re-appears before the Committee and reports back on the matter decided, as well as on his or her own line of negotiation.

When Sweden and Austria acceded to the EU in 1995, their parliaments derived inspiration from the Danish model, which was undoubtedly the strongest existing, and adopted a centralized briefing routine as well. The Swedish *Riksdag* now also features a European Affairs Committee which receives Commission proposals with explanatory memorandums from the government,[14] and which issues politically binding negotiating mandates to ministers on Fridays before Council meetings.[15] The lower chamber of the Austrian parliament, the *Nationalrat*, has assigned comparable functions to its European Affairs Main Committee and a Standing Subcommittee for European Affairs.[16] The Committees may adopt resolutions which are binding politically, or pass formal mandates which are binding legally. The Latvian parliament has adopted a centralized Danish-style model of oversight

12 See on Denmark: Fitzmaurice (1979); Arter (1995); Laursen (1995); Albæk Jensen (1996); Fitzmaurice (1999); Laursen (2001); Danish Folketing (2002); Finnish Eduskunta/Swedish Riksdag/Danish Folketing (2002).

13 Raunio (1999), p. 191.

14 Chapter 10, Article 2 Swedish Riksdag Act.

15 See on Sweden: Fitzmaurice (1999); Hegeland (2000); Hegeland (2001); Swedish Riksdag (2001); Finnish Eduskunta/Swedish Riksdag/Danish Folketing (2002); Hegeland/Neuhold (2002); Swedish Riksdag (2002).

16 See on Austria: Urbantschitsch (1998), p. 40 *et seq.*; Blümel/Neuhold (2001); Hegeland/Neuhold (2002).

as well, including politically binding mandates.[17] This has also been done by the Hungarian parliament,[18] and the Slovak parliament intends to follow the same centralized model as well.[19]

The advantages of centralization of scrutiny, especially where the European Affairs Committee is competent under all three EU Pillars, is the efficiency of the deliberation process. Arguably, the sectoral committees lack the necessary EU-related expertise, and their working methods are ill-suited to fulfil the special demands of monitoring EU-level negotiations, in particular confidentiality and speed.[20] The disadvantage of centralization, however, is the lack of institutionalized input from sectoral specialists.[21] The European Affairs Committees tend to be generalist, and miss out on technical expertise. To tackle this shortcoming, the Danish parliament turned to a parallel information system, distributing documentation among the sectoral committees as well, and allowing the European Affairs Committee to consult them.[22] In anticipation to the early warning system for the principle of subsidiarity, the European Affairs Committee has announced its intention to also consult the sectoral committees, but only if it finds itself that a Commission proposal may violate the principle of subsidiarity.[23] Apart from the consultation of the sectoral committees, specialist input is sought via overlapping committee membership, as the European Affairs Committee's seventeen members and eleven substitutes, who are often high-ranking MPs such as ex-ministers and party spokesmen, tend to be active on other committees as well. The Swedish *Riksdag* also stipulates overlapping committee membership, it obliges the sectoral committees to follow EU legislative developments on their own,[24] and invites them to refer reports for debate to the floor or to the European Affairs Committee. The European Affairs Committee of the Austrian *Nationalrat*, unlike the other committees which have closed membership, is open to participation by any MP who

17 See Articles 185.3 and 185.4 Latvian Saeima Rules of Procedure.

18 COSAC Secretariat (2005a), p. 43.

19 COSAC Secretariat (2005a), p. 65.

20 Von der Vring (1996), p. 403.

21 Critical of centralization: Ramstedt (2000).

22 CFSP matters may fall in the competence of the foreign affairs committee, while the Third Pillar is treated by the European Affairs Committee and the legal affairs committee. Following the Folketing European Affairs Committee Report of 20 May 1994, the affected standing committees were to be concurrently informed on EU matters concerning health, environment, labour market and consumer policy, and the scope of information has been extended to all policy areas following the Folketing European Affairs Committee Report of 27 December 1996.

23 Folketing European Affairs Committee paper of 12 November 2004 prepared for the 32nd COSAC meeting of 22-23 November 2004, see also COSAC Secretariat (2004).

24 Chapter 10, Article 3 Swedish Riksdag Act.

is interested.[25] Nevertheless, largely due to a lack of interest among the sectoral committees and their marginalized status,[26] European scrutiny remains effectively centralized in all of the above systems.

To combine the advantages of centralized scrutiny with the advantages of sectoral input, the parliament of Finland has, upon EU accession in 1995, devised its own model of oversight. While following the basic Danish approach of centralized briefing, mandating and debriefing of ministers, the Finnish Grand Committee competent for European affairs delegates the practical scrutiny work to the sectoral committees.[27] EU documentation and explanatory memorandums are forwarded by the Speaker to the affected sectoral committees, which discuss the matter with priority and then submit a report with their recommendations to the Grand Committee. The Grand Committee considers the incoming reports, and summarizes and mediates in case reports are submitted by more than one sectoral committee. On that basis the Grand Committee deliberates with Brussels-bound ministers and it may impose a politically binding mandate. This system of delegated scrutiny and centralized briefing enjoys an increasingly good reputation, as it seems to outperform the Danish model, long seen to be an archetype of oversight, in terms of broad parliamentary involvement. Finns are actively promoting 'their' model abroad.[28] Indeed, several of the parliaments of the new Member States of 2004 have adopted a Finnish model for their European scrutiny system. Thus, the parliament of Estonia features a European Affairs Committee, which already consists of at least one member of each of the sectoral committees, and which also receives opinions from the sectoral committees to serve as a basis for deliberations with Brussels-bound ministers on Fridays. The Committee is equally entitled to issue politically binding negotiating mandates.[29] The National Assembly of Slovenia has endorsed the Finnish model of oversight as well;[30] the sectoral committees of the Lithuanian parliament consider incoming EU documents and then send them to

---

25 Urbantschitsch (1998), p. 43.

26 Ramstedt (2000); Hegeland (2001); Blümel/Neuhold (2001); Laursen (2001).

27 Article 96 of the Finnish Constitution; see on Finland: Jääskinen (1997); Fitzmaurice (1999); Boedecker (2000); Raunio (2001); Finnish Eduskunta/Swedish Riksdag/Danish Folketing (2002); Hegeland/Neuhold (2002).

28 E.g. Raunio (2001), p. 197; Kiljunen *et al.* (2002); Gisela Stuart, the chairperson of the Convention's Working Group on national parliaments, paid a visit to the Finnish parliament upon the Grand Committee's invitation, see European Convention (2002d), p. 2; Brown (2003), p. 6. The Italian lower Chamber conducted an experimental session in February 2000, where the sectoral committees examined the Government's annual EU report, submitted their conclusions to the European Affairs Committee, which in turn drafted a resolution that was adopted by the plenary, see Swedish Riksdag (2001), p. 22.

29 Articles 152.1 to 152.5 Estonian Riigikogu Rules of Procedure.

30 Vehar (2004), but see COSAC Secretariat (2005a), p. 67.

the European Affairs Committee with red, yellow, and green cover sheets, depending on the relevance they have estimated, to help prioritize the scrutiny there.[31] Even the parliament of the Netherlands, an old Member State, has in anticipation to the early warning system switched to a Finnish model of scrutiny in monitoring the application of the principle of subsidiarity. A freshly established joint committee of both chambers, which is in itself an institutional innovation, will receive reports from the sectoral committees as regards compliance of Commission proposals with the principle of subsidiarity, and will then draft reasoned opinions for adoption in the chambers where appropriate.[32]

The other extreme, opposed to centralization of European scrutiny in a European Affairs Committee, even if the substantive work is delegated, would be decentralized parliamentary treatment. Following the slogan 'Europe is everywhere', and considering the fact that EU proposals will eventually become domestic law, the appropriate locus for scrutiny in that field would simply be the affected sectoral committees. Thus, a Commission proposal concerning agriculture would fall within the competence of the committee for agriculture, just like a domestic bill in that sector would. We should however see the term decentralization somewhat more critically than that. While decentralization may be understood positively as an active choice, it may also simply mean a lack of co-ordination and of procedural adaptation to EU membership. Firstly, the reason for centralizing scrutiny in the first place is to establish an efficiently working parliamentary liaison body to communicate with the government. Such a device would be absent in cases of decentralization, where sectoral committees are left on their own to prioritize European affairs or not. The more appropriate term would then not be decentralization, but fragmentation of European scrutiny.[33] Secondly, where European affairs are left almost entirely to the sectoral committees, the typical observation is that the affected MPs neglect EU proposals, and instead keep concentrating on domestic bills.[34] As a result, European scrutiny is largely absent or, paradoxically, *de facto* centralized, since the European Affairs Committee remains the only committee in parliament to be interested in EU-related scrutiny at all.

Examples for such a centralization through isolation can be found in the UK House of Commons. As mentioned earlier, the Commons set up a European Scrutiny Committee to filter out the more important pieces of draft legislation from Brussels for debate on the floor.[35] In 1989 and 1990, however, the Commons

---

31 COSAC Secretariat (2005a), p. 53.

32 Dutch Tweede Kamer (2004); see for further details on the TCE early warning system 7 *infra*.

33 Hoetjes (2001), p. 347.

34 Maurer/Wessels (2001), p. 450.

35 Article 1 of the House of Commons Standing Order No. 143 (Orders of Reference of the European Scrutiny Committee).

established specialized European Standing Committees. The initially proposed number of Committees was five, but since there were not enough MPs interested in membership, the number was reduced to three, Committee A, B and C.[36] The European Standing Committees specialize in particular sectors of EU policy, such as agriculture and fisheries, social security, customs, home affairs, foreign affairs, education and employment, culture, media, sport and health.[37] What is seemingly another hybrid between centralization and sectoral specialization, is arguably a way to ban European affairs from the floor, and from the sectoral committees. Valuable time and resources can thereby be allocated with domestic matters, and the two major political parties can avoid the embarrassment of constantly making visible their internal splits over Europe.[38] Also in the parliament of Ireland, the European Affairs Committee is in charge of considering incoming EU documents, and is rather alone in this.[39] Even scrutiny systems that are roughly modelled after the Danish blueprint at times bring about an isolation of European affairs if the sectoral committees keep out of the process while the actual mandating routine in the European Affairs Committee remains low-key. This appears to be the case in the parliaments of Hungary, Latvia and Slovakia and in the lower chambers of the parliaments of Poland and the Czech Republic.[40] In any event, that described above is to show that decentralization does not necessarily mean effective European scrutiny by sectoral specialists, but can mean fragmentation of scrutiny and otherwise isolation of the interested few.

Another middle way between centralization and fragmentation is the model of co-ordination. Thus, while the treatment of European affairs is left in principle to the sectoral committees, the respective European Affairs Committee can assist them and co-ordinate their efforts. The approach taken by the lower chamber of the Dutch parliament, the *Tweede Kamer*, is particularly telling. Its first European Affairs Committee was set up in 1986. Following a debate on whether such a Committee was needed at all, since after all 'Europe is everywhere', the Committee was nevertheless reinstalled in 1994 in the form of a General Committee, which has a cross-departmental scope of competences and is temporary, so that it requires re-establishment after new elections.[41] As it would raise the awareness of EU matters among MPs on the sectoral committees, the Committee's function

---

36 The Commons is again considering raising that number to five, see COSAC Secretariat (2005a), p. 74.

37 Article 6 of the House of Commons Standing Order No. 119 on European Standing Committees.

38 Holzhacker (2004).

39 O'Halpin (2001), Conlan (2004).

40 See COSAC Secretariat (2005a).

41 Articles 16 and 17 Second Chamber Rules of Procedure.

was intended to fade out with time.[42] However, the European Affairs Committee has been kept in place to date, and even turned into a permanent committee. The Committee draws attention to particularly important Commission proposals, it may hold joint meetings with sectoral committees[43] or question ministers on its own. A similar approach is taken by the two chambers of the French parliament, where the European Affairs Delegations, which are not fully-fledged standing committees, monitor EU developments.[44] Upon receipt of EU documentation they can clear an item, adopt informal conclusions, submit an analysis, with or without policy recommendations of their own, to the affected sectoral committee, table a draft resolution there and envoy a *rapporteur* to join committee deliberations.[45] The European Affairs Committee of the German *Bundestag* even has a constitutionally privileged role, as it is one of the four committees to be mentioned in the Basic Law itself,[46] and can be authorized to speak on behalf of the plenary.[47] The Committee itself is competent for cross-departmental integration issues, while for sectoral matters it co-operates and co-deliberates with an appointed sectoral committee-in-charge.[48] As a special feature, the Committee reserves seats for German MEPs to join deliberations, a feature also adopted by other national parliaments in order to import additional EU-related expertise. Later on, under the heading of inter-parliamentary co-operation, we will discuss in greater detail this measure's constitutional implications, as well as the practical question whether MEPs in fact do attend meetings in the national parliaments.[49]

The above overview along the centralization-decentralization line illustrates that institutional and procedural adaptation reflects the way in which European affairs are qualified: as quasi-domestic affairs, foreign affairs or a *sui generis* hybrid with a bit of both. Accordingly, scrutiny mechanisms vary between centralized deliberations with the government, with varying degrees of involvement of the sectoral committees, sectoral specialization within European affairs, and sectoral fragmentation of scrutiny, with varying degrees of stimulation and co-ordination

---

42 Hoetjes (2001), p. 349.

43 Attendance at joint committee meetings tends to be poor, however, see Holzhacker (2004), p. 19.

44 See on France: Rizzuto (1995); Dubois (1996); French Assemblée Nationale (1997); French Assemblée Nationale (1998); Hourquebie (1999); Sauron (1999); Nuttens (2001); Szukala/Rozenberg (2001); critically Dimitrakopoulos (2001).

45 Rule 151-1, 151-2 (1), 151-2 (6), 151-3 National Assembly Rules of Procedure. The Senate features largely identical rules, see Article 73bis of the Senate Rules of Procedure; see also Sauron (1999), p. 176 *et seq.*

46 Article 45 German Basic Law.

47 Article 93a (2) Bundestag Rules of Procedure.

48 Article 93 (1) and (3) Bundestag Rules of Procedure.

49 See 4.2 *infra*.

by the European Affairs Committee. The overview also shows that institutions can hardly be seen out of context with the procedures under which they operate. Our third thread shall therefore focus on the various methods of European scrutiny.

2.4 THE METHODS OF SCRUTINY

Instead of focusing on the institutional arrangement of the parliamentary committee system or the effect of scrutiny in terms of strong, medium and weak impact, to which we will come shortly, we may distinguish national parliaments on the basis of their method of scrutiny.[50] Such a distinction would be reflected in a categorization into three groups of parliaments. The first group of parliaments would be the 'mandate-givers', which would cover the parliaments of Denmark, Sweden, Finland, the Austrian *Nationalrat*, as well as the parliaments of the new Member States which have adopted a Danish or Finnish model of oversight, such as those of Estonia, Latvia and Slovenia. What they all have in common is that they put the procedural emphasis on briefing the competent minister immediately prior to a Council meeting, and on adopting a more or less binding negotiating mandate on a regular basis. The second category of parliaments would comprise the 'systematic scrutinizers', which carry out a systematic sifting of all incoming EU documents while reserving the right to pass resolutions where appropriate. This would include the German *Bundestag,* the French *Assemblée Nationale* and the UK Commons. The remaining parliaments, falling into the category of 'informal influencers', would finally only consider and debate those EU matters which they consider important, raising them in a more or less informal dialogue with the government.

This method-based categorization is intended to provide an alternative to usual strong-moderate-weak models. Admittedly, the placement of parliaments into the respective categories largely coincides in both models. Thus, the mandate-giving national parliaments tend to find themselves on the stronger end of the scale, while informal influencers are typically labelled as simply weak. Nevertheless, the method-based approach takes into account that a mandate which is worded in a broad manner might be no more binding upon a minister than an informal but concerted parliamentary effort.

An interesting example to illustrate the above point is the mandating practice in the Austrian *Nationalrat,* which has the power to issue legally binding instructions to ministers. Theoretically, ministers can even be prosecuted before the Constitutional Court for violating their mandate.[51] However an incident that occurred shortly after Austria's EU accession in 1995 showed the practical limits to such far-reaching

---

50 See Fraga (2000) and Fraga (2001); the COSAC bi-annual reports on European scrutiny developments are drafted with a similar categorization, see COSAC Secretariat (2005a).

51 Article 142 (2) c Federal Constitutional Act, see Urbantschitsch (1998), p. 40.

powers. The minister for agriculture had been tied to a mandate not to agree in the Council to any set of animal transportation standards which would be lower than the Austrian ones. At the end of a long day, reportedly a compromise could have been achieved, but the minister, who called back to Vienna to request a modification of his mandate, could only get in touch with the parliament's night-watch. In the end the minister stuck to his mandate and was outvoted in the Council under QMV. The outcome was even less favourable to Austria than the compromise would have been.[52] Since this incident, mandates are worded in a broad manner, in terms of 'shall work towards' or 'shall make a strong effort to', so as to leave the minister sufficient space for manoeuvring in the Council. Today, the *Nationalrat* also features a small 'fire brigade committee', consisting of the chairman of the European Affairs Subcommittee and one member of each political party group, to quickly adapt mandates.[53]

Mandates may be the method of choice in a parliamentary scrutiny system, but they need not be hand-tying at all. Even where they are, the fact that ministers have violated their parliamentary mandate in the Council bears no legal consequences for the validity of their Council vote for EU purposes. Conversely, even a parliamentary resolution, which is binding politically, cannot be entirely without weight. After all, its adoption will have required the consent of at least a part of a majority government's own party group in parliament.[54] This puts the employed formal or result-based distinctions into a relative perspective. It also affects our assessment of the practice in the other mandate-giving national parliaments, which rank highly in terms of strength. The institutionalized briefing of ministers in a European Affairs Committee may for instance convey the impression of adversarial relations, while it is not, or not necessarily so. Firstly, in the Danish mandating model, ministers do not need to assemble a majority in favour of a policy. Instead, as mentioned earlier, they seek to avoid the formation of a majority against it.[55] Secondly, even in the Danish model, mandates are not imposed upon a minister by the parliament acting on its own initiative. It is the ministers themselves who orally submit a draft mandate for tacit approval. Thirdly, in more than ninety percent of cases, the mandate finds approval as initially proposed by the government.[56] Of course, the smoothness of the briefing may be seen as a sign of parliamentary strength, as ministers try to anticipate the opinion of the European Affairs Committee and to adapt their draft mandate accordingly. Nevertheless, a certain discrepancy between written rules and the impression they can convey, on the one hand, and their practical implementation, on the other hand, can be observed.

---

52 See Urbantschitsch (1998), p. 54 *et seq*.

53 See Swedish Riksdag (2001), p. 21.

54 Weber-Panariello (1995), p. 307.

55 See 2.2 and 2.3 *supra*.

56 See Fitzmaurince (1999), p. 338 on Denmark, Raunio/Wiberg (2001), p. 72 on Finland.

Another example of scrutiny methods which do not necessarily imply any guaranteed substantive result are the so-called scrutiny reserves. If a national parliament is to have an influence on the content of EU decisions via its own government, it must become active *ex ante*, which has led some parliaments to insist that agreement should not be given prematurely. As pointed out earlier, the first national parliament to introduce such a scrutiny reserve was the Parliament of the UK. The respective resolution, adopted in 1980 and renewed in 1998, states that ministers may not give their consent in the Council to matters which are still awaiting completion of parliamentary scrutiny. This is the case when the responsible European Standing Committee, A, B or C, has not yet completed its work, or, if a matter had been referred to the floor, no resolution has yet been adopted. The minister may however proceed in the Council if the European Scrutiny Committee has waived the reserve for urgency reasons, or for the sake of protection of the national interest, or if the matter at hand is 'confidential, routine or trivial or is substantially the same as a proposal on which scrutiny has been completed'.[57] Ministers may also proceed in the Council 'for special reasons', in which case they have to explain these reasons 'at the first opportunity' to the European Scrutiny Committee or, if the matter had been awaiting consideration on the floor, to the House.[58] The Commons intends to bring down the number of overrides, many of which occur under the Second Pillar, by forcing ministers to appear in Parliament before they move ahead.[59]

In 1994, the government of France agreed to observe a scrutiny reserve as well,[60] and formalized that statement in a circulaire.[61] Applicable to both the *Assemblée Nationale* and the *Sénat*, the *réserve d'examen parlementaire* gives parliament one month to decide whether it wishes to adopt a resolution. If it does wish to do so, the government, until the reserve is waived for urgency reasons or a resolution actually passed, has to delay the voting in the Council, either by objecting to the matters being placed on the Council agenda or by seeking to delay the voting informally, depending on how much time is left.[62] The two chambers of the Dutch parliament enforce a scrutiny reserve with regard to matters falling under the Third EU Pillar and the Schengen *acquis,* where, unlike the case in other areas, national parliamentary assent is required. The Dutch parliament may even adopt negotiating mandates in this area. However, the assent procedure is based on tacit

---

57 Article 3 (a) and (b) House of Commons Scrutiny Reserve Resolution of 17 November 1998.

58 *Ibid.*, Article 4.

59 COSAC Secretariat (2005a), p. 73.

60 Statement of Prime Minister Edouard Balladur before the National Assembly of 29 June 1994.

61 Circulaire of the Prime Minister of 19 July 1994 on the taking into account of the position of the French parliament in the elaboration of Community acts.

62 Szukala/Rozenberg (2001).

approval, so that if parliament does not react to a proposal within fifteen days, approval is assumed, the reserve is waived and the government is free to proceed.[63] The Schengen and Europol Committee of the Italian parliament imposes a tacit assent, mandating and scrutiny reserve mechanism similar to the Dutch one in Third Pillar matters.[64] As to the other areas, from 2000 on it operated under a so-called 'floating scrutiny reserve', a new if somewhat unconvincing tool. Parliament is notified of the date when a Council voting is scheduled, and if no resolution is passed by that date, the government is free to agree to the proposal.[65] Since 2005 the system provides that the government is free to proceed if parliament failed to make known its views within 20 days of notification.[66]

In systems of centralized briefings of Brussels-bound ministers, parliament makes known its opinion prior to the Council meeting as a matter of course. Still, the Finnish parliament's Grand Committee for instance imposes a reserve until the sectoral committees have completed their scrutiny.[67] Yet again, the described scrutiny reserves are merely flanking measures which do neither guarantee nor indicate any particular outcome. The tool merely freezes Council decision-making, at least to the extent that it is accepted in the Council and cannot be simply overridden by the government, until parliament has voiced its opinion. The actual weight or binding effect of that opinion is another matter.

2.5 The legal basis for scrutiny

The fourth thread in our brief comparison of different European scrutiny systems in the national parliaments concerns the statutory, constitutional or otherwise legal basis for such parliamentary oversight. In the absence of any specific legal provisions, parliamentary oversight over a government's EU policy derives from general notions of parliamentary democracy, whether they be codified or not, such as ministerial responsibility and parliamentary confidence. Most national parliaments have formalized their EU-related oversight mechanism by statute, or by amending their rules of procedure. Some Member States have even changed their Constitutions to lay down the basic rules of European scrutiny. The first to do so were Germany and France. The new Article 23 of the German Basic Law was inserted in December 1992, stipulating the involvement of the *Bundestag* as well as the *Bundesrat* in German EU policy formulation. Article 23 (2) states that the federal government

63 See Del Grosso (2000); Hoetjes (2001); Holzhacker (2002).
64 Bindi Calussi/Grassi (2001), p. 293.
65 Bindi Calussi/Grassi (2001), p. 290; Pera (2002).
66 Law no. 11 of 4 February 2005, see COSAC Secretariat (2005a), p. 47.
67 Raunio (2001).

shall keep the two chambers informed about EU matters 'comprehensively and at the earliest possible time'.[68] Paragraph 3 goes on to state:

> Before participating in legislative acts of the European Union, the Federal Government shall provide the Bundestag with an opportunity to state its position. The Federal Government shall take the position of the Bundestag into account during the negotiations. Details shall be regulated by a law.

The involvement of the *Länder* governments through the *Bundesrat* is meanwhile more nuanced. Since the *Bundesrat* is to reflect federalism, rather than parliamentarism, its participatory powers in European affairs depend on the extent to which the *Länder* or the *Bundesrat* are affected by EU measures.[69] The *Bundesrat's* views are taken 'into account' when *Länder* interests are affected or when the *Länder* have legislative powers in a policy area, and they are given 'the greatest possible respect' when a matter *primarily* affects the *Länder's* legislative powers or administrative structures or procedures. In issues of exclusive *Länder* competence, a representative appointed by the *Bundesrat* assumes Germany's seat in the Council, while closely co-operating with the federal government to ensure consistent representation of national policy. The above codification was achieved in the ratification process to the Maastricht Treaty, which required a constitutional amendment and therefore assent by both chambers.

The French parliament found itself in a similar double vetoing position as regards the Maastricht Treaty,[70] and it insisted on the inclusion of the new Article 88-4 of the Constitution.[71] The Article initially provided parliament with rights to be kept informed, and with possibilities to pass resolutions on EU matters, however only in those fields which would fall under parliamentary law-making competence as being *législative* in nature, and not on matters for autonomous regulation by the government.[72] The French parliament succeeded in widening the scope of the right to pass resolutions in the ratification process to the Amsterdam Treaty, which again required parliamentary assent and a constitutional amendment. Since then, Article 88-4 of the French Constitution read:[73]

> The Government shall lay before the National Assembly and the Senate any drafts of or proposals for instruments of the European Communities or the European Union containing

68 Citations from the English translation of the Basic Law published by the German Bundestag in 2001.

69 Article 23 (2) to (6) German Basic Law.

70 Constitutional Council decision of 9 April 1992, no. 92-308.

71 Constitutional Law of 25 June 1992, no. 92-554.

72 See Articles 34 and 37 French Constitution.

73 Citations from the English translation of the French Constitution prepared jointly by the National Assembly and the Ministry of Foreign Affairs.

> provisions which are matters for statute [*lois*] as soon as they have been transmitted to the Council of the European Union. It may also lay before them other drafts of or proposals for instruments or any document issuing from a European Union institution. In the manner laid down by the rules of procedure of each assembly, resolutions may be passed, even if parliament is not in session, on the drafts, proposals or documents referred to in the preceding paragraph.

Thus, all proposals which are *législative* in nature have to be forwarded to parliament, the transfer of non-*législative* matters remains optional, yet parliament may pass resolutions on all of them, even on those which are not 'matters for statute'. Two new Articles, numbered 88-5 and 88-6, are to take effect in order to prepare the French parliament for the receipt of powers under the early warning system and the passerelle veto mechanism, as set out in the relevant EU Constitutional Treaty provisions, as soon as that Treaty would enter into force.[74]

Apart from Germany and France, Belgium,[75] Portugal,[76] Finland[77] and Austria,[78] as well as the Czech Republic,[79] Slovenia[80] and Hungary,[81] have amended their Constitutions to stipulate the principle of parliamentary oversight in European affairs.[82] However, once more we should note that there may be discrepancies between the impression conveyed by written rules or their status, and their practical impact. The constitutional status of legal provisions neither indicates nor guarantees parliamentary strength in real terms. The German and French provisions merely stipulate that the views of the respective parliament are to be taken 'into account', or that 'resolutions may be passed', which by itself says little about the political weight of parliamentary opinions. The Austrian provisions are far-reaching on paper, but are applied leniently in practice,[83] while the parliaments of Belgium and Portugal are even considered to be among the weakest in the EU.[84]

---

74 The amendment was triggered by the Constitutional Council decision of 19 November 2004, no. 2004-505.

75 Article 168 Belgian Constitution, on the parliamentary right to be informed on Treaty amendments.

76 Article 161n Portuguese Constitution, on the parliamentary right to give opinions on pending EU decisions.

77 Article 96 Finnish Constitution.

78 Article 23e and 23f Federal Constitutional Act.

79 Article 10b Czech Constitution.

80 Article 3a (4) Slovenian Constitution.

81 Article 35/A Hungarian Constitution.

82 Sweden and Austria have statutes with constitutional rank; see generally on national constitutional adaptation to EU membership in the new Member States: Albi (2003), as well as a critical review of the old Member States in Albi (2005), p. 9 *et seq*.

83 Hegeland/Neuhold (2002).

84 See 2.6 *infra*.

Conversely, the Danish prototype of a strong oversight mechanism does not have a constitutional basis, and its core is not even based on statutory law. While Article 6 (2) of the Danish EEC Accession Act generally provided the basis for information and consultation of the *Folketing*, the actual mandating system derives from a Report that the Market Committee adopted in 1973,[85] following an incident in which the minister for agriculture had agreed to an unfavourable pricing agreement for Danish bacon in Brussels:[86]

> The Government shall consult the Market Committee of the Folketing in questions relating to EC policy of a major importance so that the regard for the influence of the Folketing as well as the freedom to negotiate are respected.
>
> Prior to negotiations in the EC Council of Ministers on decisions of a wider scope, the Government submits an oral mandate for negotiation to the Market Committee. If there is no majority against the mandate, the Government negotiates on this basis.

The bacon crisis almost brought down the incumbent minority cabinet, and only this arrangement, which was supported by two opposition parties, helped the cabinet to survive a motion of no-confidence. Ever since, the Danish government has first to consult the *Folketing* on all EU policy matters of 'major importance' and to obtain a mandate for decisions 'of a wider scope'. In practice the criteria of 'major importance' and 'wider scope' are interpreted broadly, so that all EU matters are in fact submitted to the European Affairs Committee for a mandate. Constitutional codification may of course strengthen the position of a national parliament by giving it competences that it would not have otherwise, as was the case in France. It may also symbolically increase the weight, and underline the constitutional significance, of European scrutiny.[87] Yet again, codification itself does not guarantee any sharp or adversarial scrutiny practice.

2.6 The 'strength' of parliaments

The above overview already illustrates the heterogeneity of the national parliaments in their treatment of European affairs. Emphasis may lie on *ex ante* briefing for ministers or calling to account *ex post*, the treatment may be centralized in, or abandoned to, a European Affairs Committee, or left to the sectoral committees, with varying degrees of co-ordination. What we have so far left largely unattended is the role of the upper chambers in bicameral parliaments. The senates may either

---

85 Folketing Market Relations Committee Report of 29 March 1973.

86 Translation taken from: Danish Folketing (2002), p. 2.

87 See Raunio (2001), p. 197 on the benefits of constitutional codification of the Finnish model of oversight.

conduct scrutiny of their own, as is the case in the UK and Germany, or be involved in the lower chamber process by way of a joint European Affairs Committee, as is the case in Ireland and Belgium. The methods of *ex ante* influencing of the government then may range between informal pressure and institutionalized mandating, sometimes including a suspensive scrutiny reserve. However, the choice of methods, just like the constitutional, statutory or non-codified legal basis for scrutiny, does in itself not necessarily imply any particular weight of parliamentary opinions.

What all the national parliaments of the EU have in common is some form of institutional adaptation to European integration itself, especially in the period following the Maastricht Treaty.[88] Furthermore, Rometsch and Wessels (1996) argue that responses of national institutions to the integration process are gradually converging, as more attention is paid to the European dimension, cross-border and cross-layer co-operation is enhanced, and similar constitutional, procedural and behavioural innovations are adopted. The national parliaments have all, as said, established European Affairs Committees, or have re-assigned the duties of already existing committees to deal with EU matters.[89] Nevertheless, we should bear in mind that the differences between these European Affairs Committees are considerable, not to mention those between the parliaments themselves. Norton (1995b: 188) even found the very term 'European Affairs Committees' deceiving, as using it 'is to convey an impression of a uniformity that does not exist'. Yet in spite of the described heterogeneity, it would be helpful, as a last thread in our overview, to categorize national parliaments according to their relative strength.

So far the words 'strength' and 'weakness' have been used with great moderation since, as stated at the outset, they imply an adversarial relation between government, on the one hand, and a unitary parliament, on the other hand, which may not be warranted in a parliamentary system. Still, the notions of separation of powers and checks and balances do include a controlling task for parliament as regards the government. For our purposes, a categorization into strong and weak parliaments is again not a goal in itself but merely a means to expose the existing variations whose underlying reasons we seek to identify in order to draw broader conclusions. At the same time the inherent methodological problems with such categorizations should be kept in mind.[90]

A straightforward way to roughly categorize Member States parliaments in terms of relative strength is the impact they have, or can have, on their governments'

88 Norton (1995b), see also Judge (1995). The adaptation process continues after the subsequent treaties, see Maurer (2002).

89 Raunio (1999), p. 188; Weber-Panariello (1995), p. 306.

90 See 2.4 *supra*.

policy-formulation. In the context of European decision-making this would relate to the parliamentary contribution to the national standpoint in the Council. For the purposes of his own analysis, Bergman (1997) considered as a major criterion the degree to which national parliamentary opinions or instructions are binding upon a minister, as well as who the involved actors are, such as the plenary or visiting MEPs, and which EU Pillars fall under European scrutiny. Raunio and Wiberg (2000) employed the binding effect of parliamentary opinions as identified by Bergman to create their own categorization. In addition to the indicators mentioned, they considered the strength of the European Affairs Committees as reflected by the frequency of their meetings, as well as the degree of involvement of the sectoral committees as adding to the expertise in, and quality of, the European scrutiny process. Norton (1995b) distinguished three types of parliaments as well: strong policy-makers, who can amend government policies and substitute them with their own; moderate policy-influencers, who can reject or amend government policies but not substitute them; and parliaments with little or no policy effect. Maurer and Wessels (2001) based their own analysis on this categorization, adding to it as criteria the scope of parliamentary participation, the timing and management of the scrutiny, from proactive to reactive, as well as the impact of the opinion of parliament on the government's position. Translated into the authors' matrix on the performance of national parliaments as players on the national and the European arena, the scenario becomes more differentiated.

From the literature outlined in the above paragraph, we can amalgamate the following picture of the national parliaments of the EU-15. Eventually the parliament of Denmark, where ministers are briefed and mandated by the European Affairs Committee, emerges as being undisputedly strong. The parliaments of Finland and Sweden and the Austrian *Nationalrat*, which have adopted a Danish-style briefing routine, are considered strong or moderate. The strength of the Finnish model mainly derives from its optimized input from the sectoral standing committees in the scrutiny work. The German *Bundesrat* appears to be moderate or strong, especially in EU matters where *Länder* interests are affected. The Dutch parliament, whose assent is required for measures under the Third EU Pillar, is qualified as moderate in that area, while being weaker in the other areas of EU policy. The UK Commons and the German *Bundestag* are moderate, the French parliament moderate or weak, and the rest of the national parliaments of the pre-enlargement EU, the ones of Belgium, Luxembourg, Ireland, Portugal, Spain, Italy and Greece, turn out weak. Weakness in the present context is mainly indicated by a passive or reactive parliamentary attitude as regards the government's policy formulation, a low level of expertise among MPs in European affairs, and little interest in scrutinizing this policy area. Scrutiny tends to be fragmented among the sectoral committees or effectively isolated in the European Affairs Committee, and oversight is carried out *ex post*, if at all.

2.7 Explaining Variations

Triggered by the adoption of the Amsterdam Protocol on the role of national parliaments in the European Union, a fresh round of research in political science sought to identify the underlying reasons for national variation in European scrutiny procedures among the national parliaments. A consensus seems to have emerged as regards the basic factors contributing to a parliament's relative strength and activity in that field, but a large variety of complementary factors is put forward as well. An innovative and often-cited approach in this respect was taken by Bergman (1997). He identified five factors taken from competing political schools of thought – culture theory, institutionalism and rational choice theory – and combined them to complement each other in forming an integrated picture. The degree and effect of national parliamentary involvement in European affairs would thus firstly depend on whether public opinion is integration-friendly or rather Eurosceptic. The second factor, national political culture which, like the first one, originates from culture theory, would describe the relation between citizens and elites, especially whether EU policy is treated as foreign policy, and thus as a matter of discretionary government domain, or not. The third and fourth factor meanwhile stem from the institutionalist approach. The impact of a national parliament would thus further depend on the existence of a federal state structure in a Member State, with sub-national units having an institutionalized influence on the federal level. In addition, the general rules governing government-parliament relations as prevailing in a Member State would play a role. That factor refers to the question whether parliamentarism is well-developed, and how often the government in power is a minority cabinet facing a stronger parliament. Thus, a parliament which is reconciled under a permissive pro-European consensus, or which offers loyal support to a stable majority government, is not likely to be too critical of the government's EU policy. Conversely, a Eurosceptic and self-assured parliament is likely to be more active in that field, especially when it can exert pressure on a fragile minority government. When institutionalism and culture theory are thus combined, a north-south dimension emerges: scrutiny tends to be stricter north of an imaginary line running through Ireland and Belgium, and it tends to be more lenient south of that line – at least as far as the EU-15 is concerned. As a fifth factor, Bergman defined evidence for strategic action under the rational choice theory, when parliamentary rights are claimed in a domestic struggle for power. This can, for instance, be observed when powers for parliament are extended or codified in the ratification process to a treaty. Bergman also suggested additional criteria to be developed and considered. He pointed to the timing of EU membership, with later accession tending to lead to stronger European scrutiny, the 'Northern-ness' of a Member State, which refers to the Scandinavian culture of transparent governance, as well as traditional domestic patterns of interaction to which path-dependent institutions like parliaments tend to stick when challenged.

Raunio (1999) explained existing variations mainly on the basis of two factors: the position of parliament in the national setting and public opinion *vis-à-vis* European integration. A parliament's being weak in general, combined with a pro-European public opinion, would thus lead to modest European scrutiny. In a more elaborate analysis, Raunio and Wiberg (2000) again assumed public opinion on European integration to be a decisive factor, and combined that with the positions of national political parties on that issue. Maurer (2002) provided a quite comprehensive overview on the existing views in the literature for the European Convention, and named several factors playing a role for the character of European scrutiny in the Member States parliaments: domestic government-parliament relations, party systems, party positions, internal organization of parliaments, the role and style of parliamentarism, relations between European Affairs Committees, the sectoral committees, the plenary and cross-party working groups, attitudes of parties and individual MPs, as well as public opinion on European integration and on democracy and representative institutions in general.

To briefly illustrate the applicability of the mentioned factors, we may for instance take the case of Austria.[91] The relatively late accession to the EU in 1995 allowed the Austrian parliament to learn from the experience of the old Member States, and to adopt a Danish-inspired model right away. The two-thirds majority that was required for a constitutional amendment prior to EU accession placed opposition parties in a vetoing position in 1994. Indeed, the strict model of oversight was mainly pushed by the Greens and the Liberal Forum, even though the latter was not even opposed to EU accession, unlike the initially sceptical Greens. Furthermore, the federal structure of Austria made involvement of the *Bundesrat* and the *Länder* imperative. The *Bundesrat*, which is elected by the *Länder* parliaments, as well as the *Länder* themselves, by a majority of five out of nine with no votes against, can issue mandates to the federal government as well. Primacy is however awarded to the lower chamber of parliament, the *Nationalrat,* which can bind the government in more areas and must be consulted before the government may deviate from the mandate under an escape clause.[92] The *Nationalrat* itself applies the formally strong rules moderately in practice. In the light of the factors that influence the strength of European scrutiny, we may for instance observe that Austria has a consistently integration-friendly public opinion.[93] This is reflected in a

---

91 See Neuhold/Hegeland (2002); see also Urbantschitsch (1998), p. 24 *et seq*.; Blümel/Neuhold (2001).

92 The Austrian Bundesrat may issue mandates if the matter concerns a proposal that will have to be implemented by a constitutional change with the Bundesrat's assent; deviation from a Bundesrat mandate is possible for 'compelling reasons from foreign or integration policy'. See Article 23e (2), (3), (4), and (6) Federal Constitution Act.

93 The Austrian 1994 accession referendum for instance resulted in a 66% 'yes' vote. See further Hegeland/Neuhold (2002).

pro-European consensus among the major political parties, in spite of the rise of the right-wing populist Freedom Party in 1999. Furthermore, we may note that Austria is not too 'Nordic' in terms of governance culture, and that governments rely on stable majorities, with, for instance until 1999, lengthy periods of rule by grand coalitions holding two-thirds majorities against a weak opposition in parliament. Fitzmaurice (1999: 339) aptly remarks that 'Austria, with the weakest parliamentary tradition among the new members [of 1995], has gone the furthest first', yet pre-existing patterns of government-parliament relations in Austria have eventually resulted in a lighter model compared to the Danish blueprint. The Danish model in turn can be explained by the mentioned factors as well. In fact, several of the existing generalized factors are derived from exercises to find something that does exist in Denmark, and that does not exist anywhere else, so as to explain the Danish uniqueness.

Pahre (1997) defined three factors which determine the relative effectiveness of a European scrutiny model on the basis of three Danish particularities. Firstly, he observed the Danish tradition of having minority governments. Especially since the 1973 general elections, which fragmented the Danish party landscape by boosting the number of represented parties in parliament from five to eleven, minority governments have been the rule. The first cabinet to have its own majority since then was Poul Nyrup Rasmussen's four-party coalition formed in 1993, which however lost that majority again in 1994. Under the principle of 'negative parliamentarism', a cabinet does not need an own parliamentary majority to stay in office, as long as it has no majority against it.[94] This rule is also reflected in the tacit approval procedure in the European Affairs Committee. Since a minority cabinet depends on pragmatic coalition-building, opposition parties are able to exert pressure.[95] As noted earlier, the government which agreed to the setting up of the famous mandating system in 1973 was a minority cabinet facing a vote of no-confidence. Secondly, we are to bear in mind the notorious Euroscepticism of the Danish public. In other words, a significant part of the population prefers the status quo to further European integration beyond the internal market. This is prominently reflected in the Danish 'no' votes in the referendums on the Maastricht Treaty in 1992, and on Denmark's participation in the EMU in 2000, as well as the success of the Danish anti-EU lists participating in EP elections. Thirdly, Pahre pointed at peculiar party behaviour. During the 1973 bacon crisis, the social-democratic minority cabinet was backed by the social-liberal *Radikale Venstre* and the Socialist People's Party, in exchange for the setting up of a hand-tying mandating system. Thus, these two parties preferred staying in a strong opposition over entering into a government coalition themselves. Especially *Radikale Venstre,* although often a potential coalition partner later on, kept declining office.

94 See Albæk Jensen (1996), p. 39 *et seq*.

95 Arter (1995), p. 119 *et seq*.

To summarize, the high frequency of minority governments, the Euroscepticism of the public and at least one significant political party, and the existence of a significant political party which prefers to stay in opposition to a minority cabinet, led to the exceptionally strong parliamentary oversight practice over European affairs in Denmark. These particularities are at the same time used to dismiss the Danish model as being non-transferable to any other Member State, where majority governments, less Euroscepticism, as well as different party behaviour are the rule. Dutch parliamentarians, for instance, reportedly reject the idea of hand-tying parliamentary oversight in European affairs, and have no interest in introducing '*Deense toestanden*', a term which might be translated as 'Danish situations' with a derogatory note.[96] In Germany, Danish-style mandating would possibly violate constitutional law on government-parliament relations. Binding mandates could theoretically be only imposed by way of passing a statute.[97] Even for the otherwise very much Eurosceptic UK Commons, a Danish-style mandating system would not seem realistic to adopt as that would go against established traditions of how to hold ministers to account.[98] Yet even if exact adoptions of the Danish model by other national parliaments are unrealistic, it still can serve as a reference when discussing demands for stricter European scrutiny in the other national parliaments. Indeed, as Fitzmaurice (1999: 336) points out, '[t]he Danish case is an obvious choice because it is the oldest and most developed model, which has become the reference point – for good or ill – against which all others tend to measure themselves'.

We should add one last remark concerning the Danish model. The high centralization of European scrutiny in the European Affairs Committee, the fact that the Committee is staffed with senior politicians, and the need for the government to maintain a workable alliance of tacit supporters, calls into question the parliamentary character of the scrutiny procedure itself. Weber-Panariello (1995: 308) notes that meetings of the European Affairs Committee in fact appeared to be 'extended Cabinet meetings'. After all, the leaders or spokesmen of opposition parties who eventually support a minority government might as well be called *de facto* coalition partners. Von der Vring (1996: 401) argues along the same lines. He describes the Committee as a 'small privileged executive committee' whose powers go at the expense of the rest of MPs, who remain outside the scrutiny process and who reportedly call the Committee 'their House of Lords'. Later on we shall pick up on this point again, when discussing the possible transfer of MPs to be directly active at EU level, and the consequences for the parliamentary character of their work.[99] But now, having examined what makes the *Folketing* 'Danish', let us turn back to the

96 Hoetjes (2001), p. 349.
97 Dann (2004), p. 413.
98 Cygan (2004a), p. 15.
99 See 5.5 *infra*.

question why the other parliaments are actually not 'Danish', and revisit the factors that contribute to parliamentary weakness or moderation in European affairs.

2.8 The interest in European scrutiny

Apart from the constraints that the national parliaments are facing in scrutinizing European affairs, including the external agenda-setting and the information gap behind the government, there is, as repeatedly noted earlier, another side to the coin. Norton (1995b) distinguished factors which lead to *inability* of parliaments to scrutinize EU policy effectively, on the one hand, but also factors leading to *unwillingness* to do so, on the other hand. Unwillingness to scrutinize could, for instance, be caused by the ideological factor of a general pro-European consensus prevailing among the general public and the political parties represented in parliament. In addition, there is again the cultural factor of generally weak parliamentarism, yet also mutual mistrust and rivalry among politicians, for example between national MPs and MEPs, or between members of the European Affairs Committee and jealous sectoral committee members,[100] all of which impedes inter- and intra-parliamentary co-operation.

Pro-European consensus among the major political parties in parliament results in few incentives to scrutinize the government's EU policy. Especially when the opposition is equally, or even more integration-friendly compared to the government parties, any step towards further European integration will be preferred to the maintenance of the status quo, and will therefore meet approval.[101] For the same reason, when public opinion is integration-friendly as well, there will be little electoral reward for parties or parliamentarians if they engage in scrutinizing EU policy. Furthermore, a national parliament's pro-European position also tends to include the opinion that scrutiny of EU legislation should be a task of the European Parliament, and that national parliaments should step back as the European Parliament gains competences and political weight.[102]

The issue of electoral reward in turn points to further reasons for unwillingness to scrutinize. Parliamentarians in Greece and Ireland are, for instance, reported to be highly parochial and clientele-oriented.[103] Their own constituency can however hardly be appeased by sifting Commission proposals, which has to do with the perceived remoteness of EU decision-making, but also with the length of the EU policy cycle. Indeed, before a Green Paper or a White Paper is turned into a

100 Von der Vring (1996), p. 395.

101 Pahre (1997).

102 Katz/Wessels (1999), p. 27 *et seq.*; Wessels (1999), p. 213 *et seq*; Raunio/Wiberg (2000), p. 147.

103 See on Greece: Zervakis/Yannis (2001), Dimitrakopoulos (2001); on Ireland: O'Halpin (1995); Laffan (2001).

Commission proposal, before it is discussed in Coreper, the Council, the European Parliament and advisory bodies, before a directive is adopted, which in turn provides for an implementation period, before that deadline is reached or the directive is implemented into national law, and before the European Court of Justice has interpreted the directive in its case-law, the electoral term of a national parliament may long be over.[104] The EU decision-making process thus does not coincide with the rhythm of national elections, and parliamentary influence through scrutiny can, as is not the case with domestic legislation, only be had indirectly. This even turns out to be discouraging in a country as naturally Eurosceptic as the UK. While the re-election of an MP depends on the vote in his or her constituency, voters do not seem to reward records of work on European scrutiny.[105] The Commons had, as noted earlier, even to reduce the planned number of European Standing Committees from five to three due to a shortage in volunteering MPs. Also in the other national parliaments, the vast majority of incoming EU documents is either left unattended, is immediately cleared as requiring no further scrutiny, or is merely taken note of without debate.[106] The sectoral committees in the French parliament reportedly greet EU documents 'with a mix of scepticism and boredom'.[107] Even in the Nordic mandate-giving parliaments, as pointed out earlier, the draft mandates are usually approved of in the form as proposed by the government.

Thus, there is a more general point about the willingness of MPs to engage in European scrutiny, which is the salience of EU matters. Arguably, what voters tend to care about most are education, health care, pensions, taxes, employment or law enforcement, which all still happen to be predominantly matters of Member State competence.[108] When discussing the factors that impede effective national parliamentary scrutiny of European affairs, practical or procedural constraints should accordingly not be the only issues we should consider. The reasons why national parliaments may actually not *want* to engage in stricter scrutiny should be taken into account as well, and should not be dismissed or ignored.

2.9 Conclusion

The conclusions that may be drawn from our discussion so far are to provide a background against which we shall contrast demands for greater national parliamentary activity in EU affairs. To start with, the scrutiny of the governments' EU policy by their respective national parliament derives from national constitutional

104 Thanks to Rob Widdershoven for that remark.
105 Miller/Ware (1996), p. 190.
106 Maurer/Wessels (2001), p. 450.
107 Szukala/Rozenberg (2001), p. 241.
108 Donnelly/Hoffmann (2004).

notions of ministerial responsibility and parliamentary control. In a parliamentary democracy, the electorate decides on the composition of parliament in general elections, and the majority party, or a coalition of parties forming a majority together, and in exceptional cases a minority, then goes on to form a government. This government is democratically legitimized as it enjoys the support of a majority of elected MPs. Its policies may also be subject to debate, criticism and control, primarily by opposition parties or intra-government challengers, but in principle by parliament as a whole. The way in which EU policies are debated and controlled in practice however differs from one Member State to another.

Oversight mechanisms vary between centralization of European scrutiny in a European Affairs Committee, isolation of scrutiny therein, sectoral decentralization or fragmentation of scrutiny and co-ordination of sectoral activities. Methods range from weekly briefings of ministers, to the occasional adoption of a resolution, from the issuing of legally binding mandates to informal influence. The participation of the upper chambers in bicameral systems takes the form of full co-operation in joint committees, or complementary scrutiny of their own. Where upper chambers represent sub-national entities in federal states, their input depends on the degree to which the entities or the chambers themselves are affected by European affairs. The intensity of European scrutiny depends to a large extent on the prevailing political culture, and the institutional role that parliament already plays in purely domestic politics. Parliamentary culture, and the dominance and stability of the government, are important factors, and so is the parliament's general attitude towards European integration, ranging between benevolent support and sharp Euroscepticism. Where scrutiny is modest, parliamentarians might be reluctant to fulfil a function they believe the European Parliament should fulfil, or might otherwise not be interested in dealing with European affairs. The effort it takes to specialize in EU matters might not be rewarded accordingly by the electorate in general, or by the individual constituency in particular. Even when parliamentarians *want* to engage in stricter oversight, the practical constraints they are confronted with are typically the same: the complexity, remoteness, intransparency and the transnational character of EU decision-making, the resulting information gap, as well as qualified majority voting in the Council, which can deprive the tightest of mandates of its effect if the minister gets outvoted. These, as well as other considerations shall now be used to scrutinize the various demands for a greater role for national parliaments in the European Union, in the light of the different purposes that it might serve in the first place. Again, as a more general point, we should bear in mind that before we demand greater activity on the part of national parliaments, it is worth looking closely to see that there are reasons, even good reasons, why at least some parliaments do not do what we might expect them to do. Those who are eager to see 'strong' national parliaments may find out that 'strength' is not even the most appropriate of notions to start with.

3 The call for sharper European scrutiny

3.1 Introduction

Demands for sharper or more active European scrutiny in the national parliaments are frequently voiced. Actually, with few exceptions, this demand is put forward, implicitly or explicitly, wherever the effect of European integration on the national parliaments is analyzed and weakness quickly diagnosed. In the course of the debates in the Convention about the role of the national parliaments in the EU, a strengthening of oversight systems was consistently advocated as well.[1] The conclusion that national parliaments must make greater efforts to overcome their marginalized position has by now become something of a truism. The purpose of our discussion here is to critically review this conclusion, taking into account the findings of the previous chapters. But in order to do that, the actual rationale of the demands needs to be clarified first: what is it that stronger or more active European scrutiny is supposed to achieve? Once we have established that, the rest will follow with a far greater clarity of argument.

The most obvious response to the question what purpose national parliamentary scrutiny of EU matters should serve is also the broadest: stronger European scrutiny by national parliaments can help increase the democratic legitimacy of the European Union. This apparently self-explaining statement can actually be seen from two different angles: the European perspective, as well as the national constitutional perspective. From the national constitutional perspective, a lack of effective accountability of national governments for their EU policy to their national parliaments would mean, simply speaking, a de-parliamentarization at Member State level. European integration allows the government to participate in the adoption of EU legislation, which is binding upon the national parliament, while the latter has not participated in the process in the way it might have in the case of domestic legislation. EU membership thus curtails the powers of parliament, which is essentially the reason for calling the national parliaments the 'losers of integration' in the first place.[2]

From the European perspective, poor parliamentary oversight over the governments' EU policy may essentially mean an interruption of the chain of democratic accountability that leads up to the decision-making in the Council. Since the Council as such is neither directly elected nor accountable to any single parliament,

---

1 See e.g. Andriukaitis/Kutraite-Giedraitiene (2002), Basile (2002), Hübner (2002), Kiljunen, *et al.* (2002), Kreitzberg/Kelam (2002).

2 Duina/Oliver (2005) actually contest the notion of national parliaments as 'losers', arguing that European integration has helped expand the parliaments' regulatory capabilities.

its accountability can only be construed via the accountability of the individual ministers to their respective national parliaments at home, which are in turn elected by the citizens of their Member States. There are also other reasons to draw on the national parliaments, both for 'national' as well as 'European' purposes, and to stimulate their activity. One might argue that is it not accurate to strictly distinguish between a purely European and a purely national perspective, since the EU consists of Member States who themselves negotiate and conclude its constituent treaties. Nevertheless, even if the two dimensions are inter-related, a sharpened conceptual distinction is both useful and justified. Firstly, the EU with its permanent institutional structure includes bodies which enjoy a high degree of autonomy from the Member States, such as the Commission, the ECJ, the European Parliament, and even the Council itself with its consociational dynamics.[3] Secondly, we may see the European perspective as being parallel to, although not always coinciding with, a supranational view on European integration, which would qualify the EU indeed to be more, or at least something else, than just a permanent gathering of sovereign countries. What is in the end important to show is that national parliaments may be of a certain appeal not only to national sovereignists, or observers of domestic constitutionalism, but also to the European Union as an emancipated entity, its supporters as well as its critical observers.

3.2 The National Constitutional Perspective

There are several ways in which the national constitutional dimension of European scrutiny in the national parliaments can be approached. That is to say, a call for stronger parliamentary oversight in EU affairs might make sense for several reasons. Our analysis shall, taking the discussion to a certain level of abstraction, distinguish between four possible lines of reasoning: a static positivist approach, a dynamic positivism, an approach based on the notion of deliberative democracy, as well as one based on pragmatic ministerial advantage. Of course, just like the national constitutional dimension of European scrutiny is inter-related with its European dimension, so are the following sub-aspects within the national constitutional dimension itself.

To demand strengthened parliamentary oversight in European affairs implies, also from a national constitutional point of view, a stronger stance of the national parliament *vis-à-vis* the individual national government. In the absence of European integration, it might be argued under the heading of static positivism, parliament would remain the central law-maker in all the areas in which the EU is now competent to exercise regulatory powers. Now, it is in fact the government in the Council (together with the other governments) which has taken over these

3 See Lord (1998), p. 31.

powers. Accordingly, the European treaties, initially put before parliament for ratification in a classical take-it-or-leave-it manner by the government, constituted a large-scale delegation of legislative competences to the executive. Delegation however presupposes some sort of subsequent supervision over the exercise by the recipient of the delegated competences. We might note that the term 'delegation of powers' typically implies a relationship with a subordinate agent, as opposed to one with the more neutral or even opposite term 'transfer of powers', and the choice of wording can reveal general views on the relation between Member States and the EU.[4] To continue the main point, the way in which a government escapes supervision after delegation makes it a quasi-autonomous legislator in an increasing number of policy areas, at the expense of the national parliament, and to the detriment of the principle of parliamentary democracy in general. Stronger oversight in European affairs would thus merely be a means to restore, to a certain extent, the national constitutional balance of power in which parliament is ultimately in control of law-making, even in the areas of delegated regulatory powers. Another, related point can be derived from the national parliaments as being the 'Masters of the Treaties'. It is they who have conferred defined powers to the EU institutions, or so one might argue, and they consequently should have an interest, or even a duty, to ensure that the recipient of these powers stays *intra vires*. This point would also make the national parliaments the natural guardians of the principle of subsidiarity,[5] and it would primarily address the legitimacy of EU action in formal competence terms, as opposed to its democratic legitimation.[6] The above approach may be qualified as both positivist and static (as well as statist, as it stresses the priority of the Member State in the EU), for it would emphasize European integration as a singular treaty-based and therefore conditional removal of domestic powers, which retain a clear and fixed scope, and the exercise of which calls for continued parliamentary supervision to that very same extent.

While following the basic assumption that the ratification of European treaties by a national parliament is in fact a delegation of powers to the government, a second approach would add a substantive, democratic, as well as a dynamic dimension to it. Thus, it remains an inherent task for parliament to exercise supervision over the government anyway, even where a policy area happens to be European in nature. In other words, it is parliament's task to ensure that the connection between the citizens and the body which is now exercising their sovereign powers is not disrupted. Parliament itself, specifically its composition, is subjected to a direct expression of the political preferences of the citizens by way of general elections. Its own

4 Albi (2005), p. 118 *et seq.*

5 See Peters (2005); Cygan (2004b), see also Dashwood (2004), p. 356.

6 Ronge (1998), p. 61, noting that usually these two notions are equated.

domestic legislative activity therefore broadly reflects voter preferences. Foreign affairs or European legislative activities, which are exercised by the government, would need to have an 'imprint' in terms of voter preferences as well,[7] in particular an imprint from the otherwise invisible parliamentary opposition,[8] assuming that opposition input is stronger at domestic policies than it is at foreign or European affairs. Parliament is to ensure that voter preferences are translated into government policies, especially when, as is the case in EU law-making, ultimate national parliamentary intervention in the drafting stage of laws is no longer possible.

Apart from its legislative and its controlling task *vis-à-vis* the government, parliament also has a communicative function as a central arena for the exchange of opinions, and as a locus for public discourse. Parliament is a forum for competing political arguments and a core institution in a deliberative democracy. Under Habermas' deliberative democracy theory, even minorities accept the outcome of a majoritarian decision-making process as long as they feel that their opinions have been duly heard in an open discourse. Public deliberation in a familiar and well-established forum such as parliament, if this deliberation precedes the adoption of EU legislation, would thus increase the acceptance of this legislation. Since parliament, where the EU is competent, is no longer adopting laws itself, it would need to extend the reach of its deliberation to the locus where these laws are adopted. Thereby, the impression may be prevented that decisions are made by an obscure and detached Brussels machinery.

As already hinted, the national constitutional rationale for strengthening European scrutiny in the national parliaments cannot be seen but in relation with the logic of European integration as a whole. In fact, strengthening parliamentary oversight over the governments' EU policy on the national level must inevitably be seen in connection with, even in contrast to, the idea of developing a form of parliamentarism on the EU level itself. The perceived necessity to ensure control over delegated competences, the translation of voter preferences into policy outcomes, as well as an open parliamentary discourse via the national parliaments, arguably correlates with the assumption or observation that the European Parliament is not capable of fulfilling these functions, at least not alone. Indeed, there is a strong, although not very new case for questioning the European Parliament's capacities in these respects. As to the control over conferred powers, the European Union is not self-constituting or 'self-authenticating',[9] but treaty-based, and the European Parliament as a treaty institution is therefore itself a recipient of powers that have previously been delegated from the national level. As to the imprint of voter preferences into policies, it may just be noted that, firstly, the European Parliament is not

7 Cf. Ameller (1966), p. 310 *et seq.*; Raunio (1999), p. 202; Raunio/Wiberg (2001).

8 Cf. Holzhacker (2004), p. 7.

9 Dashwood (2004), p. 357.

the main, let alone the sole law-maker at EU level. Secondly, even if it was, exact voter preferences can be difficult to identify. EP election campaigns are notoriously dominated by national issues, they are conducted by national political parties, and they trigger a low and decreasing voter turnout. Finally turning to the deliberative function of a parliament, it may suffice to observe the absence of a European language, of European media and, of course, the absence of an ethnically and culturally more or less homogenous European people. Since the European Union lacks these ingredients, its Parliament, or so one may argue, will hardly be able to live up to the standards of parliamentarism within a classical nation-state thus imposed.

But even without detracting from the credentials of the European Parliament explicitly, the above reasoning would be compatible with a view on the EU as an organization of Member States, whereby the Member States ultimately remain their own law-makers, be it that they act in concert. National parliaments would then form the domestic democratic extensions of those elements in the EU order that represent the Member States' individual interests, such as the Council.[10] And wherever the Member States act, the national parliaments are inevitably implicated. If Member State action is understood as paramount in the EU, the European Council being the supreme EU organ while the Commission and the European Parliament merely support and enrich the Member States' interaction, then the national parliaments would naturally retain normative priority in any thoughts on legitimacy and democracy in the EU. Such priority would not even necessarily vanish if the EU is accepted as a hybrid with both supranational and intergovernmental elements. The preservation of the Member States as intact constituent parts of the organization would after all imply a persisting role for the national parliaments, with no prospect or inclination to step back or fade away as the European Parliament asserts itself. National parliaments should, according to that line of reasoning, never become a sort of sub-federal assemblies that have little to do with the federal level. Instead, national parliaments should, to continue that reasoning, keep their grip on decision-making inside the Member States and, by extension, the Council and, again by extension, the European Union.

To summarize, arguing from a national constitutional point of view so far, European integration means that the national parliaments have been deprived of legislative competences, and the citizens have been deprived of essential parliamentary functions. The loss should accordingly, or so it might be argued, be compensated by increased national parliamentary input.

While these motives are broadly democracy-related, we should add another, more pragmatic point why national parliamentary involvement might be worth considering from a Member State's point of view. For political reasons, such

10 See further Dashwood (1998).

involvement can also be advantageous to the government itself. Firstly, ministers who receive standpoints from different political party groups, as well as from external actors who have access to parliamentarians, can enrich the foundation of their own opinion. They may even form a new one. That in turn can help them exercise control over their own bureaucracy which to a minister may well be almost as intransparent as it is to parliament.[11] Secondly, parliamentary involvement can mean that the minister is assured of his parliament's backing. Sasse (1975: 88) gives account of how in 1974 the German government requested the postponement the adoption of a financially important EEC decision in order to secure the support of the *Bundestag*. The government thereby sought to avoid later criticism from a parliament which may at some point be composed differently. In other words, by scrutinizing proposals, parliament becomes 'implicated' in Council decision-making.[12] Thirdly, hand-tying domestic institutions, such as a mandating parliament, can increase ministers' leverage in international negotiations. They can use their domestic constraints as a bargaining chip to make their own position less negotiable.[13] Fourthly, from a long-term government perspective, involvement of the national parliament, including the opposition, can help consolidate a coherent national standpoint. On the one hand, a minister who is backed by an informed parliament can enjoy a stronger stance in the Council to begin with. On the other hand, a Member State can maintain continuity of its national policy even after the government changes, if the new government parties have previously, during the time that they have spent in opposition, been constantly kept up to date about EU affairs. A coherent national standpoint as regards the EU, even after elections and cabinet changes, should be of particular importance to smaller Member States, and opposition involvement should be especially important in Member States which tend to have multi-party coalitions.[14] These four points, which of course mutually overlap, are to show that stronger scrutiny might not only be in the interest of democracy on the national level, but also in the interest of executive pragmatism. It may not only benefit parliament itself, but also the one who is being scrutinized, namely the national government, and it may be advantageous for the effective representation of the Member State as a whole. At the same time it shows that 'stronger parliaments' can mean different things, depending on who puts forward such demand, such as 'parliaments effectively guarding delegated powers' or 'parliaments being conveniently implicated in Council bargaining'.

---

11 Weber-Panariello (1995), p. 314; Holzhacker (2004), p. 6.

12 Niblock (1971), p. 49 *et seq*.

13 Pahre (1997); Dimitrakopoulos (2001); Holzhacker (2002), p. 467 *et seq*.

14 Raunio/Wiberg (2001); see also Holzhacker (2004), p. 7.

3.3 The European perspective

In the classical federalist logic of European integration, the national parliaments of the Member States should not deserve too much attention. The efforts for developing a European parliamentarism instead concentrated on the European Parliament. The name 'European Parliament' was first adopted by the Parliament itself in 1962, to boldly replace the modest name 'European Parliamentary Assembly', and the official renaming followed only with the Single European Act. During the 1970s, the critical question was raised how the European Parliament could be taken seriously if its members owed their seats to a dual mandate, along with their mandate for their national parliaments.[15] This led to the adoption of the 1976 Decision and Act concerning the election of the representatives of the European Parliament by direct universal suffrage, and to the first direct EP elections in 1979. After that, during the 1980s, a critical follow-up question was raised: how can the European Parliament fulfil the functions of a genuine parliament if its powers, which were largely consultative at the time, do not even come close to those of its national counterparts. In response, the Single European Act introduced the co-operation procedure, the Maastricht Treaty introduced co-decision, and every new treaty since then, including the Constitutional Treaty, expanded the powers of the European Parliament. Nevertheless, its democratic shortcomings became subject to criticism, and shifted to the very centre of the debate about the EU's democratic deficit in the 1990s. Increasingly, however, the European Parliament seems to lose that central position in the debate, and the focus now shifts to the democratic deficit on the Member State level. In fact, the shifted attention towards the national parliaments is the very reason why we are questioning possible ways to strengthen them at present.

From the European point of view, to which the European Parliament itself, but also national MPs meeting in COSAC increasingly subscribe, the national parliaments can be interesting basically for the same reasons that they are interesting from the national constitutional point of view. As has been clearly spelt out in Article I-46 (2) of the Constitutional Treaty, the national parliaments are a link in the European Union's chain of representative democracy. The citizens of the Member States elect the national parliaments, to which the national governments are, according to that provision, accountable when convening in the Council and the European Council (or IGCs, for that matter). In addition, the citizens are represented in the directly elected European Parliament. While the European Parliament is at times flexing its muscles to ensure accountability of the Commission, under rights of inquiry and the sanction of censure, no such link of accountability exists, or can exist, with respect to the Council.[16] The reason for that is the fact that the

15 See Ronge (1998), p. 63 *et seq*. for an historical account.

16 Harlow (2002), p. 33.

European Parliament has no control over the composition of the Council. Since the Council is a permanent conference of national ministers, there is neither an investiture, nor a term of office, nor a possibility to dismiss or dissolve it. Accordingly, if the principle of popular representation is to be upheld with respect to all EU institutions, so as to ensure systemic stabilization and social acceptance for integration or to maintain safeguards against abuse of power, the accountability of the Council must necessarily be ensured via the national parliaments. This is what Article I-46 sought to confirm or, in the light of the priorities of the past, admit. After all, by maturing and asserting itself, the European Parliament was originally intended to make the national parliaments' role at EU level obsolete, at least in the long run.[17] Thus, in contrast to the reasoning mentioned earlier, the role of the national parliaments for EU purposes indeed should fade away with time, whereby the parliaments, in the manner of sub-federal assemblies, would be confined to purely domestic activities and would not transgress upon the domain of the European Parliament. Yet today even the European Parliament has to acknowledge a complementary function of the national parliaments in the European architecture, in as far as the latter may control the Council as the other co-legislator.

The most prominent summary of the possible contribution of the national parliaments to the European Union is undoubtedly the phrase inviting them to 'increase the democratic legitimacy of the EU, and bring Europe closer to its citizens', a phrase that can be found in different variations in the Nice Declaration, in the Declaration of Laeken and in Convention documents. It is also the basis for what can be found in the Commission's 2001 White Paper on European Governance,[18] which states:

> The European Parliament and all national parliaments of the Union and the applicant countries should become more active in stimulating a public debate on the future of Europe and its policies.

Following that line of reasoning, the transparency and accessibility of EU decision-making may be increased if it becomes subject to debates in a representative institution with which people can identify. Parliamentary debates about European integration may stimulate citizens' interest in the EU, and if they familiarize themselves with its workings, then the understanding of, and eventually the support for, the EU might be bolstered. This line of reasoning therefore essentially seeks to instrumentalize the national parliaments for the purposes of communicating EU policy downwards, to the citizens of the Member States. It is the reverse of the national constitutional reasoning outlined above, under which the national parliaments are to ensure that citizens' preferences are duly translated upwards, to

17 See Niblock (1971), p. 74; Jurgens (1993).
18 European Commission (2001), p. 30.

the level of EU decision-making. Either way, stronger European scrutiny in the national parliaments would seem desirable: as a tool for holding the governments to account, or for allowing citizens to air their concerns and preferences to the benefit of European integration and its transparency.

Apart from these democracy-related issues of closing the accountability chain to the Council, and the communication of Europe to its citizens, we should also mention a third argument which might make more active and more interested national parliaments worth considering from a European perspective. Just like a pragmatic approach to ministerial or national advantage is possible on the Member States level, the European level may have a pragmatic or technocratic interest in the national parliaments of its own. The argument would essentially be based on cross-country comparisons which reveal that those parliaments which scrutinize EU legislative proposals *ex ante* are more efficient at implementing them into national law after their adoption. Thus, the backlog of non-transposed directives in the UK and Denmark is consistently low. Countries such as France and Italy, on the other hand, tend to find themselves at the opposite end of the ranking. One might argue that the national implementation process is expedited if a parliament has already had the possibility to scrutinize pieces of EU legislation beforehand, so that it can save that scrutiny time later.[19]

Of course, we could wonder whether it is always the parliamentary process which delays the implementation of EU framework legislation. Possibly the real culprits are the governments themselves, where cross-departmental co-ordination in the drafting of domestic law is insufficient, and the implementing bills are not introduced speedily enough. More fundamentally, even if national parliaments do have the potential to delay implementation, we could wonder as to where exactly the causalities lie. A parliament may be efficient at law-making simply because it is well-organized, and it would then conduct effective scrutiny as a matter of course. An ill-organized parliament, on the other hand, may suffer from cumbersome legislative procedures anyway, and poor scrutiny may be just a symptom of its general condition. Path-dependence would suggest that where domestic scrutiny and law-making is ineffective, EU-related scrutiny and implementation processes are not too effective either. Apart from that, even a hand-tying national parliament tends to enter the scene only comparatively late in the EU decision-making process, so that to assume that last-minute *ex ante* debate can substitute in-depth implementation debate would seem unrealistic, especially if the minister concerned got outvoted in the first place. Political science research therefore focuses on rather different factors affecting the speed and correctness of national transposition measures, such as a directive's relative salience, misfits as regards pre-existing domestic legislation, the cost of compliance and the cost of non-compliance, without

19 Cf. Urbantschitsch (1998), p. 65; Fitzmaurice (1999), p. 337.

excessively drawing parliament-versus-government pictures. Nevertheless, there is a certain charm to at least the hypothetical idea of such a pragmatic approach to the national parliaments, inviting them to be more active *ex ante* for the sake of a smooth implementation of EU framework legislation when it is needed. We may apply an analogous line of reasoning to the Convention method of treaty revision, where national MPs are included in the drafting process so as to ensure that no unforeseen resistance arises at the ratification stage, at least not among parliamentarians. And again the above considerations show that the meaning and purpose of 'more parliamentary debate' varies according to author and context. It can mean 'more debate to keep Brussels at bay' or 'more debate to prevent annoying hick-ups during implementation procedures'.

3.4 Sovereignism, Federalism and a Multi-Level Union

The sovereignist lot are thus not necessarily the only natural supporters of stronger national parliamentary involvement in the EU. True, arguing from a Member States perspective, national parliaments may consolidate a national standpoint in the long run and could recover, on the national level, a greater degree of parliamentary democracy. Yet also from a European perspective, national parliaments are not, at least no longer, just a set of national actors who should be drained of powers and otherwise duly ignored. In closing the chain of accountability to the Council, and in 'bringing Europe closer to its citizens' by way of debating European issues, they now seem important and long-underestimated democratic building blocks in the EU.

However, we should still bear in mind that assigning the national parliaments a greater role in the EU keeps colliding with the original federalist logic of European integration. Long before the Treaty establishing a Constitution for Europe was agreed upon, the European Parliament had already made its own proposals for a European Constitution.[20] In each case, the European Parliament accorded itself a central place in the EU legislative process, on equal footing with the Council. This is in line with the idea of gradually developing the European Parliament to become a parliament that would be comparable to the nation-state sort. The importance of the national parliaments at EU level would, in this model, fade out with time. This idea still seems to govern the spirit of the European Parliament's contributions to the constitutional debate. Its 2002 Report on relations between the European Parliament and the national parliaments in European integration,[21] for instance, does acknowledge the importance of the national parliaments in bringing Europe closer to its citizens. The Report invites the national parliaments to scrutinize more actively their governments' EU policy, and stresses that the European

20 1984 Spinelli Report, 1994 Herman Report; see also Duff (2002a).

21 EP Committee on Constitutional Affairs Report of 23 January 2002, A5-0023/2002.

Parliament and the national parliaments fulfil complementary roles in parliamentarizing the EU, each within its own realm. However it places one crucial emphasis: for the democratization and parliamentarization of the EU, full co-decision by the European Parliament is 'essential in all legislative areas'.[22] The national parliaments should meanwhile make full use of their scrutiny powers *in all cases where there is no co-decision*.[23] The national parliaments are thus still called upon to bridge a temporary parliamentary gap, so that where the European Parliament has no say (yet), the national parliaments are to maintain oversight.[24] As soon as the European Parliament receives powers in these areas of its own, the decision whether or not to keep scrutinizing the governments any further will basically be left to the national parliaments. Only now do they still have a European function to fulfil.

The European perspective employed in the present discussion and supranational visions of Europe do not have to coincide. If they did, the discussion would be over quickly, and stall in the well dug trenches of normative thought. Sovereignists would like to see the national parliaments, or generally the Member States, return to the driver's seat, which would transform the 'losers of integration' into the real 'Masters of the Treaties'. Federalists would see the national parliaments as hindering the development of parliamentarism at EU level, while neo-functionalists would, for good measure, criticize basically any parliamentary involvement as hindering the efficiency of Council decision-making, which in itself could be justified for instance under the heading of consociational representation.[25]

This is the point at which a 'third way' in between federalism and nation-state sovereignism is usually put forward. Essentially, this approach dismisses both federalism and sovereignism as being static and state-centred. Clinging to notions of national sovereignty, and insisting that the nation-state is the only setting in which a community of solidarity is feasible, allowing for majoritarian democracy to prosper, would be inadequate in the integrated transnational setting of the EU that already exists. Federalism, on the other hand, would merely seek to transpose nation-state notions of republicanism or parliamentarism onto the European level, which is difficult to achieve since the EU is neither a nation, nor a state. Instead, we are invited to accept that the nations, the EU, and also the regions, all exist next to each other without any clear hierarchy, and that their governmental and non-governmental institutions interact with each other in what is a complex *sui generis* system of networks and countervailing powers called 'multi-level governance', a term borrowed from political science, or 'constitutional pluralism', its

---

22 *Ibid.*, Article 5.
23 *Ibid.*, Article 6.
24 This thought was also raised in the form of a question in the Laeken Declaration: 'Should [the national parliaments] have a role in areas of European action in which the European Parliament has no competence?'
25 See for critical overviews: Lord (1998); Sie Dhian Ho (2004).

non-hierarchical constitutional-law counterpart.[26] Since this perspective is global, it forms another variation on our European perspective. Where does that leave the national parliaments? Essentially, multi-level constitutionalism or constitutional pluralism, possibly complemented with broader notions of 'governance' instead of government, would require both the national and the European level to possess effective loci for interest representation. Therefore, where national parliaments are unnaturally weak, they should be propped up to adequately complement the European level of parliamentarism.[27] Accordingly, stronger national parliaments are compatible with multi-level governance and multi-level constitutionalism. What makes this approach problematic for our purposes here is that a stronger European Parliament, the battle-horse of the federalists, would be compatible with multi-level governance and pluralist constitutionalism just as well.

Pluralist multi-level models may underline the fact that a European perspective is not necessarily federalist, and that a national perspective is not necessarily Eurosceptic, but in their all-embracing and non-prioritizing approach they offer little added normative value. This is why multi-level approaches play a role as a facet, but not as a perspective of its own right in our discussion. Instead, we employ a distinction between European perspective and national constitutional perspective, which should duly accommodate all those who are theoretically in favour of a greater role for the national parliaments in the EU. Thus, stronger scrutiny there may be desirable for restoring or preserving national democracy, or for filling a temporary parliamentary gap at EU level. It may be desirable for communicating EU policy down to the citizens to overcome alienation, or in order to make sure that citizens' preferences, as reflected in the national parliaments, find their way up to the Council. It may be desirable for guarding the principle of subsidiarity, either because it may promote transparency for European purposes, or because it would keep the national parliaments in control of delegated powers, for example in preventing the phenomenon of competence creep towards the EU without explicit authorization. While we leave pluralist multi-level theories for now, we will, when we place the entire discussion into a broader framework, of course come back to this notion.[28]

3.5 How to strengthen European scrutiny

Demanding stronger oversight over EU policy requires the assumption that there is an existing weakness in the first place, and a discrepancy between the current

---

26 See e.g. Rometsch/Wessels (1996), Ronge (1998), p. 128, Banchoff/Smith (1999), Nicolaïdis (2003), Weiler (2003).

27 Hofmann (2003).

28 See 8 *infra*.

situation, on the one hand, and a desired ideal situation, on the other hand. Overcoming the perceived deficit then means overcoming the obstacles that stand in the way of more effective scrutiny. This in turn requires identifying these obstacles in the first place, which is where our earlier comparative overview of the different scrutiny mechanisms in the national parliaments comes in handy. There, the nature of the 'European challenge', as well as the factors that contribute to parliamentary weakness, or reluctance, have been pointed out. Let us sum up what would be necessary to approach an ideal situation of effective scrutiny, leaving aside for now its deeper purpose, in the form of a wish-list, so to speak. Much of this list will coincide with what COSAC has laid down in its 2003 Copenhagen Guidelines, a non-binding code of conduct,[29] and we will come back to that afterwards. We will then also duly insert the necessary qualifications as to whether it is at all appropriate to speak of any ideal prototype of parliamentary scrutiny.

3.5.1 Information

We have identified the widened information gap behind the government as being a primary impediment to maintaining oversight on EU policy. There are several actual or potential factors contributing to this information gap, the first of which is the difficulty to obtain relevant and timely EU-related information in the first place. If a national parliament has no access to, for instance, the Commission proposals to be discussed in the Council, it cannot form an opinion on them beforehand. If this parliament is then confronted with a domestic bill intended to implement a piece of framework legislation, it will possibly find out that it has missed the chance to have an impact on its substance while it was still a draft at EU level. The fundamental need for timely information, assuming effective scrutiny is desired, has in fact been addressed with priority at EU level. Thus, in Maastricht Declaration No. 13, the governments announced their willingness to ensure 'that national parliaments receive Commission proposals for legislation in good time for information or possible examination'. Article 2 of the Amsterdam Protocol on the role of national parliaments in the European Union laid down a legally binding obligation for the governments as regards the forwarding of Commission proposals. The government of each Member State was to 'ensure that its own national parliament receives them as appropriate'. COSAC requested the inclusion of a wider information scope to be adopted in the Nice IGC, so that also all Second Pillar documents would fall under the forwarding obligation.[30] Eventually, the EU Constitutional Treaty as adopted by the Convention and the IGC did broaden the scope of information, and notably switched to a new approach of document distribution.

---

29 COSAC Secretariat (2003); see also Rizzuto (2003), p. 8.
30 Swedish Riksdag (2001), p. 19 *et seq.*

Under the Amsterdam Protocol, the Commission would send its Green and White Papers and communications to the national parliaments, while its legislative proposals would be forwarded by the governments. Now, under the new Protocol, the Commission would not only distribute its consultation documents and its annual legislative programme directly to the national parliaments,[31] but also all the 'draft legislative acts' that it introduces.[32] Thus, instead of obliging the governments to forward documentation, the Protocol would oblige the Commission to send its documents to the parliaments itself.

In addition to Commission proposals, the national parliaments would be entitled to receive, under the heading of 'draft legislative acts', initiatives from a group of Member States, initiatives from the European Parliament, requests from the ECJ, recommendations from the European Central Bank and requests from the European Investment Bank for the adoption of a European legislative act.[33] The European Parliament and the Council would also forward their legislative resolutions, respectively their common positions, to the national parliaments.[34] Furthermore, the Commission would draw the national parliaments' attention to proposals to apply the flexibility clause of Article I-18 of the Constitutional Treaty, the successor of Article 308 EC; the national parliaments would have to be kept informed about the activities of Europol and Eurojust for evaluation and scrutiny subject to a European Law;[35] the national parliaments would be notified of incoming EU membership applications from foreign states under Article I-58; they would be notified of any proposed treaty amendments under Article IV-443; they would be consulted under Article IV-444 about any initiative to unanimously move to QMV or to co-decision, and the objection from any national parliament within six months from notification would suffice to prevent the adoption of the move.

Even though the maintenance of information flows may seem straightforward, the call for unlimited access to information requires a certain balance to be struck. Indeed, there may be a danger of information overloads,[36] and counter-productive effects of an 'explosion of (electronic) paperwork'.[37] The Austrian government is for instance suspected of suffocating its parliament in paper deliberately, so as to

31 Article 1 TCE Protocol on the role of national parliaments in the European Union.
32 *Ibid.*, Article 2 (3).
33 *Ibid.*, Article 2 (2).
34 Article 4 TCE Protocol on the application of the principles of subsidiarity and proportionality.
35 Articles I-42 (2), III-260, III-261, III-273, III-276 TCE; the Brussels European Council of 4 and 5 November 2004 has invited the Commission to table proposals for such a European Law; see further White (2004).
36 Swedish Riksdag (2001), p. 24.
37 Weatherill (2003), p. 911.

avoid meaningful oversight.[38] Thus, even if a national parliament receives all EU documents in time, the amount and technical complexity of the papers remains as a practical obstacle to scrutiny. To deal with the complexity, parliament would require additional information. The inclusion of explanatory memorandums from the government, which briefly outline the content and consequences of a proposal, tends to facilitate the scrutiny process. This would also help prioritize the incoming documentation, and to estimate its relevance and potential impact. An efficient sifting for pre-selection, especially in the absence of any EU hierarchy between fundamental and technical pieces of legislation,[39] is then vital for the optimal allocation of parliament's resources in the further scrutiny process, assuming that the optimum is approached as effectiveness increases. Still, reliance on explanatory memorandums attached to EU documents means that parliament essentially depends on information it receives from the own government. This might be too one-sided for the purposes of a fruitful debate or effective control.[40] Consequently, if a parliament wanted to balance this out, it would need to receive input from, for example, affected interest groups. Apart from external information originating from within the own Member State, parliament may also profit from its information sources at EU level. Contact to the individual Member State's permanent representation in Brussels, for instance via a parliamentary liaison office, can provide a helpful channel. And, of course, inter-parliamentary co-operation can be a means to extract information other than that provided by the individual government. This applies, firstly, to co-operation with the European Parliament, or individual MEPs, whose assets are their greater proximity to the Commission and the Council, as well as their expertise in general. Apart from that, maintaining contact with the European Parliament can facilitate keeping track of the co-decision procedure. Secondly, co-operation with other national parliaments could help see the individual government's position in a relative perspective, and it allows for learning the opinions prevailing in other Member States. This last issue actually points to another important aspect of European scrutiny. An essential feature of EU legislation is not only that it is complex, or that it comes in great numbers, but also that it is transnational in nature. In a decision-making process that seeks to address cross-border problems with cross-border regulation, the opinion of more than just one Member State has to be taken into account. That is of course the very essence of cross-border decision-making in the first place. And that would also have to play a role in the scrutiny process in an individual national parliament that wishes to enhance its role.

---

38 Urbantschitsch (1998), p. 47; Blümel/Neuhold (2001), p. 336; see also Raunio (2001), p. 181 on the downside of extensive information in the Finnish parliament.

39 Hofmann (2003), p. 10.

40 Raunio (2004), p. 13, Von der Vring (1996), p. 394.

3.5.2 Scrutiny

Once all the desired information has been made available, parliament can enter into scrutinizing the EU proposals themselves. Of course, the receipt of external information on the subject is already a form of parliamentary consideration. Now, however, an actual parliamentary opinion has to be formed. Here, as earlier, the question arises of who should be in charge of that process. The plenary can provide a broad forum for major issues, such as treaty amendments or EU enlargement. The specialist expertise on sectoral policy issues can be found in the sectoral committees, from agriculture and fisheries to development co-operation and gender equality. EU-related expertise meanwhile tends to be concentrated in the European Affairs Committee. In the ordinary EU legislative process, a parliament that is keen to make its scrutiny more effective would profit most from a well-balanced combination of sectoral and European expertise.

Another part of the identified information gap is caused by the fact that parliaments usually do not possess the resources, for instance, the administrative support to match the information advantage enjoyed by the ministerial bureaucracies. Especially small national parliaments tend to rely on limited research staff.[41] Sufficient resources are however necessary to manage the information flows. Here again, a certain balance would need to be struck. Munneke (2003: 62) for instance, raises concerns about a possible competition between parliamentary and governmental civil servants. The result may be too strong a focus on technical details in the political debate, which can turn out to be detrimental to the free exercise of parliament's political scrutinizing and legitimizing functions.

When a parliamentary opinion has been formed, it needs to be communicated to the government before the EU proposal is adopted in the Council if a parliament wishes to have an impact. This comprises two aspects. Firstly, there must be sufficient time for the scrutiny process to be completed. Secondly, there must be a means of communication with the government. As to the time left for parliamentary scrutiny, it was the Amsterdam Protocol that first provided for a minimum delay of six weeks between the introduction of a Commission proposal, or an initiative under the Third Pillar, and the placement of the item onto the Council agenda.[42] This was done explicitly to allow the national parliaments to become active *ex ante*. The six-weeks delay was upheld in the Constitutional Treaty, applying to all 'draft legislative acts', albeit not to non-legislative drafts such as CFSP strategies, while the respective new Protocol provision even stressed: 'Save in urgent cases for which due reasons have been given, no agreement may be reached on a draft European

41 See e.g. Bossaert (2001) on Luxembourg.

42 Article 3 Amsterdam Protocol on the role of national parliaments in the European Union.

legislative act during those six weeks'.[43] In addition, ten days must elapse between the placing of an item on the Council agenda and the voting itself,[44] and if Coreper has not finished its work within a week before the voting, the Council strikes out the item from the provisional agenda.[45] Before the passerelle under Article IV-444 of the Constitutional Treaty can be applied, the national parliaments are even notified six months in advance.[46] All of the above can be used as time windows for scrutiny and influence, ideally before the Council rushes to adopt proposals, or to rubber-stamp Coreper items, or to strike all the necessary deals behind the scenes.

If national parliamentary scrutiny should take longer than the relevant delays provide, scrutiny reserves may prove helpful to prevent premature Council action. The Convention's working group IV recommended scrutiny reserves to be given a clearer status in Council's Rules of Procedure.[47] So did the House of Commons 33rd Report on EU Scrutiny in 2002. So far, however, scrutiny reserves are not formally acknowledged on Council level.

As to the communication of parliamentary opinions to the government, there would have to be an institutionalized dialogue. If the opinion is just adopted by way of resolution without hearing the government itself, the effect may be sub-optimal, assuming that maximized effect is the optimum. If no resolution is adopted at all, the only opportunity to communicate for instance the findings of a committee to the minister would be if the minister or his staff were present at the committee meeting itself.[48] If the dialogue is not institutionalized in a committee, members of the government parties will be able to use informal, personal contacts to members of the government and its civil service, which deprives the opposition of an opportunity to articulate its views.[49] In the dialogue with the government, a balance should be struck between holding ministers to the opinions of their parliament, on the one hand, and allowing them sufficient leeway so that they can agree to a compromise in the Council. Too strict a mandate can be harmful to the national interest, if a compromise is not ideal but more favourable than being outvoted. Then again, a mandate can be stricter, the readier parliament or its European Affairs Committee is to hold urgency sessions to confer with ministers, and to adapt their mandate if needed.

After the Council meeting, if the reasoning is followed through, the government would have to report back to parliament on the course of the negotiations. It should give account about how it followed the opinions of parliament. Possible

---

43 Article 4 TCE Protocol on the role of national parliaments in the European Union.

44 *Ibid.*

45 Article 3 (5) Council Rules of Procedure (Council Decision 2002/682/EC).

46 Article 6 TCE Protocol on the role of national parliaments in the European Union.

47 European Convention (2002d), p. 9.

48 See Hölscheidt (2001), p. 138.

49 Holzhacker (2002).

deviations would then have to be subject to parliamentary sanctions, at least a reprimand, if they are not well-explained afterwards. Openness of the Council is crucial to achieve effective scrutiny *ex post,* for oversight over ministers' adherence to their parliament's opinion cannot be maintained if Council negotiations are conducted in secrecy. In that respect, Article I-50 of the Constitutional Treaty stipulated that the EU institutions should conduct their work as openly as possible, and that the Council shall meet in public 'when considering and voting on a draft legislative act'. Although it again notably excluded the Council's working in non-legislative capacity, the provision was to offer increased parliamentary oversight opportunities. In addition, the Council agendas and the minutes of Council deliberations would have to be forwarded, under the Constitutional Treaty regime, directly to the national parliaments, at the same time as they are sent to the governments.[50]

As mentioned at the beginning of this wish-list, several aspects identified herein coincide with what COSAC has included in its Copenhagen Guidelines. The Guidelines are also based upon the principles of timely information, opportunity for influence and reporting back, and they stipulate the desirability of explanatory memorandums, preparatory meetings with ministers, as well as sufficient administrative assistance.[51] It goes to show that the above wish-list can, in principle, be implemented without changing any treaty. A non-binding code of best practice is after all largely confined to naming slumbering possibilities which the addressees are capable of implementing themselves. What exactly would such an implementation then require?

3.5.3 The key to best practice

Assuming a constitutional setting of parliamentary democracy, where the government relies on the confidence or tolerance of parliament or its lower chamber, the oversight in European affairs is merely the practical materialization of a pre-existing constitutional principle. One of the most important elements in this setting is the parliamentary right of inquiry, the right to summon ministers and to demand the disclosure of information. This includes EU-related information, in as far as it is not provided by, for instance, the Commission itself. Already, Commission documents are placed on the Internet and are quickly and freely accessible to any national MP, unless he or she insists on a translated and authorized version with stamp and seal. Parliamentarians can obtain further information via the electronic

50 Article 5 TCE Protocol on the role of national parliaments in the European Union.
51 COSAC (2003).

means of existing European databases.[52] The burdening amount of EU legislation can be compensated by concentrating on certain areas only. Under the Finnish model of oversight, for example, parliament focuses only on EU proposals that concern policy areas for which parliament would have been competent if Finland were not in the EU.[53] This approach avoids unnecessary overstretching of parliamentary resources in areas which parliament would not have addressed under purely domestic standards. Further sifting of documents according to importance, as well as dealing with their complexity, is then essentially a matter of resources, time for scrutiny and money to fund support staff. The funding of parliamentary staff is an item in the national budget, which would typically lie in the hands of parliament itself. A parliament can thus in principle allocate additional money for, say, an extended research department or a European information bureau.[54] Time is then a question of priority-setting on its own agenda. The same holds true for the intensity with which European affairs are scrutinized in comparison with domestic bills. The committee structure might be optimized by amending a parliament's rules of procedure. In some cases, there might be constitutional obstacles to institutional and procedural reforms,[55] but even such obstacles could be tackled at the right opportunity, for instance, when a treaty ratification requires a constitutional reform anyway, which places parliament in a double vetoing position. European scrutiny can therefore be strengthened by the national parliaments themselves. So why would national parliaments not do what would apparently be in their own power to do? At this point, we may recall Norton's (1995b) distinction of the factors which determine a parliament's European oversight practice: there are reasons why national parliaments *cannot* scrutinize effectively, and reasons why they *do not want to* do so in the first place.

3.5.4 Why scrutiny is not sharpened

The answer to why there is not enough political will to sharpen European scrutiny has been given already. One of the most important factors was the path-dependency of parliaments. This means that responses to new challenges are heavily influenced by already existing practice. Departure from existing patterns is achieved in small

---

52 IPEX, the inter-parliamentary EU exchange and information network based on the ECPRD server is being upgraded to allow for code-protected postings by MPs; see further Weber-Panariello (1995), p. 313; Miller/Ware (1996).

53 Section 96 Finnish Constitution.

54 Raunio (1999), p. 195; Raunio/Wiberg (2000), p. 165.

55 See Article 61 (1) French Constitution, subjecting amendments of parliamentary rules of procedure to mandatory constitutional review. This might turn out to be important as Article 43 limits the maximum number of parliamentary standing committees to six per chamber.

steps only.[56] It can therefore be assumed that in the area of European affairs, a parliament plays largely the same role that it plays in domestic matters, although this may not always be accurate to state. The Finnish parliament for instance seems to be more active and assertive in EU matters than it is in domestic affairs.[57] On the other hand, equating European affairs to domestic affairs may not be justified, and the correct comparison would be that between European affairs and foreign affairs. Thus, European scrutiny may reflect a parliaments' stance in supervising foreign affairs, which is an area of aggravated information gaps and traditional parliamentary constraints. The strength of the European Affairs Committee of the Danish *Folketing* is, for instance, so remarkable *inter alia* because the European Affairs Committee is far more powerful than the committee on foreign affairs, which does not have any comparable mandating powers. Indeed, European affairs may neither be considered domestic nor foreign, but be appropriately treated as a policy area *sui generis.*[58] Even that, however, necessitates a conscious choice, and an extraordinary effort.

As far as the expression 'sharper scrutiny' of EU matters is concerned, this is a relative matter. The question is: sharper than what? European scrutiny would not only have to be sharper than it is today, but, in the light of the path-dependency argument, it would have to be sharper than the scrutiny maintained in a comparable pre-existing policy field, foreign or domestic. Basically, we would therefore be demanding EU-related scrutiny to be stronger than scrutiny of foreign affairs, as the latter is inappropriate seen the domestic implications of EU decision-making. On the other hand, we might even be dissatisfied with the way in which a parliament is scrutinizing the government on purely domestic matters. Thus, confronted with a national parliament that is a rubber-stamp in both areas, we would require it not only to be stronger than it is in EU affairs today, but also to be stronger than it is on foreign affairs in general, and stronger than it already is on purely domestic policies. These are important qualifications to make. They are not to imply that sharper scrutiny of EU affairs is impossible, but that it would have to be consciously stimulated in a setting of pre-existing patterns of behaviour and institutional arrangements. This point is particularly important to note since European scrutiny is often not rewarded by media attention, or by more votes at general elections, and since the conscious choice in an integration-friendly parliament would exactly aim in the opposite direction, namely deliberate self-constraint for the sake of efficiency or otherwise parliamentarization of the EU level itself. With this in mind, let us reconsider what exactly it is that we would expect of national parliaments when demanding stronger European scrutiny.

---

56 Dimitrakopoulos (2001).
57 Raunio/Wiberg (2001), p. 71.
58 Hegeland (2004).

3.6 What do we expect?

A demand for sharpened European scrutiny in the national parliaments can have, as mentioned earlier, different backgrounds. It may be in the interest of an individual Member State or particular national players, or in the interest of European integration at large, depending on which course is desired. Pursuing the domestic interest, a national parliament could, among other things, reclaim oversight and control over regulatory competences that it has delegated by ratifying the European treaties. European integration may in turn profit, again among other things, from the participation of democratic institutions of the Member States in linking the EU level of decision-making to the citizens. The time has come to apply the perspectives that we have distinguished, and the different angles of justification for stronger parliaments, to the identified objectives.

3.6.1 The national perspective: mind the audience

The national constitutional approach to European scrutiny, leaving aside the selfish interests of governments to co-opt and implicate their parliaments in their policies, seeks to relieve the national parliaments from their position as 'losers of integration' on the domestic arena. However, the question in how far a given national parliament is in fact a 'loser' depends to a large extent on how it has adapted to EU membership, and on what it had to lose in the first place. Critical analyses of purely domestic powers of parliament can be very enlightening, and at times sobering.[59] To recall, the form and degree of European scrutiny in a national parliament is primarily a matter of domestic history, political culture, attitudes of political parties, and the prevailing institutional balance of power.[60] Therefore, no matter how tempting it might be to picture an ideal prototype model of parliamentary scrutiny, we should bear in mind that national parliaments are a highly heterogeneous group, if we can speak of a group at all. Different election systems, for instance, lead to different modes of representation, different ratios of voters per MP, and different ways of government formation. The amount of political parties represented in a parliament varies on a scale from traditional one-party dominance and effective bipartisanism to heavy fragmentation. Some Member States tend to have single-party majority cabinets, like Greece and the UK, some tend to have coalitions of two political parties, like Germany and Austria, or of three, like the Netherlands, or even more political parties, like Belgium and Italy. In some Member States, most notably Denmark but also Latvia, even minority cabinets are not uncommon. Party discipline and mutual compatibility of coalition

---

59 See Norton (1998).

60 Norton (1995); Pahre (1997); Bergman (1997); Agostini (2001); Maurer (2002).

partners differ. In terms of political culture, even the capacity of parliaments to act as fora for public debate differs from one Member State to another. While in some Member States televised parliamentary debates, written parliamentary questions and ministers' replies attract broad public attention, in others arguments are more often exchanged outside the plenary in committees, or even outside parliament itself, in the media.

Each national parliament represents the political preferences of its own electorate in terms of composition and the placement of political parties into either government or opposition. It also reflects wider constitutional preferences. That relates to the status a parliament has *vis-à-vis* the government, which is also a matter of political culture. The activity priorities that parliaments identify for themselves with respect to EU affairs vary between domestic government scrutiny, an active role in the EU itself, and loyal regime support.[61] This again relates to the competences a parliament has on the domestic level. Thus, for each national parliament in the EU we have to ask separately: which powers did that particular parliament have in the first place? Which powers does it share with a president, in a semi-presidential system? Which powers does it share with the government, in cases where the executive has autonomous regulatory competences? Which powers does the lower chamber share with the upper chamber, in cases of bicameralism? Which powers does parliament share with sub-national entities, such as autonomous provinces, devolved regions or federal states? Which powers does it share with the electorate itself, in cases where nation-wide referendums are possible? And, when it comes to a parliament's own powers, we must ask to what extent it exercises them really autonomously. We may briefly recall the government's usual agenda-setting powers, party discipline and whip systems, the fact that most domestic bills are in fact initiated by the government, or that the government itself is often regulating actively by ordinance or decree.[62] And before we lament a decline of parliamentarism in a Member State on this basis, we would still need to add two other questions. Firstly, in how far is it true that there is a decline? Has there ever been something like a 'golden age' of parliamentarism at all? Secondly, even if we assume that the importance of parliaments once had been greater than it is today, we should ask in how far European integration has caused a decline, rather than having accentuated a general trend.

All these questions have to be answered for each national parliament, for each Member State separately, on the background of each country's very own particularities. Each national parliament is as unique as the nation it represents. The same holds true for governments and their desire to implicate their parliament or cater to the opposition. This means that for the scrutiny of European affairs the question

61 Harlow (2002), p. 104.
62 Döring (1995).

whether or not it is feasible or desirable to strengthen it, has also to be answered for each parliament individually. Suggestions to appoint a strong European Affairs Committee might collide with the principle that all standing committees should be equal. Suggestions that a national parliament should examine a particular proposal would seem misplaced if not the national level, but a sub-national level is competent in the policy area. Suggestions that small Member States with fragmented parliaments can consolidate a national standpoint by broad parliamentary involvement may seem misplaced if a Member State is not small, or if its parliament is not fragmented. Suggestions that parliaments should provide democratic legitimacy for the EU in a broad sense would seem misplaced if MPs agree that this is exactly what the European Parliament should do, rather than national parliaments. Suggestions that a parliament should help overcome the citizens' distrust and alienation as regards the EU are misplaced if a particular nation is actually just fine with the way the EU or its national parliament works. And the parliament of a land-locked Member State may simply not be interested in EU fisheries policies. To sum up, generalizations about what national parliaments should and should not do are all too easily made from a particular national perspective. While certain suggestions may be valid in themselves, and while of course one blueprint may inspire other parliaments to sharpen their scrutiny mechanism accordingly to the extent that this is possible and desired, we should remain critical about such statements.

3.6.2 The European perspective: mind the balance

Next to the national constitutional perspective, there is an all-European approach to the national parliaments, covering top-down arrangements from the EU level in favour of national parliamentary involvement. The European Union can hardly *prevent* the national parliaments from exercising a stricter oversight, if they so wish, but it cannot *force* them to be more active either. All it can do is to stimulate their interest and facilitate or even institutionalize their EU-level participation for a European purpose, depending on how that purpose is defined.

What would sharper national parliamentary scrutiny of EU affairs mean to the European Union at large? Non-Eurosceptic EU-level statements on the national parliaments tend to lay emphasis on parliamentary deliberations, rather than on parliamentary control. The slogan 'bringing Europe closer to its citizens' after all implies a communicating task between the EU, on the one hand, and the national parliaments' electorate, on the other hand. One of the most telling proposals that came out of the European Convention was, for instance, the suggestion that national parliaments should hold a 'Europe week' once a year. This suggestion was included in the final report of working group IV,[63] reiterated, on the initiative

63 European Convention (2002d), p. 9.

of the Dutch parliamentarians Van der Linden and Timmermans, in a Declaration to raise national European awareness, which was signed by fifty other Convention members[64] and endorsed by other parliamentarians in the COSAC meeting of November 2004. The idea was to have all national parliaments simultaneously debate the Commission's annual legislative programme. The intended effect was to stimulate interest in European affairs among national parliamentarians, and via them among the citizens, possibly with cross-border effects as the debate in one Member State could be compared to the ones in the other Member States. As a result, the European Union would become more familiar to the general population. That in turn is a prerequisite to active support, and to the realization that people, via their parliaments, can actually have a say in EU decision-making. It could bring about more popular participation, higher turnouts at elections to the European Parliament as a spill-over, or, to sum it all up in that other slogan, an increase in the democratic legitimacy of the European Union. This legitimizing task of the national parliaments can be understood as being permanent, complementing the European Parliament, or temporary, just until the European Parliament has asserted itself sufficiently. It is *inter alia* for the above reasons that the European Union, a treaty-based organization with the Council, the European Council and the IGCs as an intergovernmental core, 'pierces the veil' of national constitutional autonomy, reaches out into the trans-governmental area and furnishes the national parliaments with documentation to artificially facilitate their participation in European affairs.

Again, such an intervention is not at all contrary to European or international law, and one may argue that this measure is not an EU measure at all, but an agreement between Member States. However, we should recall that the EU's core is inter-*governmental*, not inter-*parliamentary*. The treaties, protocols and IGC declarations are adopted by the governments in a European capacity to the benefit of parliaments who are not present themselves. We should therefore not underestimate the unusual, innovative, if not artificial character of EU-level top-down involvement schemes for the national parliaments. Now the benefits of the recipient's boosted strength have to be weighed against the costs of the distortions that the measure might cause, especially if the benefit is expected to be a stabilization of a supranational EU, not its putting on a national leash. Let us proceed a little further along that line.

3.7 The effects of stronger scrutiny from a European perspective

If there is one statement that sums up the object and purpose of our present discussion, then it is the following remark made by Weatherill (2003b: 910): 'The risk

---

64 European Convention (2003b).

[of championing national parliamentary involvement] is the crafting of an ill-considered system that nods imprecisely to the "virtues" of national parliaments without taking sufficient account of their vices'. The virtues that would make the national parliaments interesting for the EU have been identified earlier, apart from the pragmatic idea to implicate parliaments in decision-making, in terms of 'increasing democratic legitimacy' and 'bringing Europe closer to its citizens'. Now we should ask ourselves whether either of these objectives can actually be achieved by the proposed means. That will inevitably expose the relevant 'vices' as well.

3.7.1 'Increasing democratic legitimacy'

Democratic legitimacy is a vast notion, its implications are manifold. We may boil it down to the requirement that rule-making be a reflection of popular will. This in turn is often split down into two aspects: input legitimacy and output legitimacy. Input legitimacy prescribes an institutionalized participation of representative institutions along the way of a deliberative decision-making process. Output legitimacy, as elaborated in the writings of Scharpf, is achieved if the policies that are adopted in the decision-making process do meet eventually popular approval. Thus, we can construe a functional and result-based legitimacy of efficient and cost-reducing international co-operation itself.

This distinction already puts the debate about the EU's democratic legitimacy, or in fact its democratic deficit, in a relative perspective. Crombez (2003) for instance, points out that the output legitimacy of the European Union's law-making, as well as its institutional set-up, is not lower than the one observed in the United States. This means that the policy measures adopted by the EU do not fly in the face of a substantive part of the population, and that they are not considered to be unreasonable or unjust. Alternatively, we may note that, at least to many citizens, neither the input legitimacy, nor even the legitimacy of the EU's legislative *output* is obvious.[65] We may also criticize that there is nothing democratic about the notion of output legitimacy, for then even a well-organized benevolent dictatorship may command a degree of legitimacy.[66] In any event, what pushes the democratic legitimacy debate with respect to the EU is clearly aiming at the *input* side. Since a liberal democracy comprises not only government *for* the people, but also *by* the people,[67] and efficiency must be put in balance with popular representation, a democratic deficit is quickly diagnosed as regards the EU.

This brings us straight to the European Parliament. The European Parliament is not fulfilling the same role one would assign to a national parliament, and

---

65 Bengtson (2003), p. 2.
66 See Thaa (2002).
67 Katz/Wessels (1999), p. 5 *et seq.*

we have already touched upon some of the reasons for that.[68] Anyway, they are well-known. The composition of the European Parliament does not have the same effect on the composition of the Commission like the composition of a national parliament determines the political colour of the government. Even if that were the case, the Commission is not the ultimately decisive actor in the legislative triangle and, what is more important, it is not the European Parliament either. The EP only has co-legislative powers, and in some areas it does not even have those; the Council is always either dominant or co-equal. Another point is either a consequence of the above, or in fact the cause of the above: the low voter turnout at elections.[69] Popular participation in EP elections has been steadily declining since the first direct elections in 1979. Those who do cast their vote in fact vote for national political parties, separately for each Member State, so that quantitative popular representation is unevenly distributed as well.[70] And of course there is no European *demos* that would share a common ethnos-based national identity, and that could then identify with the European Parliament. There are no European media that could stage a genuinely European public debate, which is caused by the absence of a European language, which is again related to the absence of a European people. Geographical distance to the constituents and the persisting lack of a single recognizable parliamentary site add to this picture.[71] The pessimistic argumentation about the European Parliament goes so far as this so where exactly do the national parliaments provide an alternative?

Disappointed with the European Parliament as we might be after reading the above lines, we might seek to infuse 'more democracy' into the EU by strengthening the national parliaments. That is what is essentially meant by increasing the democratic legitimacy of the EU. Inevitably, the underlying logic will appear to be that national representative institutions are 'more democratic' than the European institutions are. Arguably, this is also 'the general and absolute assumption' that underlies the subsidiarity principle,[72] which commands regulation at the lowest sensible level, in any event not at EU level as far as possible. If the national parliaments can increase the democratic legitimacy of the European Union, then it is because they are democratic institutions themselves. But where does their democratic character come from? As said, they are representative of the will of the electorate: the distribution of parliamentary seats into majorities and minorities reflects relative preferences for one simplified political agenda over the other. After the initial

---

68 See 3.2 *supra*.

69 See Blondel *et al.* (1998).

70 Schoo (2004), p. 64 *et seq*.

71 Shephard/Scully (2002).

72 Vergés Bausili (2002), p. 8.

distribution of seats, the parliaments remain focal points for public debate, where the opposition can articulate its views. Constant competition of ideas keeps the government under healthy pressure. Challengers enforce accountability, reveal deficiencies, propose alternative policies and try to score points in order to gain their own majority in the next elections. The crucial detail here is that all this happens in a domestic setting, on the national political arena: national political parties compete on national issues for the national vote.

This has several consequences for the usefulness of the national parliaments for European purposes. One such consequence concerns the desired closure of the chain of accountability, from the citizens to the national parliaments, to the governments, to the Council. If such a link is to be meaningful, it would require that the national political parties make their EU-related policy agenda a subject of their election campaigns.[73] The same, incidentally, holds true from the national constitutional point of view, where we require that voter preferences as represented in parliament be reflected in the government's EU policy. However European issues play, at best, a subordinate role at national elections. In fact, even elections to the European Parliament, where these issues should be appropriately debated, are said to be dominated by national agendas or the popularity of national politicians. Thus, if a government party has not announced how it intends to go about the European Union, but has been elected on other issues, where exactly is the EU-related voter preference that should be imprinted in national policy formulation?

There is of course one such voter preference that indeed deserves attention, namely general popular Euroscepticism. In several Member States, the political parties represented in parliament are reconciled under a pro-European consensus, while large chunks of the population are far less integration-minded.[74] The most prominent instances where that can be observed are 'no' votes in EU-related referendums, in spite of a united 'yes' campaign by the political elite. Examples include the first Irish referendum on the Nice Treaty in 2001, the Swedish referendum on the country's entry into the euro-zone in 2003, and the Dutch rejection of the Constitutional Treaty in 2005. But also apart from the headline-making events, pro-European parliamentary consensus is not necessarily rooted in a corresponding popular consensus.

In a comparative perspective, we may find Euroscepticism on both edges of the political spectrum.[75] Obviously, the extreme-right, such as the Austrian Freedom Party or the French National Front, is likely to campaign on a xenophobic and anti-European agenda. But also bourgeois-conservative parties might have reservations against giving up national sovereignty, which applies to varying extents

73 Holzhacker (2004).

74 Raunio/Wiberg (2001), p. 64, 75 *et seq.*

75 Raunio/Wiberg (2000), p. 155 *et seq.*

to the French Gaullists, the German Christian-Social Union and the Finnish Centre Party. On the other end of the scale, opposition to European integration may come from the extreme left, the labour wings of social-democratic parties, as well as from Greens. The reason for their opposition would be the perceived neo-liberal character of the European Union's internal-market policy. In spite of this Eurosceptic potential, however, if an opposition party wishes to retain its credibility and reliability as a possible coalition partner, it can hardly afford too extreme a rhetoric.[76] As soon as an opposition party actually takes over government, it is to co-operate with its European partners in the Council. A record of anti-European campaigns can weaken the government's stance and eventually harm the national interest. It would furthermore (such political considerations aside) be valid to justify the elite consensus on European integration with the argument that European integration as such is in the people's interest. Suffice to point to the added personal and economic freedoms under the EU, the sheer scale effects of multinational co-operation, the effectiveness of addressing cross-border problems at international level, the advantages to the Member States' own exporting industries or, mundanely, the attractive cash flows from Brussels. Although at times it tends to be forgotten, we still have reason to support European integration for the peace, stability and the rule of law that is has consolidated in what is historically a very much warlike continent. To promote these ambitious goals, politicians should not only passively execute their voters' wishes, which may be diffuse or short-sighted. After all, MPs also have a leading and educative function in society. One may dismiss this argument as paternalistic; in the end, however, it is the very same educative and communicative function of politicians which is invoked when asking MPs to debate European affairs more passionately, even though their voters may be absolutely indifferent.

Apparently, EU-related preferences – singular events like noisy referendum campaigns or the issue of Turkish EU accession aside – are not salient enough for most national political parties to pick up for a polarized debate. And while this may be the case at the national level, we should not forget that Eurosceptic voters do have a very prominent representative forum in elections to the European Parliament. It would thus not be accurate to argue that Eurosceptics are deprived of any form of parliamentary representation. Even if we agree that they are effectively deprived of routine representation at the national level, apart from singular events, if we agree that there is potential salience in mundane day-to-day European affairs and that national political parties should announce their European agendas in national election campaigns or should at least submit them to sharper popular and parliamentary scrutiny, we may raise another crucial question: from which point of view will such a scrutiny then be exercised?

---

76 Raunio/Wiberg (2001), p. 75 *et seq.*

3.7.2 The mandate of national parliaments

As previously mentioned, national parliaments are elected on national issues to represent national preferences. Their mandate is thus, democratic though it may be, a national one. For the treatment of European affairs, this has first of all a constitutional implication. As Hoetjes (2001: 346) pointed out with respect to the Netherlands, and alluding to Article 50 of the Dutch Constitution: '[I]n controlling Coreper, Council or EP/Council decisions ( ) – by requesting information, explanation and discussion – the Dutch Parliament will inevitably have to take the views and interests of other member states – the EU as a whole –, into account, and will therefore have to move beyond its own mandate, i.e. representing the Dutch people, and the Dutch people only'. Or, as Norton (1995a: 6) put it: 'No national parliament has a mandate beyond its own shores'. Now what does that mean?

Domestic parliamentary debate may well take place along established cleavages – and of course debate requires cleavage – of government versus opposition and, as far as substance is concerned, along cleavages of left and right, liberal and protectionist, authoritarian and libertarian, hawkish and dovish, pro-industry and pro-environment, and so on. In a purely national setting, political parties struggle to influence policy outcomes that are applicable to their own country (and not to any other country) by tilting the balance, broadly, to the left or to the right. Parliamentary debates may also be held in the run-up to Council negotiations; the difference there, however, is that political parties will try and influence the government not in order to achieve an immediate domestic policy result, but to get the government to heed to one agenda or another in the determination of a national standpoint. Once that standpoint is determined, it becomes the expression of the national will. The policy outcome itself in this instance directly affects not just the country concerned, as is the case with national decision-making, but the European Union as a whole, or in other words more countries than just one.

We may illustrate this with a little scenario where the national parliament of, say, Sweden, first discusses purely national legislation on maximum pollution standards for factories that are located in Sweden. The government may point out that higher standards are not in the interest of the Swedish industry; the opposition may argue that they are in the interest of public health in Sweden. The result is a Swedish national policy outcome. There is nothing spectacular about that. However, in the run-up to Council negotiations about EU environmental standards on the same matter, the scenario acquires a transnational component. Again the Swedish opposition may argue that Sweden should press in the Council for higher standards, perhaps deploying rhetoric that 'Europeans want a clean environment'. But what the Swedish opposition would in fact mean is that *Swedes*, or at least many of them, want a clean environment. What it would mean is that Sweden should not be polluted by factories in neighbouring Member States, and that Sweden itself should not be dragged down to lower standards. Delicately, and here the government and its parliamentary supporters might even concur, it would mean that

Swedish industries should not be suffering competitive disadvantages in the EU because of their above-average national environmental standards. In other words, Swedish industries, which comply with high eco-standards already, profit from the imposition of higher standards on other Member States that so far have lower standards. At the same time, parliamentary debates may of course take place in, say, Greece. There parliamentarians would discuss the high value Greeks place on jobs, rather than eco-standards, and about how the Greek industry would suffer if Scandinavian-style standards were imposed EU-wide.

In both Member States the accountability process would revolve around the question how well the government has defended the pre-determined national interest: what did the Swedish minister do to keep standards high, what did the Greek minister do to keep them low? If the minister did not achieve the set objective, what else did he or she secure: perhaps an escape clause or transition periods, or a package deal on more favourable animal transportation standards, or perhaps more EU subsidies? The question at the implementation stage would then be whether to match or to top EU standards. Admittedly this is a very much simplified scenario that uses stereotypes, but it helps to understand that as soon as ministers leave their capital, they are representing their Member State as against other Member States, and that left-right or we-they considerations in the run-up to Council bargaining are aired to consolidate a national standpoint which may or may not prevail in Brussels. Real-life examples of potentially dividing issues, although they have hardly been picked up in the respective parliaments, include German dairy farmers' protests against high quotas and low milk prices in 2004, or, turning to the new Member States in the pre-accession phase, the abolition of tax-free shopping on ships in Estonia, the rise of sugar prices in Latvia, and the issue of liberalized land sales to foreigners in several countries in Central and Eastern Europe.[77] The most famous example of an issue that had been picked up in an uncompromising national parliament was of course the 1973 controversy around the pricing for Danish bacon, with all its well-known consequences as the Danish parliament adopted the hand-tying mandating practice which it has imposed ever since. It is generally helpful to realize that 'debates in the national parliaments' is not just an abstract notion that resonates well among supporters of more democracy in the EU. It is a process that, while not altering the institutional set-up of the EU itself, expands the deliberation about the national interest, something that would otherwise take place more discreetly and pragmatically, and makes it subject to polarization in public. The outcome is not an immediate policy, but the determination of one national standpoint out of twenty-five which is then subject to negotiation in Brussels.

We have touched upon the transnational aspect of EU decision-making earlier, in the context of the information gap between parliament and government, and

---

77 See Albi (2005), p. 63 *et seq.*

noted that parliament tends to be under-informed about the preferences of other Member States. However, as Raunio (2004: 13) points out, in order to realistically form an individual opinion on an EU proposal, a national parliament must be informed about the preferences and strategies of its own government, of the Commission and the European Parliament, *and* those of the other Member States. These preferences of the other Member States are of course equally national in nature, and their parliaments' mandates are limited to their own Member State as well. Their main scrutiny criterion, which derives from both their constitutional mandate, as well as the ticket on which they in practice entered parliament after campaigning over national issues, is thus the national interest. That is logical and not at all dubious, since their re-election also depends on the national vote in the Member State concerned, and not on their popularity in any other Member State, let alone Europe as a whole. Consider the announcement of the German Christian-democrats in the 2005 election campaign to implement future EU directives 'one-to-one' without putting anything on top, thereby aiming at the red-green coalition government that allegedly created disadvantages for the German labour market by over-implementing EU equal treatment standards. Surely one may interpret the success of European integration as a victory for the national interest in the long run. But even then, the interest remains defined in national terms.[78] Also instances where the interests of other Member States are taken into account during parliamentary scrutiny remain within the scope of a national parliament's mandate only as long as the policy objectives remain ultimately focused on the own national interest. That may be perfectly acceptable from a purely national constitutional point of view. Under the European rationale for involving the national parliaments in EU affairs, however, this bears a number of consequences: for the Council, on the one hand, and for the quality of political debate on the domestic arena, on the other hand. Let us start with the issue of domestic debate.

Since national parliaments are elected and re-elected in the national interest, the national interest, as noted above, also pre-determines their criteria of European scrutiny: how well has the government defended the national standpoint, that is the position adopted at the end of internal will-formation in the run-up to EU negotiations? How does this proposal serve the national interest, even when discarding strategic bargaining of accepting one policy in return for a greater benefit in another area? These criteria will be applied to draft EU legislation affecting industries and environmental standards, transport and competition, and the distribution of regional funds and agricultural subsidies. But also issues such as enlargement, relations with third countries and – very obviously – the own Member State's

78 Emphasizing the distinction between national and European electoral mandates see Duff (1994), p. 163; Neunreither (1994), p. 313; Hübner (2002); Weatherill (2003), p. 909; Donnelly/Hoffmann (2004), p. 3.

contribution to the EU budget may be subject to sharpened parliamentary debate, as if European Council debates on that issue were not, from an integrationist point of view, disgraceful enough.

One might object that the above view on the national mandate is too narrow, or that it unfairly equates national debates with nationalism or Euroscepticism. After all, why should the determination of a national standpoint on a broad parliamentary basis be in any way suspicious, given that much of EU decision-making simply *is* international bargaining, and that the EU, for better or worse, is made up of Member States which naturally all have their own interests?

As we have already noted, the desirable degree of parliamentary involvement in the definition of the national standpoint is something that needs to be assessed for each Member State individually. The preferences that emerge at the end of this internal national will-formation may or may not collide with the preferences of other Member States, they may be short-termed or long-termed. In any event, the European Union's set-up is designed to settle conflicts in the bodies that are intergovernmental in composition, i.e. that are staffed with national delegations, such as the Council. Domestic parliamentary debate would merely extend deliberations to the domestic forum, and inflate the prominence of the national stakes that are admittedly there, but that have to be reconciled with other considerations. It would increase the salience of the own agenda for receiving, say, higher (or lower) milk quotas, more subsidies or a more important Commissioner post in the short run, or long-run consolidated market access, or a higher competitive advantage in the internal market. But are other scenarios possible as well? Is it for instance possible to have a national parliamentary debate on European affairs without a fixation on national interest protection? Could one think of a compromise between benevolent support for European integration in general, on the one hand, yet critical debates about its course, on the other hand? Here we arrive at a truly crucial question, especially for those who wish to combine the ideal of ever-closer union with national parliamentarism.

The parliamentary interaction between political parties among themselves, and between party groups and the government, depends on the respective setting. We may distinguish three modes of government-parliament interaction.[79] In the *non-party mode*, 'the' government interacts with 'the' parliament as a unitary body, which would occur in matters of very high or constitutional importance. In the *cross-party mode*, shared sectoral or geographical interests unite MPs from different parties to press ministers. The most common form of interaction is however the *inter-party* mode, where the government parties support the government, and opposition parties challenge it, sometimes in spontaneous single-issue 'floating

79 See Holzhacker (2002), p. 464 and Döring (1995), as well as the contribution on the UK by Norton (1998), including references.

coalitions' with a government coalition member. In any event, interaction and political dialogue is based on diverging and competing opinions. As we have noted earlier, a debate, whether it is stimulated by the EU or not, requires a minimum cleavage, between government and opposition or otherwise. Parties which are in agreement with each other about an issue do not enter into any meaningful debate. That is the essence of the pro-European self-constraint in integration-friendly parliaments in the first place.

While the national parliamentarians in COSAC picked up the Conventioneers' idea of holding a 'Europe week' to debate the Commission's annual legislative programme, in order to communicate Europe to the citizens,[80] some MPs noted that the exercise should not become a PR festival for European integration. During that COSAC session, Belgian MP Herman de Croo for instance stressed that Europe cannot be sold in the abstract. Instead, the concrete national interest in EU decisions would have to be exposed, so that popular opinions can form in favour and against such matters like the EU accession of Turkey, or the labour monopoly of unionized dock workers in Antwerp. Even debates that appear to address left-right choices are about national preferences when held in a national parliament in the run-up to EU negotiations: what are the effects of a proposal on the individual Member State's economy, cultural priorities, job market. Wherever a national parliament, for instance, requests an explanatory memorandum from the government on a Commission proposal, these are the questions that the memorandum is expected to address. If a national parliament is interested in an EU matter, it is interested in an impact assessment, which concerns, among other things, a measure's domestic economic and financial consequences, and the estimated effect on the national legal order. To address that should be the very purpose of national parliamentary debate, or if not, what else should it be about?

Again, debate requires cleavage. Without polarization and dissent, the exercise of a parliament's communicative function is bound to be restricted. Politicians taking turns to praise the European Union is not a debate. Of course we could imagine a case where an opposition party would criticize the government for not being pro-European *enough*. Thus, instead of accusing it of not defending the national interest over the interest of other Member States, it could accuse it of not furthering European integration by, for instance, agreeing to more compromises. There are three problems with that suggestion. Firstly, if European integration is understood as the creation of a supranational layer of government, including a proper European Parliament, then pro-European parties will see their general self-constraint as a contribution to that process, understanding that there is more than just one country in the EU. Secondly, if European integration is understood as a gradual process, then pro-European opposition parties will welcome even a policy

80 Conclusions of the 32nd COSAC, November 2004.

of small steps by, say, a Eurosceptic government. Even a small step is then preferable to the status quo.[81] An integration-friendly party will certainly not always and automatically be in favour of any Commission proposal it sees; yet when it is against, it will inevitably be inspired in its opposition by what it perceives to be in the best interest of its *own* electorate or clientele, not somebody else's. Thirdly, it is difficult to imagine how an opposition party would openly champion to make more concessions, to pay more money or to swallow more unpopular measures at EU level than is necessary. Conversely, a Eurosceptic opposition will indeed be more active in its struggle against a pro-European government in order to *preserve* the status quo. To this end, Sasse (1980: 138) observed that the 'European-minded members [of the French parliament] have recognized that more responsibility in European matters for the national parliament is not the means to promote European integration'. That Member States have agendas, and that national political parties may sometimes wish to drag the government to the left or to the right in defending domestic preferences at EU level, is undeniable. Whether making these agendas subject to routine domestic polarization in the run-up to Council negotiations is a good way to parliamentarize the European Union is a wholly different question, and we will come back to it shortly.

Let us first turn again to the question why Eurosceptic opposition parties seem to be rare in the mainstream field, even though this situation might not reflect popular sentiments. We have already considered the argument that political parties, especially where coalition-forming is flexible, do not wish to damage their credibility as possible government parties with anti-European populism. This in turn is linked to the noteworthy argument that party affiliations of political leaders should anyway not excessively overshadow the continuity of external representation in the EU. But there is another issue linked to that complex, namely that voters' national preferences do not necessarily coincide with their Europe-related preferences. Cleavages in that area do not have to run along a left-right divide, and they can in fact split political parties internally.[82] These splits would however hardly justify a formal split of parties, or the foundation of single-issue anti-Europe parties on a national level.[83] A prominent example of an intra-party split over Europe can be found in the party landscape of the UK, where the salience of the question does not seem to subside at all. Both Labour and the Conservatives are internally divided over EU policy.[84] Again, a different picture emerges when we turn to European elections: the growing success of anti-Europe lists running for the European Parliament, like the June lists of Denmark and Sweden, the UK Independence Party and the Polish

---

81 Pahre (1997).

82 Lord (1998), p. 52; Raunio (1999), p. 202.

83 A rare example of a formal intra-party split over EU membership was the secession of the pro-membership wing from the Centre party in Estonia in 2004.

84 Raunio/Wiberg (2000), p. 157.

League of Families in the 2004 elections, offers Eurosceptic voters and politicians a due share of public attention. What is more, European elections allow for left-right voter alignment at EU level which, under co-decision, complements the national preferences as they are represented in the Council.

To summarize, even if we desire that parliamentary left-right alignment or otherwise also takes place on a domestic level with respect to EU affairs, we should bear in mind that the mandate of national parliaments is limited to the national interest, and sharpened scrutiny and debate will in one way or another question the desirability of European legislation and integration measures in that interest. Does such a sharpened scrutiny bring Europe closer to the citizens?

3.7.3 Twenty-five times transparency

Probably the most important added value, from a European perspective, of what sharpened European scrutiny in the national parliaments can contribute is a greater transparency of the European Union, in that it could unveil the character of EU decision-making mechanisms. One of the greatest aspects of the intransparency of 'Brussels' is the very habit of calling it that way. It depicts the European law-maker as a faceless machine of unaccountable bureaucrats, symbolized by the Commission as the Union's power-house. Making the legislation process accessible to the public could reveal that it is actually *not* the Commission which is the decisive law-maker in the adoption of acts, but that it is – notwithstanding co-decision – the Council, in which the individual minister is a participant. In the absence of such transparency it is too easy, and too tempting, for a government to scapegoat the EU for policy failures or unpopular legislation.[85] In fact, even a national parliament may blame 'Brussels' while transposing framework legislation into national law.[86] It is this unsanctioned scapegoating of the EU as an external actor which effectively interrupts the accountability chain from the national public to the Council, since it allows governments to escape taking responsibility for their actions.[87] It also makes the EU democratic deficit more acute, since having allocated guilt with 'Brussels', the citizens cannot punish those responsible by voting them out of office. As a result, adverse feelings are concentrated on institutions, rather than individuals.[88]

Therefore, if the Council's, and the individual government's contribution to a policy became visible, it would make it difficult to argue that 'Brussels' is forcing it to, say, liberalize the electricity market or to cut subsidies. It could limit the impression of the EU as being an anonymous technocratic body. From this, the EU

---

85 See Neunreither (1994), p. 299; Raunio/Wiberg (2001), p. 78; Brown (2003), p. 3; Donnelly/Hoffmann (2004), p. 4; Banchoff/Smith (1999), p. 18.

86 De Gucht (2002).

87 Smismans (1998), p. 51.

88 Katz/Wessels (1999), p. 232 *et seq.*

could profit enormously. However, the blade cuts both ways. Revealing the intergovernmental or national-delegation-based character of Council decision-making, combined with parliamentary scrutiny minding the national interest, means making the EU in general appear like a bazaar of national profit-seeking. This would be particularly evident under qualified majority voting, where the question would be whether or not a minister succeeded in assembling a blocking minority, or whether he or she secured a more profitable deal elsewhere. The European interest would thus seem to be a mere accumulation of national interests. From a European perspective, unless this is exactly our idea of what Europe should be all about, it is doubtful whether this is still the same Europe that we would want to bring closer to the citizens.

Of course, we could remark that, for better or worse, this is simply the EU as it is. While that may or may not be true, the described national-interest orientation of national parliaments in fact merely forms part of a larger picture, which raises yet more problems as regards the usefulness of national parliaments for European communication purposes.

As already stated, national parliaments represent national voter preferences. They are therefore oriented towards their own electorate. The national public in turn focuses on its own parliament. This mutual attention takes place, due the exclusiveness of the electorate and the Member States' linguistic delimitations, in politically and culturally isolated entities: the public of Member State A identifies with the parliament of Member State A, and not with the parliament of Member State B. Conversely, the parliament of Member State B has neither the electoral incentive, nor the constitutional mandate, to pay attention to public opinion in Member State A. Stronger parliamentary scrutiny of EU policy in one Member State will therefore not increase the legitimacy of EU decision-making in the eyes of the public of another Member State. To pick a nation for argument's sake, the French will not feel any closer to the EU knowing that the Danish parliament is a merciless scrutinizer. Conversely, they will not feel any worse about it when believing that the Greek parliament is a yes-shop. The only thing that will matter to the French, in as far as it does matter at all, is the way in which *French* EU policies are debated in the *French* parliament.[89] Lord (2003) duly notes that as long as national parliaments are uneven in their scrutiny capacities, how well citizens are represented in the Union arena will depend on their Member State of origin and the qualities of its parliamentary politics. Indeed, this point is important to bear in mind when invoking the assistance of national parliaments to increase the EU's legitimacy or transparency in the Member States.

We should be wary of the implication that the national parliaments form a horizontal grid of institutions, neatly placed as a collective in the European

89 Kiiver (2005b).

constitutional architecture, just below the Union and just above the regions. As pointed out earlier, the parliaments are not a homogenous group, and we shall later see more clearly that they are not likely to act as a collective in solidarity either.[90] What is crucial to note here is that there are no cross-border, especially no cross-language-border spill-over effects in terms of legitimacy perception of the European Union. For the public of any given Member State, strong scrutiny in ten out of twenty-five Member State parliaments will be no better than strong scrutiny in five, and no worse than strong scrutiny in fifteen out of twenty-five. Even if all parliaments from Central, Eastern and Southern Europe after enlargement turn out to be weak, it will have no adverse effects in any existing Member State in that respect. It would be deceiving to assume that each national parliament forms one-twenty-fifth of collective European parliamentarism. A detached or Eurosceptic public will not be reconciled by being presented with the parliamentary practice in any Member State other than the own. Even if parliamentary scrutiny is sharpened in its own Member State, what is achieved is, initially, not a more transparent EU as such, but only a more transparent EU policy of the government concerned. Again, that transparency is brought about by questioning that policy under the heading of the Member State's national stakes. It might be enlightening to note that thirty years of relatively active parliamentary scrutiny of European affairs in the United Kingdom and in Denmark do not seem to make the EU any more popular there.[91] From a European perspective, all of the above devaluates the national parliamentary 'virtues' if national parliamentarism is to be reconciled with an otherwise progressive stance on European integration.

3.7.4 The effect on the EU legislator

We can sever the national constitutional perspective on national parliaments from the all-European view, and this has been done. Yet stronger national parliaments in more Member States will in practice have repercussions at EU level. Meanwhile, from a European perspective, we have pointed out the dubious, at least not universally defensible impressions that salience over the best pursuit of the national interest in Brussels may convey. However, and this applies to both headings, sharpened national parliamentary scrutiny of European affairs may not only make the EU *appear* like a bargaining arena for national egoisms, but it can actually *turn* it into one as well. Why is that so?

Toughened accountability of national governments to their parliaments, whose mandate it is to act in the national interest, would inevitably have an impact on Council negotiations. As previously stated, national debate does not have to mean

90 See 4.4 *infra*.
91 Cygan (2004a), p. 6 with reference to the UK.

Euroscepticism, and Euro-friendliness does not mean approval of all Commission proposals. But scrutiny requires a minimum degree of salience, debate requires cleavage, and opposition to EU policy measures or the own government's opinion on it will hardly be triggered by altruism, certainly not if there is an election coming up. Instead, the government would be held accountable for not heeding to the wishes of the opposition, or even those of the parliamentary majority – for instance by not insisting on higher EU environmental standards or, conversely, by not fighting for lower environmental standards in order to protect the competitiveness of the domestic industry; or the government would be held accountable, if it did heed to these wishes, for not having succeeded in having the domestic agenda prevail in the Council, or for not having prevented policies that are inconsistent with the national standpoint.

Even if we leave this substantive aspect aside for a moment, we should note that at any rate sharpened national parliamentary scrutiny raises concerns about the continued efficiency of Council decision-making. These concerns would be based on the fact that such a development can potentially introduce another twenty-five players, the national parliaments not counting individual upper chambers and regional assemblies, in addition to the national governments, who have to work in a group of twenty-five already. Thus, while EU enlargements arguably decrease efficiency in the Council by introducing new ministers to the table, introducing the national parliaments to the process alongside would automatically at least double the number of concerned parties. At this point, the old joke from the Brussels corridors may be recalled. When the EU still had twelve members, it was actually considered to have thirteen, namely the Member States themselves, plus the European Affairs Committee of the Danish *Folketing*. Also today, Danish ministers are reportedly so restricted by their parliamentary mandates that they are hindered from finding compromises in the Council speedily. After all, they have to confer with their European Affairs Committee first. Incidentally, this practice, as Fitzmaurice (1999: 338) notes, may well have harmed broader Danish interests.[92] What is more, if twenty-five national parliaments were now to aspire to Danish standards, the efficiency of Council negotiations, which require informed bargaining under time pressure and flexibility to adopt compromises and package deals, would be effectively disrupted.[93] In addition, it would disrupt not only the smooth adoption of compromises in the Council itself, but also the validity of compromises which may have been already reached at the consultative pre-legislative stage.

As to the European Parliament in its capacity of EU co-legislator, the impact of sharper national parliamentary scrutiny with respect to the Council is more

92 See also Sasse (1975), p. 124; Raunio/Wiberg (2001), p. 79 *et seq.*

93 See Sasse (1975), p. 126; Von der Vring (1996), p. 397; Hayes-Renshaw/Wallace (1997), p. 291; Urbantschitsch (1998), p. 60; Höreth (1999), p. 300; Dann (2004), p. 413.

indirect, and also more nuanced. On the one hand, if the European Parliament succeeded in convincing a number of national parliaments to subscribe to its own agenda on the substance of a particular legislative proposal, the result would be that it could confront the Council on two fronts simultaneously, namely both in Brussels and, through its allies, in the Member States.[94] A crippled Council could furthermore have trouble resisting the European Parliament in formulating or amending common positions.[95] Yet it is, on the other hand, far from evident why the European Parliament would have an interest in disrupting the efficiency in the EU legislative process, and to have a co-legislator that is unable to act pragmatically, in particular if such a situation is brought about by inflating national stakes in the Member States. And here we come to our earlier point, which is in fact far graver than the efficiency argument. There is a concern which relates to the sphere in which Council negotiations are conducted, and EU inter-institutional relations are maintained.

Even in an EU of twenty-five, Council deliberations are usually consensual in nature. Ministers speak up only when a measure strongly affects their national interest. The Council does not vote either, as usually the absence of a blocking minority under QMV is concluded, after weighing the national votes, by the Presidency. Admittedly, this does not make scrutiny by the national parliaments any easier. Another point is that ministers, when they enter the Council, themselves often have only a vague idea of how a Commission proposal might affect its own Member State. The national standpoint in the Council is then determined spontaneously, after the minister has heard the views of his or her colleagues, and the deliberation itself offers an opportunity to reflect upon his or her own standpoint.[96] The Council sphere is governed by a co-operative setting of repeat games, where the same players meet in the same composition and setting on a regular basis.[97] And the more often a game is repeated, the less likely the players are to cheat. A sense of familiarity emerges, the 'Council's ethos remains consensual',[98] and that atmosphere, although it may have been cosier in the European Economic Community of the Six, can still be traced today. Taking this aspect into account, the Council has arguably become more than the mere sum of its component members.[99] That not only makes the idea of any form of aggregate legitimacy of Council members problematic. Stronger national parliamentary control, for the already mentioned reasons, also bears the danger of disrupting the co-operative atmosphere prevailing in the Council.[100] As pointed out earlier on, hand-tying domestic institutions

---

94 See on the feasibility and further implications of such inter-parliamentary alliances 4.6 *infra*.
95 See Dashwood (2004), p. 376.
96 Lord (1998), p. 28.
97 Hayes-Renshaw/Wallace (1997), p. 247 *et seq*.
98 Dashwood (2004), p. 375.
99 Lord (1998), p. 31.
100 Hayes-Renshaw/Wallace (1997), p. 291.

strengthen ministers by making their standpoint more rigid. They may then in fact not only scapegoat 'the EU' when dealing with their own parliament, but also use their unforgiving parliament as a scapegoat when dealing with their peers in the Council.[101] The more stringent domestic parliamentary scrutiny really is, the more credible this argument becomes,[102] and the more disruptive its effect on the Council decision-making process will be.

While some national governments may have, for pragmatic or political reasons, an interest in promoting national parliamentary involvement – to deliberately tie their hands, implicate the domestic opposition in their policies, or merely appease Eurosceptics with empty rhetoric about the primacy of national parliaments – the Council as an EU institution has little to gain from this process. Furthermore, it is the European Parliament as a co-legislator that has most cause to fear that sharpened debates about national stakes might eclipse the left-right divisions on which it so much depends as an all-European parliamentary forum. In that respect, it has more to lose than the Commission does. The Commission can, in times of crisis, arguably also function as a civil service with trimmed political ambitions; the European Parliament, however, relies heavily on notions of a European identity, and on political cleavages that defy national borders. This reliance is coupled with a perception that, just like the Council is more than the sum of its members, the European Union is more than the sum of its countries. While it is not suggested here that national parliaments should immediately cease all EU-related domestic scrutiny, there remains a question of constitutional and normative priority-setting. As noted before, the EU cannot simply decree the desired level of national parliamentary involvement, it can adjust it neither upwards nor downwards; all it can do is encourage parliamentary activity, if so desired. At the same time, the more national parliaments are encouraged to subject EU decision-making to domestic political battles in the run-up to, or aftermath of, Council sessions, the less likely it is that European political cleavages might emerge from the shadow of national interests, and the less convincing the argument would be that national parliaments can safely afford to be as lenient as they wish to be with respect to parliamentary oversight over the European Union.

Decision-making efficiency is not a holy good, and a little inconvenience is readily acceptable if it means a significant boost to parliamentarism; allowing national parliaments to eclipse the European Parliament by catching and enhancing attention to national stakes, even if all national parliaments would want that in the first place, which they do not, is however a path that not everyone should be willing to walk. This is what the above discussion was intended to show. A modest achievement, one might contend – yet in a debate where the mere mentioning of the word 'democracy' buys support, analytical sensitivity is in fact priceless.

101 Weber-Panariello (1995), p. 317.
102 Dimitrakopoulos (2001).

3.7.5 A legalistic intermezzo

Especially from a European perspective, stronger national parliaments deliver questionable results at a high price, i.e. results that cannot please everyone, with effects that can be qualified as a price in the first place, a price that not everyone may be willing to pay, as we will conclude hereafter. Yet before we do, let us, for the sake of completeness, look at national parliamentary scrutiny and its relation to the Council with some degree of legal sophistication. At the beginning of our discussion we implied that Article I-46 (2) of the Constitutional Treaty, which stipulated that the governments in the Council are accountable to their respective national parliaments, was merely of a declaratory nature, making explicit pre-existing constitutional relations. One might however argue that this provision actually would contain an *obligation* for the national parliaments to give effect to this construct on the domestic scene. Thus, EU/EC law, which enjoys supremacy over Member State law with or without the Constitutional Treaty, would compel the national parliaments to engage in substantive scrutiny of their governments, or it would at least make it unlawful for parliaments not to enforce the described accountability in practice.

There is a worthy legalistic rebuttal to this claim. While Article I-46 (2) might require a minimum level of national parliamentary scrutiny, the loyalty clause of Article I-5, read in conjunction with Article I-23 on ministerial representation in the Council, might command a minimum level of ministerial *flexibility* for the attainment of the Union's objectives. Both provisions already exist in the form of Articles 10 and 203 EC, respectively. Thus, 'a system (a practice) of parliamentary participation which systematically hinders the decision-making in the Council' would be incompatible with EC law,[103] or EU law under the Constitutional Treaty. Restrictive parliamentary mandating should, under the principle of supremacy of Community law, or EU law as explicitly codified in Article I-6 of the Constitutional Treaty, be held inapplicable.

Admittedly, the field of constitutional law sometimes reaches into the domain of political and social sciences, yet sometimes, like here, it also reaches into the very core of pure textual analysis of legal provisions. Our discussion so far shows that relevant arguments can drift towards either side of the spectrum. Legal scholars need to maintain a balance. They must not get carried away too much into political or philosophical debates when assessing a polity's constitutional arrangements. This is the reason why we have considered a comparative overview of national scrutiny practice and, above, its practical effects on the EU legislator. However, legal rights and obligations in this area can hardly be construed in a sterile manner, as if a constitution existed in a political vacuum. The above legal constructions would

103 Urbantschitsch (1998), p. 64.

possibly find supporters as well as enemies, but both would essentially base their choice on underlying political arguments. Both would accuse the other side of using techniques of legal interpretation in order to promote their own not-so-hidden agenda. Since neither construction is likely to be submitted to judicial review, and since no parliament is likely to be impressed by either reasoning even if it did lead to a court judgment, the argument remains largely academic, and rather outlandish at that. Still, as such it may very well describe a facet of a broader political and constitutional debate. It is the very same debate which triggered our own discussion in the first place, and to which our discussion seeks to contribute itself. So let us summarize what we have seen as regards the vices and virtues, the costs and the benefits of national parliamentary involvement in the EU, the effectiveness of its stimulation, as well as the side-effects that come with it, depending on the viewpoint of choice.

3.8 Conclusion

To demand a greater role for the national parliaments of the Member States in European affairs means to address a set of national institutions which do in principle not play any formal role in multilateral international relations. To demand a sharper parliamentary scrutiny of EU policy on their domestic arena means to demand a level of activity which is higher than what the parliaments achieve so far. To stimulate and facilitate such activity by virtue of EU-level arrangements, such as symbolically recognizing the parliaments' role in treaties, providing them with information, consulting them or inserting time delays to wait for their substantive contributions, is a form of artificial intervention. That is not problematic just by itself, but it requires a justification like any conscious effort that has constitutional implications.

The justification for granting powers and privileges to national parliaments depends on the preferred point of view. From a national constitutional point of view, it may be desirable for national parliaments to supervise the exercise of those legislative powers of which they no longer dispose themselves, and which they have conferred upon the EU institutions by way of ratification of the European treaties. Furthermore, it may be desirable for parliaments to maintain a democratic representative imprint on the governments' EU policy formulation, to keep providing a forum for public deliberation which is not available in that form at EU level, or to broadly support a consolidated national standpoint in the EU. These national justifications, however, should not be generalized, since each national political system, and each national parliament, features its very own particularities. Different national parliaments have different historical backgrounds, they differ in terms of links to the electorate, form, composition, competence, relation to the government and, generally, in terms of their self-perception. They also differ in what they define to be in their Member State's interest as regards the European integration process. Stating that, on close inspection, the Belgian parliament is too permissive in EU affairs may or may not be justified; concluding that, as a consequence, *all* national parliaments in the EU should be more proactive in any case requires a generalization of experiences and broader constitutional preferences which would be inappropriate to make.

Meanwhile, arguing from a European, or top-down perspective, such generalizations about the role, interest and capacities of the national parliaments as a group of institutions seem almost inevitable. Again, they should be seen critically for the very same reason that they convey false impressions of homogeneity. It is easy to draw up a list of what is considered a national parliament as an autonomous concept of EU law, assign these parliaments European functions and furnish them with privileges, but that would mean the imposition of a crude standard based on at least partly inaccurate ideas of what these parliaments are, of what they can and what they should do, and of what they want themselves. Generally speaking from a European perspective, national parliaments may seem attractive for the purpose of closing the chain of accountability from the Council down to the citizens, and of using them as fora for public debate to raise awareness of, and familiarity with, the EU decision-making process. For these purposes, the exercise may cause a revelation of the intergovernmental bargaining processes in the Council, which would prevent governments from scapegoating 'Brussels' as an external and faceless actor, or a revelation of what the EU in fact should be like, if the European perspective coincides with intergovernmentalism. Yet the accountability and proximity-related achievement would come at the price of EU-level distortions, as sharpened scrutiny and tighter national parliamentary control over ministers decreases the efficiency of Council negotiations, disrupts its co-operative sphere, and re-nationalizes European politics. The accountability would focus on the extent to which a government has included the preferences of some political parties in the national standpoint, and how well it has defended that national standpoint as against the other EU Member States. A credible translation of voter preferences in that context could only be secured if national political parties would announce their EU-related agendas in election campaigns, again inflating the stakes and emphasizing and reinforcing the intergovernmental element of EU decision-making. That intergovernmental element of course remains valid and necessary, but it is not the only one in the co-decision procedure, and has the potential to eclipse the European Parliament as a co-legislator to the detriment of the consolidation of cross-border political left-right preferences.

Even more generally, the European justification for stronger national parliamentary scrutiny for the sake of democracy and accountability contains an inherent flaw, in that it implies that each national parliament constitutes one-twenty-fifth of an aggregate legitimacy scheme for the Council, and that twenty-five national parliaments, each with its own national mandate to represent the national interest, will somehow add up to a collective form of European parliamentarism and be adequate to legitimize transnational decision-making. Not surprisingly, such a view would be compatible with a sovereignist logic, which would seek to re-nationalize control over the EU anyway. The more intriguing question, however, would again be whether support for sharper European scrutiny in the national parliaments could be reconciled, in one way or another, with otherwise general support for ever-closer union. Our discussion has revealed that more assertive national parliaments on the domestic arena would not only slow down the progress of European integration, but are even capable of changing the status quo that has been achieved already, and of shifting the centre of gravity in the EU closer towards the nation-states. To be sure, there is nothing filthy about national interest as such, and the EU obviously still consists of Member States. It is just that there are appropriate fora for negotiation, and there are appropriate loci for parliamentarization. Lofty claims that more domestic debate will enrich European will-formation without bringing to the fore national stakes and without affecting the Council in any significant manner quickly reach the limits of their validity when the constitutional mandate and incentive structure, the nature and the purpose of national parliaments is recalled. We should only lament the wide-spread reluctance, constraint and deliberate self-constraint of national parliaments in EU context if we are also aware of the underlying reasons for these phenomena, and of the price tag that is attached to unleashed or deliberately boosted national parliamentarism, at least if we choose to perceive Europeanization as a benefit and re-nationalization as a cost.

4 The call for more inter-parliamentary co-operation

4.1 Introduction

The demand that the national parliaments of the Member States of the European Union, as well as the European Parliament, should co-operate with each other more actively touches upon a vast complex. Like everything else concerning more active national parliaments, inter-parliamentary co-operation can be justified from different angles of thought. According to the identified purpose, it can materialize in different ways. Let us for instance assume again a national constitutional perspective: from that point of view, exchange of information with other national parliaments, and the sharing of experience about how to deal with the effects of European integration, may strengthen a parliament in its position *vis-à-vis* its own government domestically. Such benchmarking would therefore be an extension of our previous discussion about the sharpening of individual national parliamentary scrutiny of EU affairs in general. A similar picture can be drawn as regards bilateral co-operation between a national parliament, on the one hand, and the European Parliament, on the other hand. Inviting MEPs to join national parliamentary deliberations for instance would mean to access EU-related insider knowledge for individual domestic purposes.

Turning to a more global European view on national parliaments, inter-parliamentary co-operation as a domestic tool may also be just as desirable, or indeed undesirable, as a sharpening of domestic scrutiny of EU affairs in general. Yet in addition, a broader perspective on the EU as a whole allows us to pay increased attention to the substantive networking effects of such co-operation. Co-ordinating efforts on a particular subject-matter with other national parliaments, so that each parliament can put pressure on its own government along agreed lines, allows a larger share of the Council to be subjected to more effective national parliamentary steering. If the parliaments go on and involve the European Parliament in their co-ordination as well, the Council can even be squeezed from two sides, both at EU level, and on the home front. Here we may already discern an overlap with what is usually identified as the collective role of the national parliaments. Such inter-parliamentary networking would, incidentally, neatly fit into the approach of multi-level governance and constitutional pluralism, where it envisages dynamic inter-parliamentary alliances throughout Europe, and dual legitimacy theories seeking to reconcile both European and national parliamentarism. Finally, we should also consider the less noble motives that institutions might have to encourage inter-parliamentary co-operation: the European Parliament, for whom 'co-operation' can mean 'co-option, pre-emption and implication', or IGCs, for whom 'co-operation' can be a well-sounding but unthreatening concession to supporters of national parliamentarism.

4.2 Sharing best practice and inviting MEPs

Co-operation among national parliaments for the purpose of identifying best practice for European scrutiny set-ups is closely connected to a parliament's individual scrutiny role. Exchanging information on how to deal with the effects of European integration, and sharing experience, may after all strengthen a parliament's domestic scrutiny position *vis-à-vis* the own government. It enables it to adopt new scrutiny mechanisms from abroad. Such inter-parliamentary exchange of information may take place on a bilateral, regional,[1] or Europe-wide multilateral basis. Information can be shared via European databases such as IPEX, or through the European Centre for Parliamentary Research and Documentation (ECPRD). Inter-parliamentary fora allow for personal cross-border contacts. Thus, since 1963, the Conference of Speakers of the national parliaments and the European Parliament, which operates in a rather informal manner, meets biennially.[2] Yet the most prominent and overarching institutionalized multilateral forum for inter-parliamentary exchange of information in the EU is COSAC, the Conference of the European Affairs Committees of the national parliaments, which meets along with a delegation from the European Parliament.

Since 1989, COSAC has held meetings twice yearly in the Member State holding the rotating Presidency. Each national parliament is represented by a maximum of six MPs, and the European Parliament envoys a six-strong delegation as well.[3] The organizational tasks are carried out by a troika of the Presidency of the preceding year, the current year and the following year. Since 2004, COSAC also has its own long-demanded permanent secretariat.[4] The Conference's primary function is the exchange of information between parliaments about how they deal with the effects of EU membership.[5] Under the Amsterdam Protocol, COSAC was also recognized as a forum for direct collective parliamentary participation at EU level, which we shall turn to later on under the heading of creating a congress of parliaments or a 'Third Chamber' at EU level.[6] Yet already in terms of benchmarking, some effects of co-operation within COSAC are indeed noteworthy. For example, the introduction of a scrutiny reserve in the French parliament in 1995, which bars ministers from giving assent in the Council until parliament has completed scrutiny,

---

1 The national parliaments of the Nordic Member States, for example, entertain regular mutual contacts, see Finnish Eduskunta/Swedish Riksdag/Danish Folketing (2002).

2 Smismans (1998), p. 71.

3 Article 4.1 COSAC rules of procedure as of 4 November 2004, OJ C-270/2.

4 See European Convention (2002b); Brown (2003), p. 6; more generally Raunio (2004) footnote 5.

5 Article 1 COSAC Rules of Procedure; Weber-Panariello (1995), p. 312; Urbantschitsch (1998), p. 17.

6 See 5 *infra*.

was arguably influenced by a comparison with the practice in the Parliament of the UK.[7] In other words, the French government could not withhold such a tool from its own parliament, who may have wondered why the British practice could not work in France as well. Also, several of the parliaments of the new Member States derived their information on existing European scrutiny mechanisms from their pre-accession observer status in COSAC. Finland seems to have been very successful in exporting its scrutiny mechanism, which closely involves the sectoral committees in the process while keeping the dialogue with the government centralized.[8] Another prominent result of COSAC benchmarking was the adoption of the already mentioned Copenhagen Guidelines, a non-binding code of conduct for European scrutiny procedures identifying best practice.[9]

Benchmarking among the national parliaments is a matter of 'horizontal' inter-parliamentary relations, in that national institutions, which find themselves in a comparable situation due to EU membership, seek to identify a best practice of dealing with that situation. Co-operation between the national parliaments and the European Parliament now adds a 'vertical', cross-layer dimension to the discussion. The form which corresponds best to benchmarking, as regards constitutional implications, would be the practice of some national parliaments to involve MEPs from their own Member State in the domestic scrutiny process. The reason for this correspondence is that it too emphasizes the purpose of strengthening an individual national parliament which would draw on additional external EU-related expertise. The expertise and information which MEPs can offer to their colleagues from the national parliaments results from the former's experience with, and proximity to, the EU decision-making process itself. For these reasons, the European Affairs Committee of the German *Bundestag* formally reserves, next to the seats for thirty-three MPs, fifteen seats for German MEPs.[10] The MEPs are appointed by the Speaker according to relative party strengths within the EP, upon nomination by those political party groups of the *Bundestag* which are represented in the European Parliament as well. The MEPs thus appointed may participate in deliberations in the European Affairs Committee, but may not vote. This example was followed by the parliament of Belgium, whose European Affairs Committee, resurrected by the lower chamber in 1985 and turned into a joint advisory committee together with the senate in 1990, today includes ten members of the lower chamber, ten senators and ten Belgian MEPs. The same approach was followed by the parliament of Ireland, whose joint European Affairs Committee includes MEPs from

7 Weber-Panariello (1995), p. 312.

8 See 2.3 *supra*.

9 OJ 2003/c 154/01.

10 These figures apply to the 2002 Diet; because of the election system, the size of the Bundestag and its committees usually varies from one term to another.

the island of Ireland, including MEPs from Northern Ireland. MEPs have a seat in the European Affairs Committee of the unicameral parliament of Greece and in that of the parliament of Malta.[11] In total, 19 parliamentary chambers uphold standing invitations to MEPs to join deliberations.[12] Other national parliaments invite MEPs on special occasions.[13] In those national parliaments where they have a seat, however, MEPs rarely attend committee meetings in practice, mostly due to overlapping schedules, time pressure and the burden of travelling.[14]

To provide an additional incentive for MEPs to participate one could treat their involvement as an intra-party affair, instead of an inter-institutional one. In the absence of all-European political parties, elections to the European Parliament are still based on the Member State party infrastructure. It is national political parties that compete for seats in what are initially national delegations of MEPs, which only upon arrival in the European Parliament disperse into European party families. Independent candidates, small parties and single-issue lists running for the EP aside, the national parties represented in the European Parliament are usually also represented in the national parliament, and MEPs from these 'established' parties depend on the nomination by their party for the next EP elections. This applies to the placement as a party candidate in a winnable electoral district, as well as to the placement on a promising place on the party list, depending on the electoral system. It is then not so much the national parliament as an institution, but the political parties represented in that parliament that have a potential tool for convincing MEPs from the same party to co-operate on the national level.[15] The potential sanction would be, for instance, a lower rank on the party list for the next EP elections. For example, while the parliament of Denmark usually excludes MEPs from deliberations, the Danish social-democrats regularly invite 'their' MEPs to preparatory meetings.[16] Conversely, the European Parliament itself encourages links between EP party groups and their national counterparts, for instance through separate party family meetings preceding plenary COSAC sessions.

4.3 Inter-parliamentary networking and collective contributions

National parliamentary scrutiny of European affairs *ex ante* is a process of determining the national standpoint on a broader basis than internal ministerial policy-formulation would permit. However, to an individual parliament, co-operation

---

11 Article 120F Maltese House of Representatives Standing Orders.
12 COSAC Secretariat (2005a), p. 95.
13 Raunio (1999), p. 187; overview by Maurer (2002), p. 24.
14 Von der Vring (1996), p. 395; Hofmann (2003), p. 10.
15 Neunreither (1994), p. 310; Raunio (1999).
16 Fitzmaurice (1999), p. 339.

with other national parliaments or the European Parliament can offer more than merely first-hand information about the preferences of other Member States or the EU institutions. Horizontal and vertical inter-parliamentary co-operation can offer a tool to more effectively press the Council, in general, and the individual government concerned, in particular. Here the individual and the collective role of national parliaments in the EU overlap. If several national parliaments join arms, possibly together with the European Parliament, to make a collective concerted contribution addressed to the Council, their own governments will necessarily be among the addressees. Conversely, if several parliaments agree on an inter-parliamentary standpoint which each parliament goes on to defend individually, the result is that a share of the Council is subjected to concerted, co-ordinated and *de facto* collective pressure. All too sharp distinctions between individual and collective roles of the national parliaments in the EU may therefore seem artificial.[17]

Issue-based co-operation, where it does not cover the formal role of parliaments as such, is essentially sectoral co-operation. Thus, it may cover a concerted action in the field of transport or environment, foreign affairs and enlargement, the four freedoms or human rights. Again, a national parliament would profit from such co-operation in terms of effectiveness. The same is usually said as regards the European Parliament, which could build up a network of allies on the Member State level to help it confront the Council. The tools for such sectoral inter-parliamentary co-operation are typically joint committee meetings. Thus, there is an annual joint session of defence committees, and a conference of committees on women's rights, hosted by the respective sectoral committee of the European Parliament. In fact, by now each EP committee reserves seats for interested national parliamentarians to attend meetings.

For more overarching or fundamental matters, the forum of choice would again be COSAC. For apart from exchanging information, the Conference could provide the infrastructure for a collective parliamentary contribution. This is what part II of the Amsterdam Protocol on the role of national parliaments in the European Union recognizes by awarding COSAC the right to make contributions on draft EU legislation in general, on matters concerning the area of freedom, security and justice in particular, as well as on the principle of subsidiarity and fundamental rights. In that, COSAC may be seen as inheriting the role of the Rome *Assizes*, the one-time gathering of national parliaments and the European Parliament which debated the future of Europe in the run-up to the Maastricht IGC. Indeed, the institutionalization of inter-parliamentary assemblies at EU level is one of the most prominently recurring items in the current debate, and we shall come to that later. But before we do, let us take another very critical look at what we have just discussed.

17 Cf. European Convention (2002b).

4.4 On the Solidarity of Parliaments

Let us start our critique with horizontal co-operation among national parliaments for the purpose of identifying and trading in best practice. Since it comprises a more or less informal exchange of information which is hardly binding, it appears to be of a low level of constitutional intrusiveness. Nevertheless, it should not escape an important qualification. The very term 'best practice' contains the same implication that we put into question earlier. 'Best' points to the notions of 'strong' and 'weak', which tend to blind out the idiosyncrasies of each individual set of government-parliament relations, and the particularities of each individual political system.[18] Thus, not all recipes for 'strong' oversight in one parliament can be simply transferred to another parliament. Appointing a strong central European Affairs Committee or turning to hand-tying mandate systems could be incompatible with parliamentary traditions or domestic constitutional law.[19] Parliaments appearing to be 'weak' might not even want to sharpen their scrutiny in the first place because they, or their electorate, are just fine with a more permissive stance on EU affairs: either because they feel well-represented by their government, or because they appreciate bargaining flexibility over hand-tying on behalf of their Member State, or because they do not wish to increase the domestic salience of national stakes and thereby compete with the European Parliament. Benchmarking can safely be considered as an appendix to the discussion on whether or not it is desirable, from an individualized national point of view, to optimize national parliamentary scrutiny of European affairs at all. This question would have to be answered for each Member State individually, as potential generalizations reach their limits where benchmarking practice itself reaches its limits, namely in the heterogeneity of national parliaments. That is, a parliament that does not wish to receive a constitutional transplant or adopt a new scrutiny mechanism, even if it could, cannot be forced to do so. From a European perspective, meanwhile, sharpened national scrutiny of EU matters, enhanced via inter-parliamentary co-operation, in any event seems to offer results that fit into some agendas better than into others.

Taking inter-parliamentary co-operation a step further, we would touch upon the issue of networking and concerted pressure. Here the constitutional frictions grow exponentially. As far as horizontal co-operation among national parliaments themselves is concerned, we can bring these frictions under what are by now familiar headings of heterogeneity and executive dominance. Thus, the question arises whether we can really assume that national parliaments are mutually compatible in their status and interests, and whether they can be assumed to act as unitary institutions independently of their governments. As far as vertical co-operation

---

18 See also Swedish Riksdag (2001), p. 23.

19 See 2.7 *supra*.

with the European Parliament is concerned, we can introduce new concerns: the question of overlapping constitutional mandates, and the question of structural rivalry. Let us have a look at whether an inter-parliamentary cross-layer alliance is constitutionally feasible, in the light of the basis on which MEPs and national MPs are elected, as well as in the light of their position as members of distinct representative bodies.

Under the Amsterdam Protocol, as well as under the Protocol on the role of national parliaments attached to the Constitutional Treaty, COSAC is recognized as a nucleus for concerted inter-parliamentary contributions addressed at the EU institutions. Justice and fundamental rights, as well as the application of the principle of subsidiarity, are stressed as probably being of particular common concern. To realize such contributions, COSAC requires a consolidated infrastructure and procedural framework. Indeed, it has already established a permanent secretariat, and has amended its Rules of Procedure in 2003, allowing for the adoption of resolutions by a three-fourth majority, instead of consensus.[20] Nevertheless, COSAC is still mainly used for a non-binding exchange of information. Also during the Convention, it was 'generally considered to be a useful talking shop but an ineffective forum for inter-parliamentary co-operation'.[21] Even as a talking shop, COSAC is sometimes qualified as holding 'useless meetings'.[22] If this is the case then why is it so?

Firstly, COSAC does not unite a homogenous collective of institutions sharing the same interest. As we considered earlier on, the European Affairs Committees of the national parliaments, who are represented in COSAC, are not of a mutually corresponding status.[23] Their set-up and function in their own parliaments varies considerably, from central and powerful parliamentary spearheads to isolated advisory bodies which accommodate the usual suspects interested in the EU.

Secondly, as well as in line with their lack of corresponding status, different parliaments or committees have different views on the desirable role of COSAC itself. While for instance the French senate keeps promoting the idea of turning COSAC into a veritable 'Third Chamber' at EU level, Finnish parliamentarians are satisfied with a more informal arrangement.[24] Indeed, much of COSAC's discussions revolve around the definition of the role of COSAC itself, as a mere forum or at least as a co-ordinating body.[25] At the first COSAC meeting after the signing of the Constitutional Treaty, in The Hague in November 2004, even the suggestion that the COSAC secretariat could monitor and co-ordinate the raised objections

20 See Article 10.5 COSAC Rules of Procedure, OJ C 270/2.
21 Brown (2003), p. 7.
22 Hoetjes (2001), p. 357.
23 The same holds true for the Conference of Speakers, see Bonnamour (1995).
24 Swedish Riksdag (2001), p. 14.
25 See also Maurer/Wessels (2001), p. 21.

under the early warning system for subsidiarity met resistance from the delegations of *inter alia* Italy, Spain, Belgium, the Netherlands as well as from the European Parliament. COSAC should not try and collect as many votes as possible, it was argued. Only a neutral platform for mutual notification and exchange of information was desired.[26]

Thirdly, and again in line with the previous points, the delegations sent to COSAC cannot bind their home parliaments. Both the Amsterdam Protocol and the Constitutional Treaty Protocol, while inviting the adoption of collective contributions, stress that such contributions are not to bind the national parliaments or prejudge their position.[27] The same is stated in Article 1 of the COSAC Rules of Procedure. Thus, there is still an open question concerning exactly in what capacity national MPs attend COSAC meetings: are they representatives, or delegates, or are they present in a personal capacity?[28] When asked to support a draft COSAC declaration condemning in a sharper manner the election fraud in the second round of the 2004 presidential elections in Ukraine, UK MP Jimmy Hood noted with barely concealed anger that neither did he have a mandate from the House of Commons to support any such condemnation, beyond the expression of concern, nor was COSAC itself in any position to issue condemnations.

It was initially one of our preliminary caveats that speaking of 'the national parliaments' as a catch-all denomination is deceiving. That caveat applies here as well. As regards further sources of friction when attempting to upgrade COSAC to a mighty collective institution, we may recall our other preliminary caveat, namely that speaking of national parliaments as unitary institutions can be deceiving to a similar extent. Indeed, what the proposals for inter-parliamentary networking and collective parliamentary contributions all have in common is that they seek to activate parliaments independently of their governments. Or, to put it differently, in adopting a common parliamentary position, the national parliaments are expected to bypass their own governments. Only that explains the alleged value of concerted domestic efforts under an agreed inter-parliamentary agenda, or the adoption of a COSAC resolution addressed to the Council, and thereby to the individual governments.

We can split our objections in that context under two headings. Firstly, in a parliamentary democracy in which the government is not elected directly, but remains accountable to parliament, the basic government-parliament relation is that of an agent accountable to a principal. Parliament does not need to engage in executive activities itself as long as it remains the government's principal. What is more, it

26 See on the application of the early warning system 7 *infra*.

27 Article 7 Amsterdam Protocol, Article 10 TCE Protocol on the role of national parliaments in the European Union.

28 Smismans (1998), p. 60.

would distort a fundamental constitutional relation if the principal became active next to, in competition with, or even in opposition to, its own agent.[29] The successful conclusion of an inter-parliamentary alliance with a foreign third party against a Member State's own government, or against a body of which that government forms part, provokes a friction with internal constitutional law. Another question is whether such an alliance is likely to be successful in the first place, which brings us to the second objection we should raise. In a parliamentary democracy, the parliamentary majority supports or tolerates the government. The political colour of the cabinet and the government party group, or groups, coincides. Even a minority cabinet commands a *de facto* coalition of supporters to stay in office. Depicting parliaments as routinely independent actors, particularly in foreign relations, would therefore not only ignore the fact that they already have agents to act on their behalf, but that these agents enjoy the confidence of what is the majority in a partisan assembly. Of course government parties are not always unquestioningly loyal to their cabinet, and parliamentary majorities may sometimes be united against a government. But trans-national inter-parliamentary alliances eventually require inter-parliamentary solidarity, and possibly Europe-wide accords of parliaments.[30] The question is whether such a solidarity can exist, not merely sympathy in a general way, but specifically a bond of alliance that bypasses individual governments. In other words, the question is whether a domestic cleavage between a parliamentary majority and a government can be sufficient to support a sustainable solidarity between that parliamentary majority, on the one hand, and the parliament of another country, on the other hand. Answering this question in generalizations would again be misleading, for in the Member States different issues are of different domestic salience.[31] But it is important to ask the right questions in the first place, so as to avoid unwarranted hopes and subsequent disappointments. Our conclusions here should be very helpful when we discuss, a little later, the occasionally floated option of setting up a 'Third Chamber' made up of national parliamentarians at EU level. As with concerns raised earlier on, the above critique, which was targeted at feasibility rather than desirability of inter-parliamentary co-operation, could be countered with the argument that COSAC or other fora might work nonetheless, i.e. in spite of all academic wisdom. Yet again, we would first need to agree what exactly we mean with 'work', and then to recall that our critique is not at all intended to *refute* the workability of inter-parliamentary alliances, but to explain the lack thereof. At present, COSAC is helplessly low-key. The above considerations should help us understand why this is so, and also to appreciate the evolution should COSAC suddenly gain high profile in the future. Now let us turn to the desirability of such possible high profile.

---

29 Raunio (2004).

30 See Harlow (2002), p. 104; Cygan (2004a), p. 22.

31 See on the salience of human rights as a possibly uniting agenda item: 4.6 *infra*.

4.5 Minding the Mandate

The reason why national parliaments are brought to the European agenda in the first place, whether as a genuine cause or as a pretext, is that they are democratic institutions, and their democratic character derives, not exclusively but as a *conditio sine qua non*, from the fact that they are elected at regular intervals. They thus receive a mandate to represent the citizenry. This mandate is, however, not boundless or randomly interchangeable, it has its limitations. Parliaments are elected for a purpose. One such limitation we have just touched upon is that national parliaments are not elected to engage in foreign relations with other countries, or their institutions, themselves. This task is delegated to the government as an agent. Parallel contacts between parliaments among each other, next to governments, would distort this principal-agent relationship. Furthermore, if a parliament's opinion is in line with that of its own government, we may ask where exactly is the added value of inter-parliamentary standpoints. A second limitation, which is closely related to the first one, is that a parliament is elected to represent its own people, and only them. The much-lauded responsiveness of parliaments to the wishes of the population is targeted at their *own* populations.

Earlier on we sketched a scenario refuting the idea of cross-border spill-over effects in transparency perception as regards the EU, as the citizens of Member State A follow the policy formulation of their own government. They may demand the dismissal of incompetent ministers of their own Member State, but they have no constitutional basis, nor the necessary amount of information or emotional attachment for demanding the dismissal of a minister in Member State B. Even if they did demand it, neither the government nor the parliament of Member State B would have any constitutional basis or electoral stimulus to comply. A national parliament is elected to represent the national interest, and in as far as national interests converge or collide internationally, it is the task of the Council, which is set up for that very purpose, to reach binding agreements or compromises. For a parliament, independent participation of COSAC as an alternative to the Council would therefore mean, among other things, a blurring of its constitutional mandate. Just as in other instances of EU-level activation of national parliaments, the gravity of the effects increase with the significance of the exercise. A COSAC meeting producing hot air will not make any national constitution crumble (and it is worth considering whether encouragement of COSAC is not hot air itself); real concerted action overriding the individual governments would however seriously call into question the stability of some national cabinets, and the justification of how MPs spend their time and resources, engaging in cross-border campaigns instead of keeping an eye on the domestic scene and their own ministers.

This again brings us straight to the European Parliament. For the point of blurred mandates becomes even more pronounced as regards co-operation between a national parliament and the European Parliament. Each institution has its distinct mandate. Each institution is elected for its own purpose. The cases of persisting dual mandates, where MEPs are also elected as national MPs at the same time, have become an exception since 1979. The vast majority of MEPs are elected for the European post only. In the discussion above we considered the tools of joint committee sessions, whether hosted by the committees of the European Parliament, or by national sectoral committees or European Affairs Committees. The tensions that arise in the latter case, due to the different mandates, are particularly telling.

As previously stated, several national parliaments sometimes invite MEPs to sit as a sort of expert witnesses. Some parliaments however award MEPs who are elected with respect to their own Member State a seat on the European Affairs Committee. This means that MEPs sit together with national MPs opposed to the national government. Where MEPs enjoy a right to speak, the constitutional tensions reach their peak. Firstly, the result is that a government is being held accountable by politicians to whom it owes no accountability. Single-mandate MEPs neither elect, nor dismiss any national government, either on a national level or within the Council. Conversely, no national government, neither from within the Council nor individually on the domestic arena, depends on the MEPs' confidence. The Belgian parliament for instance makes a point of stressing that the right of Belgian MEPs who sit on its European Affairs Committee to insist on the disclosure of government information has to be seen as part of the general information process, not as part of an accountability process.[32] In the light of our above considerations, it is clear why the Belgian parliament feels the need to emphasize this point. Secondly, from the point of view of voter-parliament relations, formal involvement of MEPs in a national parliament means that tasks of popular representation and parliamentary control on behalf of the citizens are carried out by politicians who are not elected for that purpose. A political party group which has a substantive share in the European Parliament could, for instance, be represented in the national parliament where the share of its mother party is smaller. Thirdly, we could make a reproach analogous to the one made earlier with respect to national parliamentarians: if a national parliament is elected to represent the national interest, and should not overstep its national constitutional mandate, why should members of the European Parliament be permitted to overstep their European mandate by acting on any national arena?

These considerations have had their effects on some of the national parliaments. When the German *Bundestag* first included German MEPs in the composition of its European Affairs Committee in 1983, it was only permissible because of the Committee's special status, as instead of an ordinary standing committee composed of MPs it was formed as an inquiry committee.[33] In the French *Assemblée Nationale*, problems arose with respect to national parliamentarians who simultaneously held

32 COSAC Secretariat (2005a), p. 95.

33 Hölscheidt (2001), p. 125, see Article 56 Bundestag Rules of Procedure.

a seat in the European Parliament. Only since a reform of 1990 may these dual-mandate MPs become a member of the European Affairs Delegations.[34] The essentially external or visitor status of MEPs in a national parliament, whether they have a permanent seat in a committee or not, can be illustrated well with the Irish example. As noted above, the parliament of the Republic of Ireland features a European Affairs Committee which includes MEPs from Northern Irish constituencies. Northern Irish MEPs are of course elected as part of the EP elections in the United Kingdom. The Irish case shows that the European parliamentary mandate defies national boundaries. There would be, by analogy, no reason why MEPs from Northern Ireland should not also have a seat in a European Standing Committee of the UK House of Commons. In fact, they could just as well be awarded a seat in the national parliament of Belgium, Germany or Poland. Conversely, the Irish parliament is not prohibited from inviting MEPs from France, Italy or Cyprus to its deliberations.[35]

The crucial link between a national parliament, on the one hand, and the MEPs from the same Member State, on the other hand, is again political party affiliation. As institutions, apparently none of the national parliaments which include MEPs in their deliberations can provide enough incentives for these MEPs to attend in practice. There is an institutional reason for this, which is related to the difference in mandates. When visiting a national parliament, MEPs can, at best, influence one government out of twenty-five. When working within their own EP party group and their own EP committee, they can influence the outcome of EU legislation directly. A similar, though inverse picture may be drawn as regards national parliamentarians who are regularly invited to join committee meetings in the European Parliament.[36] They have the right to attend, but not to vote. Save for matters of extraordinary importance, their reserved seats remain empty.[37] If they did occupy their seats, they would be visitors, who would for instance call the Commission to account, whereas the Commission is not accountable to them, as it does not depend on their vote of confidence. The people who are accountable to them are their own ministers. A national parliament is, after all, elected by the voters of a Member State to both support and control the national government. The controlling or challenging aspect is especially vital for opposition parties. The opposition or intra-coalition challengers however do not oppose the government for opposition's sake, but in order to expose its weaknesses and to present itself to the electorate as a possible alternative. Thus, while for MEPs it does not seem to pay off to influence only one national government, when they can influence EU

34 Rizutto (1995), p. 51.

35 Swedish Riksdag (2001), p. 16 actually suggests that national parliaments could establish contacts with MEPs from other countries as well.

36 See Article 123 EP Rules of Procedure.

37 Weber-Panariello (1995), p. 312.

legislation directly, for national parliamentarians the question would arise why they should attend meetings of the European Parliament, where they would be facing twenty-five national governments in the Council at a time, while they can confront their own government individually, directly, more conveniently and with greater domestic media attention at home.

Thus, to fulfil their national constitutional mandate, the domestic arena is the place of choice for national parliamentarians' activity. Just as it is the case with MEPs, it boils down to a matter of opportunity costs. Taking into account parliamentarians' workload, irrespective of where they sit, they can do more effective work in line with their mandate in their own parliament during the time that they would lose when working in any other parliament. Of course, opportunity costs are only relative to the profit one seeks to reap in the end. If a piece of EU legislation is of high domestic salience and national MPs feel side-stepped by their government, they may well feel inclined to join arms with their colleagues from Strasbourg, even if it takes time and effort. Conversely, MEPs may find it worth investing in a journey to a national capital if they could help build up a network to balance out the Council on a controversial policy issue. Again, the points made here are not to refute the possibility that inter-parliamentary alliances can materialize; they are however helpful when analyzing why they do not. This in fact brings us to the structural possibilities of alliances between national parliaments and the European Parliament.

4.6 Rivals or allies?

Parliamentarization of the European Union through inter-parliamentary alliances is a fashionable notion. In principle, there is a strong case for such an alliance between the European Parliament and the national parliaments. The national parliaments would gain an additional external source of expert information, which they could effectively drain via internal political party lines. The European Parliament, in turn, could profit from a network of parliamentary partners on the national level who, if they are in line with its own preferences, could put pressure on the governments domestically, in the Council's back yard, so to speak. Indeed, the European Parliament goes a long way to emphasize that it does not consider the national parliaments to be rivals in a struggle for exclusive representation of the European citizens.[38] MEPs even seem to have more 'downward' contact to the national parliaments than the other way round.[39] Many MEPs want national parliamentarians to play a greater role.[40] Neunreither (1994: 313) prominently stresses that the national

38 EP Committee on Constitutional Affairs Report of 23 January 2002, A5-0023/2002.

39 Katz (1999a).

40 *Ibid.*

parliaments and the European Parliament complement each other in their legitimizing tasks, and therefore should co-operate. But why stress all this?

The background of demands for inter-parliamentary co-operation is indeed a background of rivalry, historically and structurally. Historically, already in the 1970s the European Parliament was highly sceptical about promoting the role of the national parliaments. After all, classical federalist ambition aims at consolidating a supranational layer of government, with a bicameral European legislator consisting of the European Parliament and the Council, and with a Commission as an executive which is accountable to the European Parliament.[41] Even today, our discussion on sharpened national parliamentary scrutiny has revealed the inherent structural danger that national parliaments can pose to such a vision, in that they would cause a shift towards nationalization of European decision-making. Rivalry is of course not a one-way road, and suspicion thrives on national level as well. In those national parliaments where Euroscepticism falls on fertile soil, the primary source of democratic legitimacy in the EU tends to be seen in the national parliament itself. A stronger European Parliament is then perceived as just bringing about 'more Union'.[42] The European Parliament, being an EU institution itself, is therefore not the solution, but 'part of the problem'.[43] Indeed, there is a structural divergence in preferences, or a 'natural competitive relationship'[44] between the national parliaments and the European Parliament. Simply speaking, the European Parliament favours broadened EU competences and the co-decision procedure. National parliaments, however, if cornered, would favour subsidiarity and unanimity voting in the Council to enhance their control.[45] The European Parliament favours a greater EU budget, while the national parliaments of net contributing Member States favour domestic use of taxpayers money.[46] As a consequence, we may very well assume that the eagerness of the European Parliament to win the national parliaments as allies stems from the fear that, as Fitzmaurice (1999: 337) notes, the national parliaments may be dangerous if they turn hostile. To embrace them under its own conditions and on its terms is then preferable to maintaining a rivalry with an uncertain outcome.

There are examples for such an embracing on the European Parliament's terms. Famously, the Rome *Assizes*, the gathering of national MPs and the European Parliament, were strongly dominated by the latter. The European Parliament managed to determine the agenda, and even dictated the seating arrangements. Thus, national MPs were seated not by national delegations, but by political party

41 Niblock (1971), p. 73.
42 Laursen (2001), p. 99.
43 Cygan (2001), p. 4.
44 Von der Vring (1996), p. 406.
45 Harlow (2002), p. 107.
46 Smismans (1998), p. 52.

families, in which MEPs asserted leadership. In the end, the European Parliament got the *Assizes* to subscribe to its own pre-determined agenda.[47] Harlow (2002: 105) argues that the European Parliament delegation dominates COSAC as well. While delegations in COSAC are seated by Member State, not party colour, so that exact *Assizes*-type domination is in fact not discernible, the EP does indeed keep putting substantive items that should unite the parliamentarians of Europe onto the COSAC agenda. Thus, COSAC's expression of concern about the election fraud in the Ukrainian presidential elections[48] was tabled by MEP Elmar Brok. Incidentally, the Constitutional Convention, with MEPs and national MPs in a majority, also happened to produce a document that clearly implemented the European Parliament's agenda of making co-decision the standard legislative procedure.

Embracing the enemy can of course hold risks. After all, more active national parliaments, who are aware of the European implications of their domestic scrutiny, do not necessarily have to be in line with the preferences of the European Parliament. Earlier on, we pondered on what sort of matter might unite parliamentarians from different Member States, or indeed from national parliaments together with MEPs, as against the governments in the Council. One such example may be, as also mentioned by the Amsterdam Protocol, the area of freedom, security and justice and fundamental freedoms. Parliamentarians who are close to their citizens may have a common interest in putting a stronger emphasis on personal basic rights, for instance where flight passenger information of EU citizens is to be disclosed to US authorities or telephone records are to be kept under the EU's agenda for the fight against terrorism. That common concern may or may not materialize in practice, and it may be simplistic to juxtapose ministers all pursuing hawkish policies and MPs all campaigning for civil rights, but again, stimulating activity in the national parliaments for own purposes in any event can result in a situation where the national parliaments are explicitly *not* in line with the European Parliament. However, the danger of such a situation may of course not be substantial after all. If a national parliament disagrees with the European Parliament, it would probably be in line with its government, which we can presume to be the normal situation anyway. The national parliament would then just be more outspoken in case of an open disagreement with the EP. As noted earlier on, sharpened national parliamentary debate does not alter the European Union's institutional set-up as such, but it expands the basis for the determination of the national standpoint and thereby brings national stakes to the fore.

Above we have considered vertical inter-parliamentary ties as a means for the European Parliament to pre-empt uncontrolled and potentially hostile national parliamentary activity. The national parliaments, however, especially if invoking

47 Duff (1994), p. 162; Corbett (1998), p. 296.

48 Conclusions of the 32nd COSAC.

intra-party dependencies, could use an additional ally at EU level of their own, as well as some expertise imports. Yet we should see especially the last point in a more nuanced perspective. Why is this potential of involving MEPs under-used by the national parliaments? One reason is that there are Eurosceptic national parliaments for whom the European Parliament itself is part of the larger problem of de-nationalization of European politics and the ensuing de-parliamentarization of the national level. European policy may seem generally suspicious, as even fellow national parliamentarians who specialize in European affairs are often considered 'EU-ised Trojan horses'[49] and remain isolated in their scrutiny work. In addition, where the salaries of MEPs are beefier than those of national MPs, mistrust and rivalry can thrive as well. Yet there is another side to all that. For there are those integration-friendly national parliaments for whom reluctance to get involved in the EU decision-making process would stem from the desire not to interfere to the detriment of efficiency. Under a pro-European political consensus, parliamentary supervision of EU decision-making should be a task of the European Parliament. Teaming up with the European Parliament, or draining its expertise in order to have a stronger say in EU politics, would thus be contrary to these national parliaments' wider objectives.[50] The German *Bundestag* for instance would not even open a liaison office in Brussels, for it might unduly interfere with EU legislation. In addition, it would show a lack of trust in the European Parliament, whereas the *Bundestag*, unlike its British and Danish counterparts, insists on a strengthening of the European Parliament prior to a strengthening of the national parliaments in the EU.[51]

4.7 Conclusion

The demand that parliaments of all levels of the European Union should co-operate more actively with each other is of an appealing obviousness. However, as soon as we venture beyond the mere catch-phrase, and analyze its different underlying implications, the plan appears to be far less straightforward than it may have seemed.

To summarize, the possible forms of inter-parliamentary co-operation in the EU can vary between informal sharing of experience, to the creation of alliances between national parliaments, from the invitation of MEPs to national parliamentary deliberations, to agreements with the European Parliament on a common

49 Maurer/Wessels (2001), p. 450.

50 Dann (2004), p. 413 points out the national parliaments' structural dilemma: the more intensively they exercise control over their Governments in Council, the more they block Union decision-making.

51 Ronge (1998), p. 77.

line in certain sectors of EU policy, from individual but co-ordinated action in the respective domestic arena, to the adoption of collective COSAC resolutions addressed at the EU institutions. From a national perspective, inter-parliamentary co-operation can be a tool for boosting the effectiveness of an individual national parliament (as a means for parliamentary majorities to promote an agenda which coincides with that of their majority-backed government, or as a slogan for governments who are well aware that inter-parliamentary alliances are not likely to materialize in any threatening manner anyway). From a European perspective, it may give effect to the notions of the two-tier accountability of the EU institutions, cross-border public deliberation or multi-level governance, or it could simply reinforce the stance of the European Parliament if it can dictate the agenda. Yet in the end, the entire complex raises more questions than it answers. For instance, why should competing or concurring opinions of different Member States as regards EU policy meet in a national parliament, which is elected by and for its own Member State only? Where is the added value to the meeting of the representatives of the Member States, and in fact the agents of these very same national parliaments, in the Council? What would be the relation between COSAC and the European Council, and where would it leave the individual governments, not to mention the European Parliament?

Next to desirability concerns, there is the question of feasibility. Thus, what kind of controversial issue could open a domestic divide between government and its parliament, instead of the usual intra-parliamentary split along the left-right dimension? The constitutional frictions that arise are multiplied when the European Parliament enters the realm of vertical inter-parliamentary co-operation. National parliaments can have cultural or ideological reasons to shy away from entering into a full alliance with the European Parliament, either because it provokes Eurosceptic suspicion as it is part of the EU itself, or because it meets integration-friendly sympathies which are expressed in conscious self-constraint. The structural dilemma is that the further national parliaments push, or are pushed, onto the European arena, the more they obstruct the efficiency of Council negotiations, and the more they bring about a rediscovery of the national interest. Even if certain topics like human rights may unite the parliamentarians of Europe, not all EU matters concern such fundamental values, but may simply imply redistribution of wealth or harmonization measures which affect different national industries to varying degrees.

Another constitutional friction arises where MEPs and national MPs join each other's committee meetings, for that introduces external parliamentarians who are elected for different purposes to an accountability process, whether with respect to a national government or the Commission. Generally, the further inter-parliamentary co-operation is developed or even institutionalized, the more the different electoral mandates of parliamentarians are blurred. This concerns a national mandate of one Member State as opposed to the national mandate of another Member State, or the national mandate to represent a Member State as opposed to the European Parliament's mandate to represent the citizens of Europe as a whole.

On the scale of institutionalization of inter-parliamentary co-operation, the informal and pragmatic exchange of information for the purpose of benchmarking seems least intrusive, yet even here the practice should not be seen too uncritically. Since every national parliament is unique and has its distinct historical, cultural and institutional setting, we should, even though some common elements can surely be distilled, be careful with promoting one-size-fits-all models of scrutiny mechanisms. In the end, it is the same heterogeneity of national parliaments that we should bear in mind when considering an effective and collective stance for COSAC, as opposed to the other EU institutions. Different national parliaments have different ideas of what their roles should be in inter-parliamentary fora. Add to that their different positions and attitudes *vis-à-vis* their respective governments, which can vary from critical to loyal support, and we can draw a more realistic picture as regards the potential for sustainable inter-parliamentary solidarity. To recall our two caveats from the very beginning, national parliaments are neither a homogenous group, nor a collective of independent actors. If we keep this in mind, we can treat and assess COSAC and other fora in a much more realistic, and in a much fairer way.

5 The call for a congress of parliaments

5.1 Introduction

How can we ensure parliamentary oversight over EU decision-making if the European Parliament is not delivering, and the national parliaments are bound to be weak when tied to the domestic arena? A prominent and recurring suggestion is to ensure a direct and collective role for the national parliaments at EU level, in the form of a new parliamentary chamber. Such an idea can take different shapes in reality. One could establish a permanent chamber where national parliamentarians, equipped with a dual mandate, would act as European parliamentarians. Such a chamber could then complement the existing directly elected European Parliament as a 'Second Chamber', or actually as a 'Third Chamber' if we count the Council as an already existing senate.[1] Alternatively, such a chamber could replace today's European Parliament altogether. Yet another option would be to create an assembly or congress comprising MEPs as well as national parliamentarians, which would resemble the *Assizes* and which would meet less frequently, to discuss fundamental issues of European integration. The Convention that drafted the Constitutional Treaty could be seen, due to its membership, as a largely inter-parliamentary assembly as well. Whatever its task, such a congress would not merely exchange information, but act as an EU institution. Of course there are variations between these possible models. What they all have in common, however, is that they would create a European parliamentary body which would re-introduce the concept of a dual mandate, a national and a European one, for members of the national parliaments.

5.2 Congresses, chambers and *Assizes*: an overview

Proposals for creating a European chamber of national parliamentarians, resembling a senate, or a joint congress of national parliaments together with the European Parliament, based on the *Assizes* or the current COSAC model, have been put forward by both political actors and authors. The former French minister Roland Dumas suggested creating regular *Assizes,* which would consist half of national parliamentarians and half of MEPs, to meet thrice a year to discuss major EU policy guidelines and the application of the principle of subsidiarity.[2] David Millar suggested fully integrating such an *Assizes*-type congress in the

---

1 Cf. Swedish Riksdag (2001), p. 17.
2 See for an account Smismans (1998), p. 62.

European legislative process.[3] As to senate models, in 1989, British ex-minister Michael Heseltine suggested setting up a 'Second Chamber' of national MPs with a dual mandate, next to the directly elected European Parliament and with similar powers.[4] Commissioner Leon Brittan advocated in 1994 at least a 'committee of the national parliaments'.[5] During the Amsterdam IGC, the French government suggested a dual-mandate 'Second Chamber' to guard the principle of subsidiarity.[6] This is also consistently a priority issue for the French parliament.[7] Tony Blair, during his speech before the Warsaw Stock Exchange in October 2000, suggested awarding such a 'Second Chamber' the role of monitoring the division of powers between the EU and the Member States, as well as the conduct of the Common Foreign and Security Policy. French prime-minister Lionel Jospin advocated the revival of the *Assizes* to discuss the 'State of the Union', to monitor the application of the principle of subsidiarity, and to approve minor treaty amendments. His Spanish colleague José Maria Aznar suggested that the national parliaments should collectively approve the transfer of such competences to the EU which had not been mentioned in the treaties.[8] Convention chairman Valery Giscard d'Estaing, albeit unsuccessfully, proposed the creation of a 'Congress of the Peoples' as well. Convention member Andrew Duff (2002a) envisaged a Congress of MEPs and an equal number of national MPs to elect and impeach the Commission President.[9] The German minister of foreign affairs Joschka Fischer, in his Humboldt University speech in Berlin, raised the idea of replacing the directly elected European Parliament altogether in the long run. Instead, he suggested returning exclusively to the dual-mandate model as it existed prior to the first direct EP elections of 1979.[10]

The nucleus for an *Assizes*-type congress could be found in COSAC, the half-yearly Conference of national and European parliamentarians, which is already invited to adopt collective inter-parliamentary contributions under the Amsterdam Protocol. What is the rationale behind all these ideas? In fact, they can all be seen as extensions of the demands for a greater involvement of the national parliaments in European affairs that we have reviewed so far. Also, they are based on largely the same initial observations and assumptions, depending on the point of view. Thus, the national parliaments have given away legislative competences without

3 Millar (1995).
4 See for an account Smismans (1998), p. 63.
5 See for an account Norton (1995a), p. 7.
6 See for an account Raunio (2004), footnote 7.
7 See Swedish Riksdag (2001), p. 14; see further Layer (2001) with references to the French debate, as well as Barrau (2002).
8 For further overviews see Agostini (2001), p. 35-37; Hansen (2002), p. 17 *et seq*.
9 See on the proposals to have national MPs elect the Commission: 6 *infra*.
10 Fischer (2000).

ensuring continued accountability, or so one might argue, and if they are confined to their own Member States their substantive impact is doomed to be marginal. The European Parliament meanwhile is not, or at least not on its own, providing the amount of democratic legitimacy to the EU that one would expect from a federal nation-state. National issues remain closer to the citizens, national political parties and politicians remain more recognizable, not least because they speak the same language as their Member States' citizens, and national representative institutions remain more familiar and easier to identify with. These features are sought to put to use for overcoming the barrier between the EU institutions and the citizens. Elevating national parliamentarians to the European arena by giving them a direct influence in EU decision-making would, according to that line of reasoning, boost national public attention, do away with federalist utopias of a European nation with a single parliament, and give the national parliaments back some of the control they have lost. Arguing from a benevolently pro-European perspective, it might kill two birds with one stone: it would bring Europe closer to the citizens *and* increase the Union's democratic legitimacy. Or, arguing from a national constitutional point of view, it would ensure a direct, rather than indirect, imprint of national voter preferences upon EU legislation *and* turn the national parliaments from powerless losers into key actors, as befits their status as the true Masters of the Treaties, in as far as such notions are fashionable in a given Member State. In addition, the national parliaments could automatically reap the benefits of having expert dual-mandate MEPs within their ranks. Governments could, again, appreciate a new EU body which is not toothy enough to be a real threat, but prominent enough to be co-opted into their policies, a point to which we shall return shortly. So far the rationale which, in the light of our previous discussions, can be kept comparatively short here.[11] Now we can devote our full attention to its critique.

5.3 THE DUAL MANDATE: BACK TO THE FUTURE?

Whether one favours a dual-mandate European Parliament, a dual-mandate 'Third Chamber' next to a directly elected one plus the Council, or an *Assizes*-type congress of parliaments at EU level, the proposals all boil down to creating an inter-parliamentary assembly for the European Union. This allows us to draw parallels with other inter-parliamentary assemblies of international organizations in Europe, past or present. Examples for such bodies are the Parliamentary Assembly of the Council of Europe, the Parliamentary Assembly of the OSCE and the Inter-parliamentary European Security and Defence Assembly, originally established under the WEU and now overseeing the area of defence and armament policy

11 On the rationale for a Third Chamber see further Donnelly/Hoffmann (2004), p. 1.

within both the WEU and the European Union. And of course we can draw a parallel to the European Parliament as it existed prior to its first direct elections in 1979, when it still consisted of MPs delegated by their national parliaments. In fact, the pre-1979 European Parliament should be our preferred point of reference, for several reasons. Firstly, the WEU, the OSCE and the Council of Europe are all international organizations with a relatively narrow scope of activity. The EU, and the former EEC, on the other hand, cover far more aspects of international and domestic policy-making. Secondly, the assemblies of the WEU, the OSCE and the Council of Europe share a self-perception as being meetings of otherwise independent parliaments. The old-style European Parliament, on the other hand, already understood its role as being the representative body of a *sui generis* entity, a pre-federal parliament for a state in the making.[12]

The automatic dual mandate for national parliamentarians was abandoned with the Decision and Act on direct EP elections. In order to evaluate a possible re-introduction of the dual mandate, let us recall what it was that led to the abolition of the dual mandate in the first place. One line of arguing in the 1960s and 1970s criticized that the European Parliament, at the time still officially called European Parliamentary Assembly, could not exercise genuine parliamentary functions if it was not even directly elected. Another line of arguing was more practical in nature. A dual mandate meant an excessive drain on the time and energy of MPs.[13] Even in the 1970s, when the scope of competences and flow of legislation at the European level was comparatively moderate, parliamentarians would opt to concentrate on just one of their mandates.

This last point also had implications for the 'educative effect' of dual-mandate MEPs, where they were expected to share their first-hand expertise with their fellow national parliamentarians. Firstly, double workload of dual-mandate MEPs led to absenteeism in the national parliaments. Just like today's directly elected MEPs, where they are invited to join meetings in national parliaments, the dual-mandate MEPs were rarely around to share their knowledge. Secondly, we should note the very small number of dual-mandate MEPs that each national parliament could delegate out of its total membership.[14] At the time of the abolition of the dual mandate, the German *Bundestag*, for example, delegated merely thirty-six out of its then total of 519 MPs. Of course today, in the current directly elected European Parliament, Germany boasts a ninety-nine-strong delegation, almost three times the size compared to the old dual-mandate times. However, let us not forget that today's MEPs are elected on a full-time basis. Under a revived dual-mandate scheme, a delegation of 99 German parliamentarians would be unsustainable. Due to the absenteeism

---

12 Niblock (1971), p. 67, 74.

13 See European parliament (2002), Sasse (1975), p. 87.

14 Niblock (1971), p. 66.

of the 'Europeans', the *Bundestag* would effectively forfeit one-sixth of its total membership, which corresponds to the combined membership of about four of its permanent committees. For the parliament of the Netherlands, which delegated eight MEPs in the 1970s, the burden under the current Dutch delegation size would be 27 MPs out of 150. Furthermore, as to the educative effect, not only were the relative numbers of dual-mandate MEPs small in the 1970s, but these MEPs tended not to be high-ranking politicians domestically either.[15] To expect an enhanced link of European parliamentarians to national politics would therefore hardly be justified on that basis. We may recall the isolation of the interested few who staff the average European Affairs Committee today.

Then, instead of having an educative and integrative effect on the rest of national MPs, the dual mandate could even have an effect quite to the opposite. Sasse (1975: 86) for instance remarked how under-informed and disinterested German MPs were as regards European affairs: 'For [the average *Bundestag* member] the 36 members of the Strasbourg parliament almost have something of an alibi function'. We can therefore conclude that on the national arena, a dual mandate is unlikely to create, let alone re-create, a direct link to the European level. Parliamentarians who focus on their European workload, which today is far heavier than it was in the 1970s, neglect their national mandate. Those who remain in their national parliament neglect their MEP functions and provide little added value for either arena. Electing separate MPs at national general elections for European tasks only would create two-class parliaments where the EU-MPs would not provide any added value to the MEPs we have today.[16] Especially when the rest of national MPs take comfort in completely delegating European affairs to the 'usual suspects', scrutiny of these matters in the national parliaments would be even weaker than it is today.

5.4 The collective revisited

Permanent parliamentary chambers based on a dual mandate are not the only suggestions put forward. *Assizes* and similar constructions would meet less frequently, and deprive MPs less of their time. Still, even such models, whatever their purpose, would meet objections of a fundamental nature. Just like the idea of turning COSAC into a forum for substantive inter-parliamentary contributions, which we have discussed before,[17] the institutionalization of a body along the same lines inevitably comes with the implication that the national parliaments are a sort of homogenous collective which can boost the EU's democratic legitimacy if only

15 *Ibid.*
16 See Raunio (2004), p. 9.
17 See 4.3 *supra*.

they could be fused and upgraded to form a nexus of European parliamentarism. And again, we must recall that the national parliaments are neither homogenous, nor a collective. Their historical backgrounds vary between 19th century bourgeois emancipation in constitutional monarchies, to re-democratization processes in 20th century post-authoritarian settings. This goes without mentioning the even more centuries of tradition in the UK Commons. In terms of political and constitutional systems, flavours of parliamentarism range from moderately adversarial government-parliament divides to strong executive dominance, from full parliamentary systems to semi-presidential systems, from formal government investiture to pragmatic workable majority rule, from proportionate representation to first-past-the-post district systems, from unicameralism to bicameralism, from a unitary state structure to devolution and federalism, from multi-party governments to single-party governments, from bipartisanism in parliament to heavy fragmentation, from rationalized parliamentarism to rule by fragile coalitions or minority cabinets, from working parliaments to talking parliaments, from sharp-tongued scrutiny to loyal regime support, from stability to volatility, from majoritarian to consensual policy-making. Member States can be Nordic or Mediterranean, large or small, rural or industrial, they can be part of 'Old Europe' or 'New Europe'. And then, of course, there is the range between integration-friendly consensus and deep-rooted Euroscepticism. Crucially, apart from not being homogenous, which might not even be such a big problem in itself, their general views on the role of national parliaments in the EU differ as well. Thus, integration-minded parliaments would not be eager to engage in any sort of competition with the European Parliament.[18] To complete the picture, the national parliaments cannot easily be assumed to have sufficient potential for a solidarity which would bypass their own majority-based governments. Therefore, before we try and upgrade COSAC to a 'Third Chamber' at EU level, we should remember the different plans' inherent flaws, the effect of which can be witnessed already today.

5.5 THE IMPORTANCE OF BEING ELECTED

How would the members of a dual-mandate chamber or *Assizes* interact? Would they sit along political party lines, for instance along the divides of left and right, libertarian, social-democratic and conservative, or perhaps along the line of federalism and sovereignism? Or would they sit by national delegation, the French group next to the German, the Italian and the Polish delegations? It is important to ask that question, for its answer tells us something about the added value of the entire exercise. Thus, if national MPs sit in groups divided by political colour, where is the added value to the European Parliament, where such arrangements exist already

18 Raunio (1999), p. 199.

today, and are consolidating? Conversely, if the MPs sit in groups divided by country, where is the added value to the Council, the EU's international bargaining forum par excellence? This especially since the political colour of government and parliamentary majority normally coincides anyway.[19] Speaking about the Convention which drafted the Constitutional Treaty, Bengtson (2003: 4) refers to 'anecdotical evidence [suggesting] that parliamentary and government representatives from the same countries often followed the same line of argument'. Niblock (1971: 72) illustrates this phenomenon with respect to the old dual-mandate European Parliament prior to 1979, when a cleavage arose over agricultural policy between free-marketeers, on the one hand, and protectionists, on the other hand: '[I]n so far as opinion within the [dual-mandate] European Parliament does divide on these traditional lines, it is clear that the attitudes prevailing among those members who in their home Parliaments belong to the Government parties are likely to be closely related to standpoints taken up in the Council of Ministers by the individual Council members. The simple fact that the majority of any national delegation is drawn from the parliamentary majority which supports the policies of the Government of the moment is sufficient to ensure this in most cases'. A dual-mandate European Parliament asserting itself against government positions would mean that a national government would heed to the opinions of delegates of other Member States, or to the influence of domestic opposition parties, neither of which is probable.

So why would it be desirable to have national parliamentarians duplicate the activity of either the European Parliament or the Council? The obvious response to this question, whatever the respondent's agenda, would be that national parliamentarians have a stronger electoral mandate than governments and MEPs do. As to the latter, one might argue that MEPs are elected under very questionable circumstances, in national campaigns dominated by national issues. Of course, we could note that if the national electoral basis is a problem for MEPs, then this can only be worse in the case of national parliamentarians, where such a national bias is even very much intended. Turning to the national governments, we can indeed acknowledge that they are only elected indirectly in a parliamentary democracy, while MPs are elected directly. This thought, concerning the electoral basis of the Council members, is an interesting one. In fact, it provokes another question: why would politicians be 'better' just because they have been directly elected?

What is the difference between, say, a social-democratic minister and the leader of the social-democratic government party group in the national parliament? Both are from the same political party, which is typically chaired by the Prime Minister anyway. Both eventually depend on re-election, the minister maybe more so than the MP. For an MP can re-enter parliament even as a member of the opposition,

19 Cf. Harlow (2002), p. 104; Raunio (2004), p. 8 with references.

while a minister can only re-enter the cabinet if his or her party remains strong enough to stay in power. Either way, the views of the two individuals are not likely to diverge. And if they do? The constant challenge by the parliamentary opposition, and dissent within the rank-and-file of the government parties, is exactly what fuels parliamentary debate. That is the essence of the deliberative aspect of parliamentarism. However, that property is linked to the domestic arena, where it is subject to popular scrutiny itself. It cannot be simply detached, moved and re-installed at EU level. It is based on familiar institutions and procedures, and the presence of opposition. This opposition is opposing the national government, and not a group of twenty-five governments, certainly not in coalition with twenty-four other parliamentary minorities. As far as parliamentary majorities are concerned, we may seriously question whether 'more democracy' will be infused into the EU if MPs duplicate the activities of their very own agents in a 'Third Chamber'. Indeed, for the purpose of national interest representation, the European Union already *has* a chamber, namely the Council.[20]

The idea that directly elected parliamentarians are democratically 'better' than indirectly elected governments are, finds prominent expression in the suggestion that national MPs should accompany ministers to Council meetings.[21] The parliamentarian is however not at all 'better' or 'more democratic' than the minister is. He or she is a colleague, only one who tends to be worse informed. His or her mere presence does not ensure parliamentarization just by itself, for the communicative tasks of a parliament are not fulfilled by MPs' attending confidential meetings.[22] The attractive representative and majoritarian-democratic aspect of parliamentarism cannot be imported to the Council if opposition members are left outside.[23] After all, as noted at the very outset, it is not parliament as such that is interesting, but its composition. Cramming ever more MPs into the Council meetings, and letting them all openly debate there, in a European Union of twenty-five and counting, would clearly bring the kiss of death to the efficiency, and to what is left of the intimacy, of Council negotiations. Decreased efficiency as a price to be paid for democratization is only acceptable if that democratization can in fact be achieved. Perhaps the *activity* of the Council is indeed undemocratic, as in intransparent and unaccountable. But it is not the actors who are undemocratic, and MPs will not exceed the democratic properties of a minister in the Council if they engage in the same activity that the latter engages in today.

---

20 Einem (2002).

21 Suggested *inter alia* by French European affairs minister Lamassoure in 1995, see Agostini (2001), p. 38.

22 Weber-Panariello (1995), p. 308 *et seq*.

23 In COSAC, the number of delegates per national parliament is, for instance, intended to allow for representation of different political parties, see Swedish Riksdag (2001), p. 7.

Quite to the contrary. Setting up a dual-mandate chamber or congress next to the existing EU institutions would make the institutional landscape and the decision-making process even more complex and intransparent than it already is.[24] To avoid mutual blocking between the European Parliament, the Council and the new assembly, enhanced bargaining behind closed doors would be necessary, which would again diminish transparency. The possibility of being outvoted under majority voting, if that is already deemed problematic in the Council, would persist in a dual-mandate assembly as well.[25] National parliaments which want to retain control over delegated MPs who speak on their behalf would have to insist on much the same mandating routine that exists today in some Member States with respect to ministers. A further decrease in democratic content can be linked to the above proposition to have national MPs accompany ministers to the Council itself. This would allow the government to take parliament 'hostage', by claiming that the accompanying MPs have accepted the government's conduct in the Council. As a result, national parliamentary scrutiny would be impeded.[26]

Even more fundamentally, we may again pick up the theme with which we started our discussion, namely that involving national parliaments in the EU to a greater extent, for whatever purpose, than what is inherent to a treaty-based organization, is a form of artificial exercise. Desirable as it may be from various points of view, the exercise produces side-effects and causes distortions. One of the gravest distortions that a new dual-mandate assembly at EU level would bring about would affect national constitutional settings. As Weber-Panariello (1995: 311) observes, in Western parliamentary democracies, government and parliament are intimately connected to each other. The attempt to again separate these two powers with a new body at EU level therefore appears questionable and *wirklichkeitsfremd*.

To this detachment from reality we may add another observation from the very beginning of our discussion. Reaching out to national non-governmental political institutions in a top-down manner requires the application of a crude standard. With a rough approximation of which national parliaments or chambers should qualify for a dual-mandate scheme in the first place comes a distorted perception of domestic government-parliament relations. Not all chambers in Europe are elected, not all chambers can dismiss the government, not all chambers are always competent law-makers, and not all of them are truly parliaments. As before, the

---

24 See Neunreither (1994), p. 306 *et seq.*; Weber-Panariello (1995), p. 311; Swedish Riksdag (2001), p. 17; European parliament (2002); Harlow (2002), p. 107 picturing the inclusion of regional parliaments in an unwieldy forum; Dann (2004), p. 412; Donnelly/Hoffmann (2004), p. 2; Raunio (2004), p. 7; Brown (2003), p. 4 notes that the national parliamentarians in the Convention were 'almost unanimous in rejecting any idea of a Congress or similar new institution' on EU level.

25 Höreth (1999), p. 301.

26 Swedish Riksdag (2001), p. 25.

only convincing solution from a methodological point of view would be to reserve a number of seats to national delegations, to be filled by the Member States as they see fit. Still, few parliaments would fit into simplified adversarial government-versus-parliament models, if any.

5.6 The Convention method of treaty revision

One of the most prominent innovations in the EU's approach to the collective involvement of national parliaments, as well as to the process of drafting pieces of primary EU law itself, was the introduction of the Conventions. So far in the history of European integration there have been two Conventions, the one that drafted the EU Charter of Fundamental Rights, and the one that drafted the Constitutional Treaty. Since a Convention comprises not only government and Commission representatives, but also MEPs and, importantly, national parliamentarians, they could provide a useful addition, if not a substitution, to the traditional IGCs.[27] Conventions are intended to offer an open forum for public debate, as opposed to the usual secretive intergovernmental bargaining. What is more, Conventions may offer an avenue for direct and collective national parliamentary participation in the process of treaty drafting, as opposed to the mere take-it-or-leave-it ratification scenario following IGCs. Since MPs and MEPs together hold the majority of Convention members, 72 out of 102 in the Constitutional Convention excluding chairmen and observers, the forum bears a similarity to the *Assizes* in membership, which is why we can fit it, for the sake of convenience, into our discussion of inter-parliamentary congresses complementing intergovernmental negotiation. Also our earlier conclusions on chambers of MPs at EU level are largely applicable to the Conventions as well.

The superior democratic properties of especially the Constitutional Convention are usually advanced with references to some core notions. As previously stated, the Convention, unlike an IGC, offered openness to the public. The Convention, unlike an IGC, directly involved national parliamentarians in the pre-ratification stage. This means that, unlike an IGC, the Convention included MPs from opposition parties who provided a corrective to government representatives.[28] The democratic legitimacy of the actors was more immediate, their link to the national parliaments stronger, their distance to the electorate shorter. It is beyond doubt that the Convention was a unique and highly exciting experiment, and it will be the subject of many studies that will evaluate it from different angles, and with increased objectivity as time passes. As to its inter-parliamentary aspect, however, we may already

---

27 Brown (2004), p. 3.
28 Brown (2003), p. 5.

now insert some important qualifications. As to the Convention's desired openness to the general public, only with the notable exception of the refreshing debate whether the Constitutional Treaty should contain a reference to God, can we seriously question whether it has really attracted any significant attention 'outside the usual circles'.[29] The national parliaments did not seem to pick up any domestic debate matching the deliberations in the Convention. More fundamental qualifications we should place with respect to the personality of the Convention members. The fact that a member is an MP does not automatically make him any 'better' if his activities are detached from the domestic setting. The Convention did not involve national parliaments as such, but only individual MPs. While the national parliaments as institutions remained where they were, on the Member State level and outside the Convention, the Convention's relative openness was originary, and not derived from the openness of the national parliaments.[30] Such originary openness however is based on the uniqueness of the exercise, and on the moment that captures attention. Regular repetition or institutionalization on such a scale would forfeit the Convention's more or less captivating effect, which would be our next qualification, namely that the legitimacy that the Convention may have provided to the Constitutional Treaty was 'genetic', attaching to its moment of genesis, and not permanent.[31]

Anyway, the fact that the Convention, essentially another EU institution, happened to comprise national parliamentarians did not even seem to give it that much legitimacy or transparency to start with, as the referendums in France and the Netherlands on what the Convention produced have clearly shown. As to ideas to make the Conventions a more or less permanent institution, our earlier qualifications apply. Congresses, *Assizes*, 'Third Chambers' or institutionalized Conventions provide little added value at best, due to their duplication of existing institutions while being detached from the national parliaments themselves, and they come at a price that is higher the more meaningful the exercise becomes. Of course, 'value' and 'price' are in the eye of the beholder, and the noted effects may be very much desired. The difference now is, however, that we ourselves as observers can assess these prices and values more objectively than we would in the absence of a critical preliminary analysis.

---

29 Brown (2004), p. 9 quoting Irish Foreign Minister Brian Cowen; Føllesdal (2004), p. 3, with references, notes that the deliberation conditions in the Convention, while being of increased transparency, were 'still far from those of Habermas' "ideal speech situations"'. On the debate about a reference to God see Weiler (2002).

30 Dann (2004), p. 410 is critical of the representativity of the composition of the otherwise interesting Conventions.

31 Cf. Peters (2004), referring to a possible referendum to legitimize the TCE.

5.7 Conclusion

The creation of an inter-parliamentary assembly, a congress of national MPs as well as MEPs, a 'Third Chamber' based on dual mandates for national parliamentarians, or a return to a dual-mandate European Parliament exclusively, are all models which seek to address two points at the same time. Firstly, these models are based on the observation that the indirect influence which national parliaments can have on EU decision-making via their governments is an insufficient way of national parliamentary participation. Secondly, the model abandons the idea that the European Parliament, at least the European Parliament alone, can provide a sufficient degree of parliamentary participation at EU level. The solution would therefore be to lift the national parliaments themselves up to the EU level, institutionalize their direct and collective input, and replace or at least complement the directly elected European Parliament. In that, the national perspective and the European perspective, which we consistently employ, converge. From both angles, the model might be justified for largely the same reasons. The objections that can be raised with respect to such plans are not only of a practical nature but, corresponding to the scale of institutional reform that the realization of these plans would require, they are also quite fundamental. To a large extent, in as far as a congress of parliaments constitutes an extreme version of older general thoughts, our objections can be based on considerations made earlier on. National parliaments each have a national electoral mandate, their majority is in solidarity with the own government, rather than with other parliaments, and they are highly heterogeneous for the rest, including their broader vision on parliamentarism, both in their own Member State as well as in Europe as a whole.

A congress based on dual mandates, which is divided along a political left-right dimension, would offer little added value to the already existing European Parliament, but instead add to the EU's institutional complexity. Historical experience with the dual-mandate European Parliament prior to 1979, the recent Convention experience as well as the current experience with the EU specialists sitting on the European Affairs Committees show that direct and meaningful links between congress delegates and the remainder of national parliamentarians are unlikely. If the envisaged congress splits up along national, rather than political colour lines, it will meanwhile offer little added value to the already existing Council.

Parliamentarians as such do not feature any better democratic properties than a national minister does, since both are eventually dependent on re-election, while both would engage in much the same international bargaining process. The deliberative properties of simplification and polarization are not attached to MPs themselves, but to the representative institution of which they form part. In that, a parliament relies on its roots in the society it represents, which would make the idea of continued operation after a transplant to the European arena highly dubious. In as far as genuine cross-border public discourse is achievable, it would be taking place in the current European Parliament already. Even more fundamentally speaking, the suggestion of linking national MPs to the European scene relies on the idea that twenty-five national parliaments, each with its own national mandate, can together constitute a form of collective European parliamentarism. However, all this model seems to achieve, in ascending order of detrimental effect, is a duplication of the functions of already existing institutions, a burdening of the EU decision-making efficiency, a worsening of its complexity and intransparency, a distortion of otherwise non-adversarial government-parliament relations on domestic level and, if democracy is our highest value, a factual decrease in parliamentary accountability. The national parliaments would after all be able to leave involvement in European affairs entirely to their delegates, while the governments would be able to pre-empt parliamentary scrutiny by making these delegates their accomplices. This might make the dual-mandate model appear attractive to governments; downgrading the EU, which now has a directly elected parliament, to something like the OSCE, which merely has an inter-parliamentary assembly, might furthermore resonate well with supporters of an anti-federalist agenda. To the rest, however, the model of an inter-parliamentary dual-mandate congress, *Assizes* or a 'Third Chamber' would seem strikingly unconvincing.

6 The call for Commission accountability to the national parliaments

6.1 Introduction

The proposals concerning inter-institutional relations that we have reviewed so far concentrated on the links between the national parliaments and the Council, and between the national parliaments and the European Parliament. Now let us turn to the parliaments' possible links with the third part of the European Union's legislative triangle, the Commission. Up until here, the Commission mainly featured as the initiator of legislative proposals, in the sense that it is a source of information and documentation which marks the starting point of the formal EU law-making process. We might however note that parliamentary oversight over the initiator of legislation, and thus the agenda-setter, is no less important than control over the body which finally adopts the legislation.[1] Apart from that, the Commission is a politically prominent institution, and its President is an important political figure, so that enhancing the respective democratic legitimacy there may add to the symbolic weight of the Commission – and the national parliaments who would be calling it to account – and may also cause spill-over effects to the citizens' perception of the EU as a whole. These two aspects also reflect the two perspectives, the national and the European one, which we employ. From a national point of view, tying the Commission closer to the Member States and their parliaments would enhance its democratic content as derived from the national democracies, and reinforce national control – in both a constitutional-philosophical as well as cynic-pragmatic sense. From a European point of view, such ties would again elevate the national parliaments to the EU arena and in the process bring that arena closer to the citizens. In the following paragraphs we shall focus on those proposals which boil down to, or which are closely related to, the idea of having the national parliaments collectively elect the Commission or the Commission President.

6.2 Election and inquiry

At present, the Commission President is nominated by the European Council and confirmed by the European Parliament, while the other Commissioners are selected by the Commission President upon proposal by the Member States and again, as a college, confirmed by the European Parliament.[2] The national parliaments are

1 Urbantschitsch (1998), p. 62.
2 Article 214 EC, see also Article I-26 and I-27 TCE.

involved in that process only indirectly, in as far as they can control the nominations which are put forward by their governments. The usual picture emerges, in that confidential compromise-finding in the European Council and the traditional executive prerogatives in foreign affairs marginalize the national parliaments. Direct parliamentary power is exercised by the European Parliament. However, if one subscribes to the thesis about the insufficiently democratic or representative character of the European Parliament, a stronger national parliamentary involvement should help bridge the gap between citizens and the EU institutions.

Hix (2002) suggested departing from the Commission investiture procedure between the European Council and the European Parliament, and instead proposed organizing elections of the Commission President by the national parliaments. This would, according to Hix, ensure direct participation of the national parliaments at EU level, and trigger domestic debates on the course of European integration. Candidates for the post would have to defend their agendas in an election campaign to win the support of the national parliaments. Duff (2002a) proposed an *Assizes*-type congress of MEPs and national parliamentarians to both elect and impeach the Commission President.[3] Even without having the national parliaments elect the Commission President, occasionally the proposal is put forward to enhance his or her accountability towards the national parliaments. Thus, the Commission President or individual Commissioners could pay visits to the national parliaments and answer their questions, for instance during the proposed 'Europe week', when all national parliaments would debate the 'State of the Union' and the Commission's annual legislative programme.[4]

6.3 Congruency and Added Value

Our critique here can set in with fundamental considerations of constitutional law, and move its way up to more practical objections. To start with the last proposals, which aim at national parliamentary scrutiny of the Commission or its President, we may observe a lack of congruency which is essential for a parliamentary system. If the system were adopted, those who scrutinize the Commission would not be the ones who elected it, and they would not be the ones empowered to dismiss it. The parliamentary right to summon national ministers, and the right of inquiry, derives from the fact that these ministers owe their office to continued parliamentary confidence. There is a congruency, in fact identity, between the institution which calls a government to account, and the institution which wields the power to dismiss it. From a constitutional law point of view, as long as the Commission does

---

3 Duff (2002a): Article 10; see also Brown (2003), p. 6.

4 See for an account of such proposals: Brown (2003), p. 7, Raunio (1999), p. 196 *et seq*. with references.

not require confidence in the national parliaments to stay in office, its touring the national capitals would be bound to be an entirely voluntary exercise. This exercise, in the present setting, would blur the distinction between the accountability of governments to the national parliaments, and the already existing accountability of the Commission towards the European Parliament, which indeed does possess the power to oust the Commission. Another concern in that respect would be the choice of parliaments to visit. If the answering of questions by national parliaments is a voluntary exercise, there would be little use for a Commission President to tour parliaments which are integration-friendly and benevolently supportive of the Commission anyway. A Commission President who would confine his or her journeys to Copenhagen and Westminster would, however, not only distort the existing links of parliamentary accountability at EU level, but would also damage the essential character of the Commission itself, namely its neutrality with respect to, and its autonomy from, the Member States.[5]

Such concerns about the Commission's autonomy, and the lack of congruency or identity between inquirer and elector or dismisser, would at first sight be of a lesser significance if the national parliaments were indeed directly involved in the Commission's election. This is where the mentioned proposals set in to organize individual voting for Commission candidates in the national parliaments, or to hold an electoral congress for that purpose. Yet again, the problem of incongruence would persist. Whether the voting is decentralized in the national capitals or centralized in a type of *Assizes*, the function of the voters can only be compared to those of an electoral college. This means that a Commission President would enjoy an initial legitimacy moment through his election by parliamentarians. The day-to-day scrutiny, and the enforcement of accountability for post-election policies, would however have to rest with a permanent assembly, notably the European Parliament. Indeed, Duff's proposal envisages the election of the Commission President by *Assizes*, as well as his impeachment by the *Assizes*, but it also provides for the continued right of the European Parliament to dismiss the Commission. Hix's proposal also included the right for the European Parliament to impeach the Commission President, even though he or she would be elected by the national parliaments. The European Parliament would thus be presented with a Commission President whom it has neither elected nor confirmed itself, but it would have the right to dismiss him, thus overriding the *Assizes* or the national parliaments, respectively, and extinguishing the legitimacy moment that was apparently sought. If such a right

5 Commissioner for Institutional Relations Margot Wallström announced in 2005 that she would pay a visit to all national parliaments in the EU, see the Commissioner's press release of 17 February 2005. As relations with national parliaments fall into her specific portfolio, an impression is duly avoided that *all* Commissioners should report to national parliaments, let alone to those of their home countries.

of ordinary censure is not granted to the European Parliament, those who favour enhanced national parliamentary control over the Commission would paradoxically find themselves supporting an extreme presidentialization of the European Union. If the right of censure remained with the national parliaments, then the Commission would be politically accountable to the Member States and lose its supranational neutrality.

Our critique is not limited to aspects of constitutional law, but it also includes practical concerns. These concerns show strong parallels to our previous discussion about the creation of an inter-parliamentary congress featuring national MPs. Firstly, we have to raise the question of added value. If the national parliaments, whether individually or assembled in a congress, vote according to political party colour broadly corresponding to a left-right dimension, where is the added value of duplicating the European Parliament? Conversely, if the national parliaments, that is the respective majorities, vote according to national preferences, where is the added value to the European Council? Political colour and national government support still coincide in cases of majority cabinets. Indeed, in a reaction to Hix' proposal of national parliamentary elections of the Commission President, Hoffmann (2002) showed that the outcome there would hardly differ when compared to the calculated outcome of an election in the European Council. Thus, the same candidate would win in either scenario.

We have already questioned earlier the alleged added value of conducting elections by, and campaigns for, national MPs. If the MPs gather in *Assizes*, they leave behind their national forum to which their power of deliberation and polarization is attached. If MPs gather in their national parliaments, meaningful debates on the course of European integration could only emerge in the presence of a real cleavage. That cleavage would, due to the parliaments' constitutional mandate and the target-group of their deliberation, inevitably stress the nation-state interest in the Commission, an office which is intended to serve the European Union as a whole, perhaps decreasingly neutral as regards political colour, but still bound to the principle of neutrality as regards its treatment of Member States and still autonomous from national instructions.[6] Anyway, in a functioning parliamentary democracy, there is no reason why a government that enjoys the support of a parliamentary majority would fail to gather support for its favourite candidate. After all, the majority of voters has given preference to one political colour over the other at national elections, which should be translated into the choices of the government and the parliament itself. And if voters' national preferences differ from their EU-level preferences, it is all the more reason to have these preferences expressed at EU level accordingly. This means that the way towards full parliamentarization of the Commission election process cannot lead through the national capitals.

6 Article 213 (2) EC, Article I-26 (7) TCE.

6.4 Conclusion

A link of accountability between the Commission and the national parliaments meets both theoretical and practical objections. Parliamentary rights of summon and inquiry are based on the rule of parliamentary confidence. In the absence of the Commission's owing the continuation of its term to the confidence of the national parliaments, appearances of Commissioners before national parliaments are voluntary political exercises which would distort the line of confidence and accountability that already exists towards the European Parliament. To replace the current Commission election procedure by turning national MPs into electors, in one way or another, produces similarly distortive effects. Singular collective elections without continued accountability under standards of parliamentarism leads to presidentialization. Preserving the continued parliamentary accountability towards the European Parliament leads to incongruence between the assembly that elects or confirms, and the one that dismisses the Commission. The apparently desired momentary legitimacy effect from collective election by national MPs would be largely meaningless if the European Parliament could overrule the MPs' choice by censuring the Commission thus elected. A collective censure right for the national parliaments would however mean a nationalization of the Commission. Practical concerns relate to the little added value that is gained in return for the described distortions. Collective elections by MPs would merely duplicate the present-day work of the European Council, without achieving deviating results in terms of winning candidates. Instead, nationalizing Commission elections calls into question the supranational neutrality and autonomy of that very institution. From an intergovernmentalist point of view, this might be desirable or at least acceptable; from a supranational perspective, the Commission's autonomy should however be cherished.

7 The national parliaments as guardians of subsidiarity

7.1 Introduction

The rejection of the EU Constitutional Treaty in the French and Dutch referendums in 2005 also meant a rejection of one of the Treaty's most prominent institutional and procedural innovations: the early warning system. The system was intended to explicitly involve the national parliaments, for the first time, in the EU legislative process. The parliaments were meant to sift EU legislative proposals, to check their compliance with the principle of subsidiarity, and to raise objections if they found that a policy area could be better dealt with at a lower level. The truth of the matter is, however, that the national parliaments do not actually need a new treaty in order to act as guardians of the principle of subsidiarity.

First of all, national parliaments can already sift EU proposals anyway as they come in, and they naturally can use subsidiarity as a criterion in their analysis: provisions concerning access to EU documentation and a six-weeks time window for scrutiny are already contained in the Amsterdam Protocol on the national parliaments. Secondly, if we look at it soberly, we have to conclude that the early warning system as it was originally adopted by the Convention and the IGC was by itself not terribly earth-shaking either. To name but the two most prominent weaknesses perceived, firstly the collective veto that the national parliaments could cast would not be absolute, it could be overridden, albeit only if reasons are provided, and secondly the national parliaments would not receive *locus standi* as privileged applicants before the European Court of Justice of their own: the ECJ would have jurisdiction to rule on annulment actions on subsidiarity grounds, but a national parliament would still have to ask its government to bring an action on its behalf.[1] Seen purely in terms of substantive power allocation with the national parliaments, we must note that nothing precludes a national parliament from asking its government to bring an annulment action, and that nothing precludes it from writing angry letters to the Commission. To raise subsidiarity concerns, which the Commission may or may not honour, the national parliaments do not require a new treaty provision. They have always been able to do that.[2]

However we would be short-sighted if we evaluated the monitoring of the subsidiarity principle purely in terms of substantive powers allocated with national parliaments, and purely in the context of the Constitutional Treaty. Firstly, the idea itself tells us something of the Convention's constitution-building ambitions,

1 Article 8 TCE Protocol on the application of the principles of subsidiarity and proportionality, Article III-365 TCE.

2 Thanks to Hans Hegeland for this remark.

and we can make conclusions for possible future attempts to address national parliaments in that area. Secondly, as already mentioned, national parliaments can be guardians of the subsidiarity principle even without a new treaty. In fact, several parliaments have already adapted to their subsidiarity monitoring task in anticipation of an eventual entry into force of the Constitutional Treaty, without waiting for the outcome of the ratification process. COSAC has already conducted a pilot experiment with the system, which yielded interesting results. Generally, just by backing it up with a new enforcement mechanism in the draft Treaty text, the Convention succeeded in awarding a higher prominence to the subsidiarity principle. Let us therefore consider what the monitoring of compliance with the principle of subsidiarity could mean to the national parliaments, and to the application of the principle itself.

7.2 National parliaments and subsidiarity

The reason why the early warning system was included in the Constitutional Treaty in the first place can be seen in the light of the mandate that was initially given to the European Convention which devised it. In as far as the role of the national parliaments is concerned, the Constitutional Treaty continued a development which started, on IGC level, with the Declarations of Maastricht which explicitly addressed the national parliaments in an individual and collective capacity. Maastricht Declaration No. 13 recognized the possible contribution of the national parliaments in the EU, the Amsterdam Treaty recognized COSAC and invited it to adopt contributions, improved information flows to the parliaments and inserted the mentioned six-weeks scrutiny delay. The Nice IGC of 2000 and the Laeken European Council addressed the subject of national parliamentary involvement again, putting the question, along with those on treaty simplification, the Charter of Fundamental Rights and indeed subsidiarity, on the agenda for the Convention that was to draft a new treaty. The role of the subsidiarity principle itself was perceived to be lacking effective enforcement in practice. What in the end happened was that the desire to overcome the peripheral position of the national parliaments in the EU, and the desire to strengthen the principle of subsidiarity, merged into one new idea: the national parliaments would receive a role in the EU legislative process as the new guardians of subsidiarity. The question of the division of competences between the Member States and the EU, debated in the Convention's working group I on subsidiarity, and the question concerning the role of the national parliaments, debated in working group IV, in fact largely overlapped.[3] The early warning system was, in a way, a composite answer to two

3 Rizzuto (2003), p. 2; Vergés Bausili (2002).

separate questions from the Nice Declaration, as it sought to provide for both: a greater role for the national parliaments, and a more effective enforcement of the principle of subsidiarity.

Indeed, there appears to be a natural link between national parliamentarism and subsidiarity in the EU. The Convention in fact addressed the national parliaments in a variety of capacities for subsidiarity purposes, although it of course never clearly defined these capacities itself. Firstly, since subsidiarity means regulation at the lowest sensible level, national parliaments are addressed as the ones who would presumably retain or inherit those regulatory powers which seem inappropriate for the EU level to wield. Secondly, since controlling subsidiarity means a policing of the boundaries of EU competences, national parliaments are also addressed as the ones who have presumably conferred these competences upon the EU by way of treaty ratification in the first place.[4] And thirdly, since a devolution of EU powers downwards makes the scope and exercise of these powers more transparent and recognizable, national parliaments are inevitably addressed as the ones who can presumably bring 'Europe closer to the citizens', especially since they are external and therefore perhaps more objective actors in the EU decision-making process, in contrast to the Commission, the Council and the ECJ.

The idea of having the national parliaments monitor compliance with subsidiarity could be appealing, both from a European, as well as from a national constitutional perspective. From a European perspective, clarity in what the EU does and does not do may increase its legitimacy in a broad sense. Both Eurosceptics and integrationist could readily agree on this ideal: enforcement of subsidiarity may increase transparency of EU action, and the prevention of unauthorized competence creeps towards the EU may have a stabilizing effect in what is a quasi-federal order.[5] And perhaps it truly takes an external actor to enforce subsidiarity, if the EU institutions themselves do not take that principle all too seriously because they can only profit from competence creeps. Apart from that, the involvement of national parliaments means an instrumentalization of their communicative value, which might again generate popular support for a more transparent EU. Having them on board could further strengthen their interest in European affairs, as well as their support for European integration, as MPs would come to have their own stake in the game.[6] Mundanely, courting the national parliaments was probably also intended to appease sceptical MPs and citizens who would have to ratify the Constitutional

4 See Dashwood (2004), p. 368; Cygan (2004b) on the notion of subsidiarity as a form of 'substitute sovereignty'.

5 See Donnelly/Hoffmann (2004), p. 3; Straw (2004); Swenden (2004); Føllesdal (2004), p. 10, see also Moersch (2001), p. 387; Nicolaïdis (2003), p. 7. Critical of the invocation of subsidiarity for legitimacy purposes: Estella (2002).

6 Donnelly/Hoffmann (2004), p. 1; Vergés Bausili (2002), p. 16.

Treaty. Furthermore, making sure that MPs read Commission proposals as they are published could mean that the eventual implementation process runs smoothly.

From a national perspective, subsidiarity once again underlines the status of the national parliaments as 'Masters of the Treaties' in guarding conferred powers, and their direct involvement in the legislative process allows for a more effective and non-mediated democratic and deliberative imprint on EU policies. Eventually, strict enforcement of subsidiarity might even lead to a 'repatriation' of competences from the EU back to the Member States, should a particular parliament (or government) desire to insist on that.

7.3 Subsidiarity Enforcement in Practice

Let us briefly recall the Convention's idea how the early warning system would work. As usual, the Commission may initiate legislation under what used to be the First Pillar.[7] The Commission proposal is sent to the national governments and the European Parliament, and it is also directly sent to all the national parliaments.[8] This would be an innovation with respect to the system under the Amsterdam Protocol, which merely obliged the governments to *forward* proposals to their parliaments. Apart from Commission proposals, the early warning system would also cover the examination of 'draft legislative acts' originating from the European Parliament or a group of Member States, as well as initiatives from the ECJ, the ECB and the Investment Bank. As soon as the relevant proposals are distributed in all language versions, the six-weeks delay for *ex ante* scrutiny and influence that we already know from the Amsterdam Protocol starts.[9] Within these six weeks, the national parliaments are to scrutinize the proposal under the criterion of compliance with the principle of subsidiarity, as well as proportionality, although the early warning system itself would only apply to subsidiarity. If a parliament or chamber concludes that a proposal violates the principle of subsidiarity, then it may send a 'reasoned opinion' to the Commission, the Council and the European Parliament, as well as the other initiator where applicable.[10] Incoming reasoned opinions would count as votes against the proposal, two votes being assigned per national parliament, one per chamber where the parliament is bicameral.[11] If reasoned opinions representing one-third of the total votes are issued (one-quarter in the area of freedom, security and justice under Article III-264 of the

---

7 Article I-26 (2) TCE.

8 Article 2 TCE Protocol on the role of national parliaments in the European Union.

9 *Ibid.*, Article 4, see also Rizzuto (2003), p. 10.

10 Article 6 TCE Protocol on the application of the principles of subsidiarity and proportionality.

11 *Ibid.*, Article 7.

Constitutional Treaty), then the initiator of the proposal, typically the Commission, would have to reconsider the proposal. The Commission could re-introduce the proposal without amendments if it wanted to, but it would have to give the reasons why.

We can already point out the weaknesses of the mechanism, some of which we have already mentioned. First of all, 'reasoned opinions' would not be of a binding nature, a triggered system would not constitute an absolute veto against a Commission proposal.[12] Secondly, the scope of the early warning system would only cover alleged violations of the principle of subsidiarity, excluding proportionality. Objections could therefore only be formal, not substantive,[13] and they would be confined to EU action falling under competences that are shared between the EU and the Member States, since there is no subsidiarity in matters for exclusive EU competence. Thirdly, the required thresholds of one-quarter and one-third of votes to trigger the early warning system are quite high, although even higher thresholds had been under consideration.[14] In an EU-25, there would be fifty votes distributed among the national parliaments, two votes each. An ordinary one-third threshold would require a minimum of seventeen votes to be cast against a proposal. That translates into a minimum of eight unicameral parliaments casting two votes each plus one individual chamber of a bicameral parliament, or nine unicameral parliaments who would reach between them eighteen votes, or eight bicameral parliaments with both chambers concurring plus one additional parliament or chamber, or nine bicameral parliaments with both chambers concurring, etc. The minimum threshold would therefore be nine parliaments, and the maximum threshold seventeen individual chambers of bicameral parliaments casting their votes separately, all this while the incoming documentation is extensive and different parliaments prioritize differently. Fourthly, six weeks is rather short for in-depth examination and external consultation. Fifthly, a national parliament's objections are only enforceable before the ECJ via the government, which still holds the monopoly of representing the Member State in annulment actions, so that the parliament depends on the government's goodwill. Even if the national parliaments did have separate standing for annulment actions on their own, the ECJ so far treats the principle of subsidiarity with great scepticism. The principle is not strictly legal but bears political implications, and moreover it has distinct

12 Also noting that the early warning system could have been broader in scope and more binding in effect: Donnelly/Hoffmann (2004); Føllesdal (2004), p. 10.

13 Vergés Bausili (2002), p. 12 and Raunio (2004) note that substantive and formal, subsidiarity and proportionality considerations cannot be neatly separated from each other.

14 See Götz (2004), p. 60; Duff (2002) had proposed for these purposes a threshold of a majority of national parliaments representing a majority of the EU population; so had De Gucht (2002).

anti-federalist connotations.[15] This does, at least so far, not provide the ECJ with incentives to apply it as a legal concept.

In response to the above critical points, we could also argue along more optimistic lines. First of all, and most importantly, the meaning of the early warning system cannot be evaluated solely on the basis of textual analysis of written rules. It may indeed be frustrating for national parliaments to see their reasoned opinions being overruled by the Commission. Yet one has arguably to take into account that objections from a significant number of national parliaments will send a political signal which cannot be ignored.[16] This holds true even if these objections do not constitute an absolute veto, and even if the objectors are short of a formal blocking minority. After all, the Commission may expect that the complaints of several national parliaments are likely to herald objections that will be raised later by the respective governments in the Council.[17] The limitation of the early warning system to the subsidiarity principle should not be a weakness *a priori* either. If the principle gains a greater legal significance, not merely a political one, the weight of objections under the early warning system would increase as well. The rather short time window of six weeks can be extended simply by starting scrutiny at an earlier stage, for instance by already considering Green Papers or the annual legislative programme. Not even the parliaments' lack of privileged standing before the ECJ should cause too much concern, one might contend. It is true that privileged standing for annulment actions is still reserved for the Member States, which are represented by their governments, yet one can assume that the Member States will find internal arrangements to ensure that the governments will bring actions upon request and on behalf of the national parliaments. Moreover, as Verges (2004) argues, if the Commission sticks to good European governance, there will be no reason for the national parliaments to interfere in the EU legislative process in the first place.

As mentioned earlier, the idea of having the national parliaments monitor the subsidiarity principle is to serve two purposes at the same time: upgrading the parliaments, and upgrading the principle. Let us start with what the new manner of enforcement could mean to the significance of the subsidiarity principle itself, before we turn to the effect on the national parliaments.

7.4 The COSAC subsidiarity experiment

The first COSAC meeting after the Constitutional Treaty was signed was held in the Hague in November 2004. The parliamentarians who were assembled there agreed to conduct a pilot project in order to start gaining experience with subsidiarity

15 Estella (2004), p. 178.

16 Swenden (2004), p. 387.

17 Dashwood (2004), p. 369.

control right away. They chose as a test case the Commission's proposal for the so-called third railway package, a legislative project including a directive on the development of the Community's railways, a directive on the certification of train crews, a regulation on the rights and obligations of international train passengers and a regulation on cases of non-compliance in freight rail contracts.[18] All national parliaments would examine the package, test it for compliance with the subsidiarity principle, and report back to their colleagues at the next COSAC meeting to see whether the monitoring mechanism would work, and whether any violations of subsidiarity could be found.

Most parliaments carried out the experiment trying to apply the procedures they would use in reality, in as far as that was possible or appropriate.[19] The procedural details are left to the individual parliaments, so each parliament for instance has to decide who is competent to review proposals: the European Affairs Committee, the sectoral committees, or both.[20] Each parliament would also have to decide who then speaks on behalf of the parliament: the European Affairs Committee on behalf of the plenary, or the sectoral committees, or the plenary upon a draft resolution from a committee.[21] In the meantime, parliaments are encouraged to post their relevant scrutiny documents and to announce the state of affairs on the IPEX database, which can be accessed by other parliaments. During the COSAC meeting in the Hague, such use of the information platform was carefully endorsed, upon a Danish initiative. Several delegations objected to turning COSAC into a co-ordinating body via IPEX or the permanent secretariat, pointing out that scrutiny should remain an autonomous task for each parliament.

Half a year later, at the 33rd COSAC meeting in Luxembourg in May 2005, the MPs presented their results. Almost all delegations pointed out that six weeks is too short a period to carry out in-depth scrutiny. Especially where efforts are co-ordinated between two chambers, or where regions are to be consulted, the time window is rather narrow. For the rest, comments about the third railway package were manifold. Several MPs from Central and Eastern Europe complained that not all documents had been translated into all languages – the railway package had been elaborated and adopted before the 2004 enlargement. They found a breach of subsidiarity on the ground that the Commission is still obliged to justify all

---

18 Com (2004) 139, 142, 143 and 144, respectively.

19 See for a summarized account of the experiment: COSAC Secretariat (2005b).

20 See Dutch Tweede Kamer (2004).

21 According to the COSAC Secretariat (2004), the parliaments of Austria, Denmark, Finland, Slovenia and Latvia have announced that they will give the power to issue reasoned opinions to their European Affairs Committee, with varying participation of the sectoral committees in the monitoring process itself; in the parliaments of the Czech Republic, Hungary, Lithuania, Portugal, the Netherlands and the UK, a reasoned opinion would be adopted by the plenary.

its proposals under that heading, that the burden of proof lay with the Commission, and that the absence of a satisfactory justification in all official EU languages would constitute a breach of subsidiarity by default. Many delegations actually complained of the lack of subsidiarity justification even in the translated versions. Some delegations criticized that the railway package regulated liability for non-compliance in freight services; they found a breach of subsidiarity of the ground that state regulation should not take place where problems could be better solved by the market itself. Some delegations complained that the package, for instance the directive on the certification of train crews, affected not only cross-border railway traffic but also purely internal traffic, and thus breached subsidiarity on that ground.

MEP Jo Leinen remarked that not all of the filed complaints truly had to do with subsidiarity. The absence of translated texts in that particular case was more something of a technicality and anyway an exception since in reality the six-weeks time period would start only once all language versions were available. Furthermore, Leinen pointed out, the choice for state regulation rather than leaving problems to free market forces was a question of economic policy, not of competence allocation. Harmonization measures that have no cross-border implications at EU level are nothing special either: an EU citizen is entitled to assume that if she gets on a train in any other Member State, the engine-driver is properly trained just like he would be in her home country, and that he has not just been operating the engine since yesterday. EU ecological standards on ground water apply all over Europe, too, even if the water does not actually cross borders. The rationale is largely the same.

The COSAC experiment revealed a number of practical problems. Time is scarce, a national parliament is under constant pressure, and six weeks is really not much; moreover, Polish proceedings were delayed because of the death of Pope John Paul II, Danish and Portuguese proceedings were delayed because of general elections. Summer recesses and other holidays – Easter holidays in this particular case – can indeed interrupt the effective monitoring of subsidiarity compliance by a parliament. Another problem is that objections about breaches of subsidiarity may be based on different grounds, and directed at different aspects of a proposal. In this particular case, 31 out of 37 parliamentary chambers participated in the experiment, of which 14 found a breach of subsidiarity – 11 of them wrote a reasoned opinion – and another three chambers expressed doubts as to whether subsidiarity had been respected; yet again, these figures represent objections aimed at different parts of the Commission proposal.[22] Furthermore, not all of the raised objections were truly related to subsidiarity, or at least the principle is difficult to separate from proportionality or in fact simple political choices. The parliaments of Finland and Luxembourg even explicitly found breaches of proportionality, only to be reminded that the early warning system was designed for subsidiarity only. By the way, the

22 COSAC Secretariat (2005b).

Finnish parliament has already conducted a review of its activity over the last few years and could not find a single instance where it would have found a breach of subsidiarity,[23] and the Finnish delegation was actually surprised to see so many subsidiarity objections during the COSAC experiment.

Moreover, not all Member States are equally concerned about subsidiarity in the first place, or are equally affected by a policy measure. The parliament of Malta had no objections against the railway package since Malta does not have a railway system. Apart from that, because of the great flow of information from Brussels, and because all parliaments have to prioritize in the allocation of their time and energy, an individual MP can never be sure whether it would make sense to focus on a particular EU item. If he is the only one in Europe who cares about it, he could never mobilize more national parliaments anyway, even if he could mobilize his own committee.

Nevertheless, what the experiment certainly did achieve is a more prominent spot on the agenda for subsidiarity, even if only for a brief moment. Even if the first COSAC exercise suffered from teething problems, even if the monitoring practice remains messy, even if the exact delimitations of this principle are hard to fix, and even if there will never be a case where a Commission proposal or a piece of EU legislation suffers shipwreck because of subsidiarity – with or without a Constitutional Treaty – what COSAC at least insisted on was that the burden of proof always lies with the Commission. The Commission is not absolved from its duty to 'consult widely' and to justify each of its proposals under subsidiarity aspects beforehand.[24] If national parliaments can force the Commission to at least include more elaborate justifications in its proposals, then perhaps proponents of subsidiarity may at last see the principle play a more prominent role in the EU. Perhaps just as lip service, perhaps only on paper, perhaps just this once or otherwise during the next COSAC pilot project and never again. Be that as it may, our discussion is primarily devoted not to the principle of subsidiarity, which may or may not see a revival, but to the role of the national parliaments. These two concepts are not quite the same thing, which complicates the matter somewhat.

7.5 Constitutional implications of subsidiarity control by the national parliaments

If we see subsidiarity as a means of strengthening the national parliaments, rather than the national parliaments as a means of strengthening subsidiarity, we can recall that the actual scope and content of the Convention's idea might not have

23 Statement by Finnish MP Heidi Hautala at the 32nd COSAC.

24 Articles 2 and 5 TCE Protocol on the application of the principles of subsidiarity and proportionality.

warranted the prominence it was given. The parliaments' veto is not binding, the scope of their veto is limited to formal subsidiarity arguments, not proportionality, and the parliaments have no *locus standi* before the ECJ. What is more, so great an emphasis on subsidiarity might lead to the impression that this is the *only* aspect under which parliaments should deal with EU decision-making, whereas monitoring compliance with subsidiarity does not of course absolve parliaments from all the other checks they might want to apply.[25]

Essentially the national parliaments can engage in the monitoring exercise, even expanding it to proportionality and other criteria, without there being any protocol or treaty provision authorizing them to do so. However the status of the exercise is arguably elevated if it is codified as a formal part of the EU legislative process, and we can and should evaluate proposals or projects on such a collective role for the national parliaments to assess not only current, but also future attempts to consolidate that role. And as often previously noted, the constitutional implications of instances where national parliaments are addressed for EU purposes are graver the more significant the exercise itself is. Sweeping statements in a political speech do not have to be all that intrusive, yet formal treaty provisions collectively addressing the national parliaments can be. This is where we need to assume a critical position, and where we may recall the caveats that we identified earlier. 'National parliaments' is a catch-all term which refers to a variety of chambers which all have their different roles, powers, preferences and self-perceptions. In Western parliamentary democracies, parliaments are not juxtaposed to their governments in an adversarial manner. Purely inter-parliamentary standpoints require inter-parliamentary solidarity. National parliaments have a constitutional mandate to represent their own Member State. Meaningful parliamentary debate requires a minimum cleavage for polarization. These caveats should help us address two questions: in how far can there be a collective role for national parliaments in subsidiarity enforcement, and how far can we go in assigning them binding veto powers and access to judicial review?

7.5.1 The phantom collective

Consider the following scenario: a national parliament reviews a controversial Commission proposal and sends a letter to the Commission complaining that the proposal violates the principle of subsidiarity. Where does that leave the national government? Of course the national government has formed an opinion itself, perhaps it has already done so during the consultation stage. In the end, there are four possible combinations with respect to objections against a Commission proposal: either the government has no objections against the proposed EU measure, but

25 Statement by Finnish MP Heidi Hautala at the 32nd COSAC.

parliament does, the government does have objections but parliament does not, both the government and parliament have objections, or neither the government, nor parliament have any objections against the measure. In the light of the typical information advantage of the national governments, and their role as the initiator of even domestic legislation, it would be very much in order to review the position of parliament in contrast with the government's initial preferences, not just as a purely pre-emptive, simultaneous or disconnected voicing of a parliamentary opinion.

It would not be surprising if, where the government had no objections against an EU measure on the grounds of subsidiarity, the parliamentary majority had no objections either. Conversely, if the government has objections already, and it has expressed them at EU level as well, there is no reason why it should not receive support for these objections in its own parliament. The really interesting options concern possible cases of dissent: after all, subsidiarity enforcement is intended as a tool for parliaments to prevent the own governments from legislating in Brussels more than they should.

The dissent scenario has two basic versions, and another, special one. In the first basic version, government has objections against a measure on subsidiarity grounds, but parliament does not, and the latter refuses to send a letter to the Commission. In the second basic version of the dissent scenario, the government has no objections to the proposed measure, but parliament does. Thirdly, and this is the special case, the government might be facing a dissenting upper chamber in a bicameral system. After all, depending on the mode of election of the upper chamber, political party affiliations of the majority therein do not have to coincide with the government's, and an upper chamber may also have an electoral bias irrespective of the political colour of the incumbent government. What these considerations should show is that the adoption of an objection on the basis of subsidiarity against an individual government's will is an act of opposition. That act of opposition, if it is to be carried out on behalf of the parliament as a whole, requires a parliamentary majority as against the government. Perhaps the government majority is divided over European integration itself, or intra-coalition dissenters join arms with the opposition, or perhaps a majority of MPs wishes to embarrass a minority cabinet on the European scene, or perhaps a senate is engaged in a domestic power struggle with the lower chamber and the government anyway. Whatever the circumstances, this act of opposition will be initiated and carried out on the domestic arena.[26]

The label of 'collective role' that seems to be attached to the early warning system is therefore highly misleading. The national parliaments continue to play an individual role, each defined through domestic government-parliament relations.

---

26 Donnelly/Hoffmann (2004), p. 3 also expect the application of the early warning system to be based on national political cleavages.

This is a conclusion that also puts the threshold of one-third or one-quarter of votes under the early warning system as devised by the Convention into a relative perspective. It is irrelevant to the public of any given Member State what degree of parliamentary scrutiny is maintained in any Member State other than its own. For legitimacy perception it is also irrelevant whether the share of strong scrutinizers in the EU is ten, fifteen or twenty out of twenty-five.[27] In the absence of inter-parliamentary solidarity as against the national governments, the reaching of the threshold can only be considered as essentially, even if parliaments kept each other up to date about their plans, a coincidental sum of otherwise unrelated events. The impression should in any event be avoided that, whatever the procedural setting, the national parliaments within the EU vote just like individual MPs do within their parliament. What may have been intended as a collective intervention device for national parliaments would in fact become another facet of intergovernmental bargaining, and of Council-Commission power struggles, or of domestic power struggles, or an additional tool for governments to mobilize national opposition to unwelcome proposals. Incidentally, for these reasons Convention members Michel and Chevalier (2002) favoured the establishment of an impartial court of arbitration to guard the principles of subsidiarity and proportionality, instead of jeopardizing European integration by giving national parliaments a tool to engage in competence struggles with the EU level and dragging domestic conflicts to Brussels. And again, the salience of the issue would increase with the degree to which national parliamentary vetoes would actually matter. Whether salient or not, twenty-five national parliaments will not form any type of collective.

7.5.2 The national parliaments' access to court

National parliamentary vetoes would matter more if they were absolute, not suspensive. But we could go even further and consider the debate about awarding the national parliaments standing before the ECJ to enforce the subsidiarity principle in court. Under the Constitutional Treaty, the national parliaments are not awarded separate standing as privileged applicants before the ECJ for subsidiarity enforcement, but the government representing the Member State could bring action on parliament's behalf. This qualification has been criticized as yet another weakness of the early warning system.[28] If the system had been taken seriously, so the argument goes, the national parliaments would have been awarded *locus standi* on their own, independent of the goodwill of their governments. However, in the light of our earlier discussion concerning crude standards and constitutional distortions that top-down recruitment of national parliaments for EU purposes comes with,

27 Kiiver (2005b).

28 Donnelly/Hoffmann (2004), p. 4; Cygan (2004a).

the relevant provision has actually just averted another distortion. Where is the potential for disharmony?

As we are persistently reminded, the national parliaments are not a homogenous group. Standing in court would imply legal capacity to bring actions. Some national parliaments do have legal capacity under domestic constitutional law, while others do not.[29] More fundamentally, as was the case with the establishment of a 'Third Chamber' of national MPs at EU level, separate court standing would have severed parliaments from their governments, to which the former tend to be intimately connected, for an artificial exercise. It would have allowed parliaments to use a capacity they may not have had under national law, and take domestic struggles, if they wished, not only to another level of government, but actually to that level's judicial system. The fact that the German government has agreed to bring ECJ annulment actions on behalf of one-third of the *Bundestag* should fill us with particular concern: this would not only allow a parliamentary majority to sue its own government, as it were, but it would give such power to the domestic opposition.[30] Otherwise, if the parliament is in agreement with its government, it would mean just another tool for the government to recruit support against a piece of EU legislation outside the political process.

Awarding more actors standing for subsidiarity purposes raises further concerns. If subsidiarity is to devolve power closer to the citizens, why not also award regions, or their assemblies, their own standing as privileged applicants? Under the early warning system, such right would be given to the Committee of the Regions as a body, where it had been consulted in the legislative process, but not to individual regions with legislative powers, and this has also been criticized.[31] Again, we must note that bringing ever more national actors to the European arena, let alone inviting them to carry out essentially political disputes in court, entails more constitutional repercussions than might instantly be visible on the drawing board.

In the absence of separate standing, a national parliament is unlikely to be accepted by the ECJ as representing a Member State, exactly because of the possible conflicts with the national government.[32] Individual MPs, or national or regional parliaments, provided they have legal personality, could theoretically seek to challenge EU legislation as non-privileged directly and individually affected individuals,[33] yet the success of that approach is highly uncertain, especially if the *Plaumann* criteria[34] keep severely restricting this avenue for non-individualizable persons as

---

29 See Claes (2005).

30 See 1.6.2 *supra*.

31 Jeffery (2004), p. 5, Swenden (2004), p. 388, Weatherill (2003a), p. 64.

32 Smismans (1998), p. 72.

33 Weatherill (2003a), p. 65.

34 *Plaumann & Co.* v. *Commission*, ECJ 25/62, [1963] ECR 95; see for instance on the implications of *locus standi* requirements for sub-national authorities: Van Nuffel (2001).

regards EU legislation of general application. It would be at least very difficult to prove why a random number of politicians are directly and individually concerned, and distinguishable from everybody else, by a subsidiarity infringement. These restrictions can efficiently prevent an uncontrolled multiplication of the amount of actors with privileged or ordinary access to court who wish to enforce a principle like subsidiarity. Firstly, it is questionable why disputes involving political institutions like parliaments should be taken to court. Secondly, it is questionable why the ECJ should be allowed to be instrumentalized by more actors. For if the avenue of Member State actions is opened to national parliaments, why not open it to regions as well, and if it is already open to regions, why not open it to municipalities, or functionally decentralized and democratically elected state entities like the Dutch *waterschappen*, the specialized boards which manage surface waters?

But even if we restrict the option of such court actions to national parliaments, we should seriously question whether an inevitably crude standard for selecting addressees would be adequate in a treaty drafting exercise. Who are 'the national parliaments' in the specific context of subsidiarity enforcement? On what basis should they be assigned formal privileges before the ECJ? There do not seem to be any selection criteria. As noted at the very beginning, leaving the determination of who is a parliament to the Member States may work with the assignment of duties, but not with the distribution of powers and privileges. If we hand out veto powers in a decision-making process, we cannot vaguely define the recipients and wait to see who shows up, for that would leave not only the game, but also the rules of the game, in spite of their being codified in an impressive-looking Constitution, at the discretion of the Member States. Methodologically the only solid solution would again be to draw up a list mentioning exhaustively all national parliaments that would have *locus standi* by name. This would prevent Belgium from unilaterally introducing its regional assemblies to the arena, it would prevent Germany from introducing its parliamentary minority unannounced, and it would also prevent the British government from ignoring the House of Lords where the latter wishes to exercise a treaty right while depending on the government's goodwill. Yet even then, we would face the already mentioned concerns of dragging domestic political battles to the EU judiciary. We would face theoretical objections of what exactly makes the UK House of Lords democratic, what makes the German *Bundesrat* a parliament, what makes the Belgian parliament a law-maker if the policy area in question is federalized, what justification there is to favour regions that happen to be represented in a senate over regions that are not, or what excuse there is to leave regional assemblies outside for purposes of subsidiarity, a principle that after all commands regulation at the lowest sensible level. And we would face the general objection of having the national parliaments interfere at EU level, which some players or observers may find appealing but others, in the light of the dubious results and unforeseeable side-effects yielded, would not. All mentioned objections may in the end of course be legitimately overruled, for instance by a new Convention or IGC in another treaty reform attempt. They may be swept aside as academic criticism that does not affect the functioning of institutions in practice, and *locus standi* and absolute veto procedures for national parliaments may be put in place anyway. Nevertheless, and it should be the contribution of academia to insist on that, Conventions or IGCs should at least consider these objections before rushing the treaty-drafting process and expanding the role of national parliaments beyond informal arrangements: poorly designed documents do not deserve to be ratified, especially documents that saw no serious preliminary debate. The present discussion is not to categorically rule out a particular design, but to show that the current consensus to endorse the national parliaments may prove rather shallow if that endorsement is taken too far.

7.6 Conclusion

In as far as the Convention envisaged a direct and collective role for the national parliaments in the EU decision-making process, the exercise turned out rather modest. Raunio (2004) criticized the early warning system's non-binding nature, and favoured an absolute 'red card', instead of a softer 'yellow card' effect of a collective national parliamentary veto. Weatherill (2003) shares the conclusion that the system features a weak design. However, he explicitly welcomes that weakness, and refers to the taken step towards direct involvement of the national parliaments as being 'gratifyingly modest'.

Indeed, as far as the national parliaments are concerned, more impressive attempts to boost their status could have been made: absolute vetoes and *locus standi* before the ECJ of their own right are but the two most prominent examples. However, having external actors like national parliaments insist on more consideration for subsidiarity, even if this happens in a non-binding manner, could give life to the principle. From a national constitutional perspective, guarding the scope of conferred powers that the EU exercises, and retaining their exercise with national democratic institutions as far as possible, might seem generally desirable, and even from a European perspective, there might be something attractive to an enhanced clarity of the scope of EU competences, and to the involvement of national parliaments to capture public attention for the EU's activities in the process.

Good news for subsidiarity does, however, not necessarily mean good news for European parliamentarism. A collective role for the national parliaments is not cultivated with that sort of exercise: neither homogeneity nor the necessary degree of solidarity among national parliaments as against their governments can be presumed, and since no uniform idea of their own role in the EU exists, the label of collective national parliamentary involvement via subsidiarity enforcement seems generally misplaced. Governments would drag their parliaments to the EU arena for individual support, or parliaments would settle domestic scores with their governments in Brussels – if any adversarial cleavage between cabinet and parliamentary majority can be assumed in the first place. Meanwhile, subsidiarity itself is, as seen, not clearly distinguishable form substantive aspects of EU legislation, such as proportionality. As argued earlier, if national parliaments discover a monitoring task for themselves with respect to the EU legislative process, reserving the right to intervene or perhaps to bring legal action on the grounds of subsidiarity and, while they are at it, other criteria, that brings about a re-nationalization and therefore particularization of European decision-making to the detriment of Council efficiency. In the light of these fundamental considerations, it is valid to conclude that the more non-binding subsidiarity monitoring turns out to be, the better. That does not mean that a re-nationalization of the EU, or government rhetoric about impressive-sounding but toothless subsidiarity enforcement mechanisms, is somehow *a priori* invalid. The intellectual achievement here should be, however, to see that there is more than just one meaning to 'subsidiarity enforcement', and more than just one interpretation of the notion of 'stronger national parliaments'.

8 The national parliaments and the locus of European parliamentarism

8.1 Introduction

We have now considered a set of suggestions on how to mitigate the effects of European integration on the national parliaments, their competence drain and marginalization. In that, we have sought to avoid lines of reasoning which follow either federalist or sovereignist approaches as to where the appropriate source of democratic legitimacy in the EU should lie. Instead, we have seen that stronger or more active national parliaments can seem desirable from a national constitutional perspective, as well as from an otherwise Europeanist point of view. However, each time these suggestions seem to form an artificial exercise which would bring about lighter or heavier national constitutional distortions. More fundamentally, they tended to shift the centre of gravity in the European Union towards the Member States and the national interest. Whether we admit it or not, this tendency ultimately points to sovereignist preferences regarding European integration or co-operation between Member States. Indeed, our discussion cannot suppress the normative approaches towards democracy and parliamentarism in Europe forever. This is the moment to face them.

The debate that shifted the attention towards the national parliaments (the debate on the constitutional future of Europe) would profit most if empirical and conceptual ground-work were fit into a broader normative frame, so that we do not resort to actionism to strengthen national parliaments without any clear vision of the purpose of the exercise. Without the necessary consideration of conceptual details, like the ones that we have examined so far, such broader visions of stronger national parliaments are bound to remain little more than platitudes of high abstraction and little practical use. Let us now consider the bigger picture.

8.2 Democracy in the European Union: the inherent deficit

The swing of attention towards the national parliaments of the Member States is intimately connected to the realization of a democratic deficit in the European Union. Arguably, the term democratic deficit is very flexible, and it is tempting to stretch it as a problem to fit one's own ready-made solutions.[1] Classically, the argument goes that the drain on the competences of the national parliaments has

1 Lord (1998), p. 11.

not been matched by an increase in power and weight of the European Parliament, or that the Council, which exercises parliamentary powers, is not a parliament itself, but is executive in its composition and working style. In the end, the European Union appears to be so undemocratic that, if it were a state, it would not even fulfil its own Copenhagen criteria. Thus, the EU would be rejected if it tried to join its own club.[2]

The dissatisfactory reproduction at the EU level of what we are used to on nation-state level in terms of democracy and parliamentarism brings us to the demand for more parliamentary involvement. Here the sovereignists – those attached to national statehood – would stress the importance of the national parliaments, and therefore the democratic Member States, in retaining and regaining control over EU activities. Here the federalists – proponents of ever-closer union – would demand even more powers for the European Parliament. However, both camps would by now have to face another alternative: what if the democratic deficit is inherent to European integration itself and cannot be solved in the present setting at all? Dann (2004) argues that the marginalization of the national parliaments is indeed inherent to the 'systemic logic of executive federalism'. In that sense, European integration, which is based on ultimately intergovernmental decision-making in a transnational setting, is bound to escape parliamentary control in the classical sense. Its foreign policy aspect makes national parliaments under-informed outsiders, and the transnational setting seems prohibitive to the development of a single European Parliament comparable to the ones of the nation-state type.

Assuming that a democratic deficit is an inevitable side-effect of European integration, we might of course boldly embrace this consequence and instead focus on the functional legitimacy of the integration project. Thus, the emphasis could shift towards the sheer advantages, and therefore the legitimacy of the output, of international co-operation and integration. Cost-reducing integration with its positive externalities, if proceeding smoothly and reaching generally acceptable results, could then outweigh the parliamentary deficit on the input side. National parliamentary involvement would for instance, in that model, only disturb the maintenance of the EU's key asset, namely the efficiency of its decision-making itself.

Earlier on, we briefly sketched the possible normative critique as regards this functionalist approach.[3] Closed-doors international diplomacy, supported by permissive domestic elite consensus, no longer reflects the realities of European integration. To justify the absence of popular participation on the input side merely by stressing the legitimacy of the policy output, similar to a benevolent dictatorship,

---

2 Thanks to Dimitry Kochenov for this remark.

3 See 3.7.1 *supra*.

no longer seems acceptable. Firstly, output legitimacy concepts might suffice for more or less uncontroversial technical matters of regulation, but fail to cover issues involving moral judgments, or wins and gains between cultural and ethnic groups. Apart from that, output legitimacy is oriented towards concrete popular support of EU decision-making for the benefit of a specific interest. It does not ensure value-based diffuse or social support for the system, so that if the quality of the output deteriorates in a time of crisis, the legitimacy framework becomes unstable.[4]

As a consequence of these considerations, new and modern concepts of pluralism and democratic participation are being developed, which might better fit the particularities of the EU as a polity which is not a state. Meanwhile, the two orthodox camps might feel inclined to push their demands even further. Thus, federalists would advocate yet greater efforts in parliamentarizing the EU level, while for sovereignists the logical step to take would be the famous 'step back', away from ever-closer union and towards national statehood. Let us consider what these different approaches have to offer, and how they would affect the role of the national parliaments.

8.3 The 'step back' to national democracy

The notion of a 'step back' essentially implies a withdrawal from the current state of European integration. It is based on the assumption that democracy is only possible in the framework of a nation-state which is culturally and ethnically more or less homogenous. This homogeneity allows a robust social solidarity which can support majoritarian rule to be maintained. Thus, even a minority which has been overruled in the course of a deliberative decision-making process will accept a policy, even if it is detrimental to itself, because this minority feels part of a larger national collective, a *demos*, sharing the same identity and a common historical memory. Genuine *demos*-based democracy would, according to that reasoning, be impossible to achieve across a continent as heterogeneous as Europe.

The reach of democratic national institutions into the realm of EU institutions and their processes is meanwhile severely restricted. Council bargaining is not transparent to the national *demoi*, and qualified majority voting allows a majority *within* a nation-state to be outvoted and overruled by a majority of *other* nation-states, while the former shares no common national identity with the latter. Consequently, the only way out of the democratic deficit would be the way out of supra-nationalism. An essential element to such a 'step back' is the return to unanimity voting, instead of QMV, so that a nation-state majority can retain a veto to reject intrusion from abroad. Another element is the return to the core of EU activity, namely economic integration, customs and trade, while leaving issues

4 See Thaa (2002).

which can polarize societies along a political left-right or other dimensions to the national level. Within the area of economic integration, the EU would further have to restrict itself to negative integration, the mere removal of trade barriers, rather than engaging in positive integration including regulative and redistributive policies. This negative integration would have to be conducted in the intergovernmental mode, with no or limited involvement of supranational institutions. Member State control, and therefore national parliamentary democracy, would at last be restored.

This 'step back' scenario meets strong resistance. Objections do not even need to be political or ideological in nature. To the contrary, since the 'step back' aims at returning to purely economic co-operation, it can appropriately be rebutted with economic arguments. What these counter-arguments would boil down to are the high costs that the Member States would incur from 'stepping back'. It is deceiving to assume that the entire area of European economic co-operation is free of transaction costs, and that it always constitutes positive-sum games. Purely voluntary confederation-type agreements, especially in a Union of twenty-five and counting, no longer suffice to efficiently and effectively address transnational problems. In addition, a return to the intergovernmental mode of decision-making, and the exclusion of the Commission and the ECJ from the game, would make 'cheating' and non-compliance with EU obligations easier for individual Member States. The fact that the game is played at two levels finally facilitates deliberate disinformation at either level.[5]

The 'step back' to unanimous intergovernmental co-operation over apolitical issues is arguably just the extreme version of what is otherwise a nation-state-oriented democracy model for the European Union. Thus, even without abandoning the current degree of integration, a greater democratic element can be sought by involving national representative institutions more closely in the EU decision-making process. This is what fuels demands for a greater role for the national parliaments, from the nation-state-oriented wing within what we have identified as the European perspective. We have discussed a range of demands, up to direct representation of the national parliaments at EU level, MPs accompanying their ministers to Council meetings, and the introduction of blocking national parliamentary vetoes in the EU decision-making process. Our critique in that respect pointed out the national constitutional distortions that such scenarios entail, where parliaments are artificially set against their governments, as well as the resulting EU-level distortions, notably decreased efficiency in decision-making, and even lower transparency through the influx of additional actors. What is left is a re-nationalization of the EU processes which, in the light of the foregoing, is a highly questionable gain.

5 Lord (1998), p. 52; see for further discussion: Weber-Panariello (1995), p. 309; Höreth (1999), p. 295 *et seq.*; Thaa (2002).

8.4 Multiple levels and multiple identities

An increasingly popular line of argument discards the above nation-state approach altogether. A return to pure intergovernmentalism would be a detrimental step to take, while enhancing the grip of Member State democracy on the EU institutions still reveals an inappropriately state-centred thinking. Also the forging of EU-level parliamentarism is rejected as following the same static and state-centred ideologies. What we are invited to accept is that the European Union is a *sui generis* polity, which is neither a mere confederation of sovereign states, nor a federal state which replaces the existing Member States.

The alternatives that are put forward can be roughly summarized as a sort of 'third way' in between sovereignism, on the one hand, and supranationalism, on the other hand. Nicolaïdis (2003) for instance makes an impressive case against the 'tyranny of dichotomies' which tends to simplify and polarize debates about European integration as a struggle between federalists and Eurosceptics, between 'in' and 'out'. Instead, the European Union should be embraced as a *demoi*-cracy, a hybrid between federation and confederation, in which different levels of representation reflect non-exclusive identities and interact with each other. Accordingly, Ronge (1998: 128) calls for a multi-dimensional legitimacy theory for the EU, instead of simply equating parliamentarism to democracy and democratic legitimation to legitimacy. Weiler consistently advocates the endorsement of Europe's constitutional status quo, instead of applying generic constitutional models on what is a unique polity.[6] After all, as also Rometsch and Wessels (1996) argue, neither a full federalization of the EU, nor a 'step back' is likely to occur, so that we are just left with an increasingly complex constitutional structure. Banchoff and Smith (1999: 2), while confirming that conventional state-based standards of legitimacy 'do not capture the dynamics of recognition and representation in the EU', advocate a re-conceptualization of the EU to acknowledge the growing acceptance of the EU as a political framework, including its pluralist forms of representation, even though the latter are not centralized in strong democratic institutions. This is where the different notions of multi-level governance and multi-level constitutionalism or constitutional pluralism set in. Instead of focusing on static forms of majoritarian and representative democracy in a hierarchical constitutional order, we should embrace what is already a reality, namely that interests and identities can be European, national, regional or even local at the same time, and while the decision-making processes that affect these levels are diffuse or at least decentralized, citizens should engage in deliberations and forms of interest representation at different levels as well.

---

6 See e.g. Weiler (2003).

If we focus on 'governance' notions in this context, then the modern form of pluralism and deliberation is not centred in a parliament, but it includes debate in the media, judicial review of legislation, as well as networks of 'civil society', NGOs and interest groups including trade unions which speak on behalf of their membership to advance particular interests. But even if we leave 'governance' aside, and focus on multi-level constitutionalism, its government-based twin concept, we are still invited to let go of traditional notions of statehood. There does not seem to be a clear dogmatic hierarchy between EU law and Member State law, as is illustrated by the fact that the supremacy of Community law can be justified on different legal bases, and that otherwise supreme Community law can theoretically be subjected to constitutional review in the Member States.[7] Similarly, the national parliaments and the European Parliament have a function to fulfil, each within its own realm, without any clear hierarchy either. As these realms are closely interconnected – the EU is installed *above* the Member States, on the one hand, but it also *consists* of Member States, on the other hand – the two types of parliaments have a joint task of parliamentarizing their own level and thus of contributing to multi-level government or indeed governance. While the national parliaments may be at a structural disadvantage with respect to the European Parliament at European affairs, as Dann (2004: 417) argues, together they still form a 'parliamentary constitutional alliance'. The national parliaments should therefore co-operate with the European Parliament and, as Hofmann (2003) argues, become more active in playing their part on the national level.

The described notions of multi-level pluralism, governance and constitutionalism purport to provide an alternative to classical notions of government and representative democracy. At the same time this is what makes them problematic and diminishes their usefulness. Multi-level governance, for instance, elevates a descriptive approach to the functioning of modern Western democracies in transnational context to the status of a normative model of legitimacy. For this purpose, it detaches the deliberative aspect of democracy from statehood, territoriality and membership of a nation, in favour of deliberation through media and civil society networks. In doing so, however, it tends to ignore the constitutional foundation which allows such networks to operate today in the first place. Civil society may or may not have a valuable consultative role in a decision-making process, but in the end, the adopted policies have to be implemented and enforced by coercion.[8] Deliberation therefore does not replace government. Even the very value of deliberation through civil society seems highly dubious. Unlike it is the case with institutionalized will-formation in a parliamentary system, where each citizen has one vote: the effectiveness of a lobby group depends on the available amount of money and

---

7 See Claes (2005).

8 Thaa (2002).

expertise. This makes it technocratic, elitist and, with increasingly exclusive membership and scope of interests, decreasingly representative.[9] A common good does not emerge by affirming, rather than transcending, special socio-economic interests, and democratic legitimacy does not derive from merely consultative processes.

Multi-level governance is a descriptive exercise, which arguably also applies to the Member States internally. Thus, also on the nation-state level, modern parliamentary democracy has become unthinkable without the complementary roles of civil society and media, municipalities and regions, which are all connected through informal networks. However, while that may all be so, the nation-state always retains the concept of parliamentarism as a matter of normative priority and constitutional foundation. A country which exclusively relies on 'governance' by unaccountable lobbyists would, if it were to apply for EU membership, be rightfully rejected for failing to meet the Copenhagen criteria of democracy and the rule of law. As to the European Union itself, civil society can play a complementary and consultative role, but without embracing parliamentarism as a constitutional foundation, the EU is doomed to be trapped in its own democracy gap.

Even without reference to 'governance', and merely underlining the need for co-operation between parliaments as central institutions in overlapping constitutional orders under the heading of multi-level constitutionalism, the description of the national parliaments and the European Parliament as being component parts of a larger multi-level scheme seeks to conceptualize reality, but it offers no normative priority comparable to the ones we find in the nation-state. Multi-level approaches may not even have the purpose of identifying any static priorities, yet without priorities it is of little use for the determination of policy objectives. A concept which accepts a stronger European Parliament, while at the same time accepting stronger national parliaments as supporting the second tier of EU democratic legitimacy, as well as co-operation between the two tiers, has a certain reconciliatory appeal, but is bound to be shallow. As mentioned above, advocating stronger national parliaments or more inter-parliamentary co-operation without doing the conceptual ground-work will hardly result in anything more than the affirmation of catch-phrases. Our discussion has already revealed the effects and side-effects of sharpened national parliamentary scrutiny of European affairs, and the structural impediments to inter-parliamentary co-operation. For normative guidance we have to look somewhere else.

8.5 Parliamentarization as a normative priority

Who or what has brought the national parliaments onto the European agenda in the first place? Apparently, with their national-interest bias, national parliaments

9 See Curtin (2002), p. 5.

are attractive as battle-horses for the Eurosceptic group. Interestingly, however, EU-level statements about stronger national parliaments tend to remain sweeping but abstract. The government of the UK, for instance, seems to champion stronger national parliaments *in general.* But when it comes to submitting British government policies to scrutiny in its *own* parliament at Westminster, British ministers are far less enthusiastic about national parliamentary involvement.[10]

As far as the other side of the divide is concerned, more active national parliaments seem useful under similarly vague notions of 'bringing Europe closer to the citizens' to stabilize the European construct. For the European Parliament, the national parliaments seem more agreeable as subordinate or temporary allies, rather than as dangerous rivals, so they are embraced increasingly closely. However, what lies at the heart of the entire debate is a disappointment with the capacities of the directly elected European Parliament to legitimize EU decision-making, and to eventually substitute the national parliaments as the EU's democratic link to the citizenry. This is what led Harlow (2002: 191) to pessimistically conclude: 'Until the political accountability to which we have, in the course of the twentieth century, become used in the nation state, is replicated at transnational level, we would be wise not to entrust transnational organizms [sic] with too much power'. Instead, she advocates the nationalization of accountability, not as a step back to the trenches of nationalism and xenophobia, but as a safeguard for democracy.

In the beginning of the European integration process, democratization and parliamentarization was not in the interest of pro-European elites. Fearing that the sovereignists would be too strong to beat in an open battle, they promoted their cause through the back door, leaving the democratic element fragmented.[11] Functionalism was to replace notions of open discourse and representative democracy. In the meantime, however, the tables have turned. Referendums are en vogue, and each new vote can spell doom to the integration process. At the same time, the European Union has moved beyond the scope of international co-operation in matters of customs union and milk quotas. It is therefore increasingly measured by nation-state standards, and the ideal level of democracy in the European Union is the level that a country would have which is not itself a member of the European Union.[12] Thus, the benchmark for the EU is a sovereign state, without the supranational drain on its competences and parliamentary control.

We have already seen that there is opposition to comparing a non-state polity to idealized 18th and 19th century standards which are derived from states, and to which today not even the states themselves can fully live up.[13] This is why

---

10 See Norton (1995b), p. 186.

11 Blondel *et al.* (1998), p. 2 *et seq.*

12 Ronge (1998), p. 69.

13 Von der Vring (1996).

Lord (1998) raises a crucial question: should we not ask whether the EU is as democratic as it reasonably can be, given the inherent constraints?[14] Parliamentarizing the EU with nation-state blueprints arguably collides with the 'problem of translation' of democracy at Member State level to the EU level.[15] However, when governed by a polity which carries out more and more state functions, it is far from being obvious why citizens should trim down their expectations as regards pluralism and popular representation. In fact, there is nothing to preclude us from demanding a genuine parliamentary democracy in the European Union as a matter of normative priority. While complementary notions of governance and output legitimacy are not invalid as such, the fundamental notions of parliamentarism cannot lose their constitutional primacy simply as a consequence of the relocation of the decision-making centre to Brussels, not even as a consequence of the mere creation of an additional locus of decision-making next to the national ones.

In spite of its treaty-based character, the European Union has become more than an international organization, and more than a free-trade area. It regulates, *inter alia,* whom a Member State must let inside its territory, whom it must extradite, how much money it can spend in its national budget, what it can subsidize with that money, and generally where and when to legislate. Justice, police, foreign affairs and defence policies, currency, environment, fisheries, agriculture, traffic, consumer protection, industrial standards, gender equality and non-discrimination, competition policy, development co-operation, citizenship and the protection of human rights are no longer policy areas or concepts that fall under nation-state monopoly. In a word, the EU constitutes a quasi-federal order, usually qualified as 'coming-together federalism', 'executive federalism' or 'co-operative federalism'.[16] The essential feature of the EU's executive federalism is its bicameral legislature which includes, next to a directly elected federal chamber, a chamber which represents the governments of its component Member States.[17]

Here we can draw an obvious parallel with the German constitutional order, which is similarly characterized as executive federalism. The institution corresponding to the Council would be the German *Bundesrat.* Both of these institutions are law-makers, but neither of them is a parliament. Instead of comprising parliamentarians, both consist of representatives of the governments of the subfederal entities, the Member States and the *Länder*, respectively. In both institutions the governments vote *en bloc*, and in both institutions the principle of sovereign

14 See also Banchoff/Smith (1999).

15 Walker (2003b).

16 Cf. Hoffmann/Shaw (2003), p. 3; Dann (2004); Føllesdal (2004), p. 3, with references; Swenden (2004).

17 Dann (2004), p. 407 *et seq*.

equality of states is balanced out with a system of weighed votes.[18] Both institutions are established to reflect federalism, not for purposes of popular representation, and in both institutions, what is important for our own discussion, the democratic legitimacy for co-legislation derives from the fact that the represented governments are each accountable to their parliaments at home.

In both orders this is to a certain extent reflected by the respective constitutional document. Article I-46 (2) of the EU Constitutional Treaty declared that the governments meeting in the Council are each accountable to their national parliaments. Article 28 (1) of the German Basic Law provides that the *Länder* must conform to the principles of a republican, democratic and social state governed by the rule of law, and that in each *Land* the people must be represented by a body chosen in general, direct, free, equal and secret elections. With respect to the Council we have already seen the practical constraints to the realization of what Article I-46 (2) of the Constitutional Treaty proclaims. With respect to the *Bundesrat*, the picture is not too inspiring either. The *Länder* parliaments have no effective control over their governments' conduct in the *Bundesrat*.[19] Instead, that conduct is generally determined by national political party affiliation. A conservative *Land* government will support a bill introduced by a conservative federal government and approved by a conservative-dominated *Bundestag*. Conversely, if the conservatives are in opposition in the *Bundestag* but dominate the *Bundesrat*, they can, and often do, obstruct the passing of federal legislation. In case of a coalition government on *Land* level, the determination of that government's stance in the *Bundesrat* is regulated in the coalition accord, typically providing for abstention on federal level in case of internal disagreement. If a *Land* government supports or rejects a bill in contravention to instructions from the national party headquarters, this is considered an embarrassing defeat for the party leadership.

All this brings us to a noteworthy observation. If the degree of democracy and parliamentarism in Germany solely depended on the democratic credentials of the *Bundesrat*, and its sixteen sets of accountability to the *Länder* parliaments, the picture would look rather grim. A Basic Law provision solemnly declaring that the principle of representative democracy in Germany is partly ensured by the fact that the *Länder* governments are each accountable to their *Länder* parliaments, would even seem highly disturbing. Yet as already stated, the *Bundesrat* is not intended to act as a popular representation in the first place, its *raison d'être* being added

18 See Articles 205 (2) EC resp. Article 51 (2) German Basic Law, which both roughly link the amount of votes to population size, as well as Article I-25 TCE which contains a population threshold for qualified majority.

19 See Hofmann (2003), p. 19; Von der Vring (1996), p. 391, footnote 5, remarks: 'If one imagines that there were no Bundestag and the Bundesrat were the only legislator in Bonn [nowadays Berlin], then this would be a system of government similar to the Brussels one'.

checks and balances to reflect the federal constitutional structure. Instead, and crucially, Germany does have a parliament proper on the federal level to fulfil legislative, controlling and communicative functions, namely the *Bundestag*, the directly elected Federal Diet. It is thanks to the central and dominant role of the Federal Diet that the democratic deficit of the *Bundesrat* does not significantly affect the democratic content of the German federal constitution as a whole.[20]

On the European level, the balance of power is of course slightly different. While the Federal Diet is the dominant law-maker in Germany, the European Parliament, its directly elected counterpart at EU level, is not. The Federal Diet can in certain cases override a *Bundesrat* veto, while the European Parliament cannot enact legislation against the Council's will. While it would be simplistic to merely demand more powers for the European Parliament to completely solve the EU democratic deficit, the above considerations should make us aware of the fact that it is far from obvious to expect such miraculous solutions from the national parliaments.

8.6 OUTLOOK: ASKING THE RIGHT QUESTIONS

The adoption of binding legislation by hardly accountable politicians or civil servants, at best interacting with lobbyists behind closed doors, is certainly not what we can understand to be an example of democratic governance. Unlike a parliament, with its polarized competition and majority rule, the Council operates on the basis of compromise-seeking negotiation and at least informal unanimity or consensus.[21] Transparency concerns with respect to the Council have been addressed by the Constitutional Treaty, stipulating Council meetings in public when acting in legislative capacity.[22] However we should bear in mind the Council's hybrid legislative and executive-bureaucratic character. As Von der Vring (1996: 391) points out: 'The Council is the continuation of national government on a European level. Indeed it plays the role of a legislature but is according to its nature executive'. Confidentiality is for instance a prerequisite to maintaining a consensual intergovernmental negotiating style.[23] That allows us to draw some analogies. Miller and Ware (1996: 185) quote UK junior foreign office minister Heathcoat-Amory, who rejected any comparison between the Council and a parliament: 'No-one is seriously suggesting that a British Cabinet should sit in public'. What ministers discuss

20 We should note, though, that a debate is going on in Germany to cut back the number of absolute *Bundesrat* vetoes, for the *Bundestag* opposition increasingly obstructs federal law-making via the upper chamber.

21 Dann (2004), p. 409.

22 Article I-50 TCE. See also Crombez (2003).

23 See also Dann (2004), p. 409.

confidentially is necessary as a stage in national decision-making, but it does not replace open parliamentary deliberations.

This brings us back to the parliamentary option for the European Union. From the early decennia of European integration onwards, mainstream opinion supported the evolution and emancipation of the European Parliament. Projecting nation-state standards, direct elections, more legislative competences and stronger powers to hold the Commission to account were demanded, and granted. Still, as the Parliament's powers grew, voter turnout declined, and during and after the Maastricht ratification debates the permissive support for European integration started to fade.[24] This tendency culminated in 2005 with the unequivocal rejection of the Constitutional Treaty in the referendums in France and the Netherlands, two old Member States, and definitely not members of the awkward squad like the UK and Denmark. In disappointment in the apparent failure of the European Parliament, attention has been turned to the national parliaments, and weaknesses are discovered there as well. By now, mainstream opinion is recognizing the need to strengthen the national parliaments in their European role. They must allegedly be turned from under-informed, disinterested, passive, slow and path-dependent rubber-stamps into active networkers, sharp scrutinizers and inspired debaters of European affairs. From a national constitutional point of view, such demands may or may not be justified, depending on the Member State and parliament at hand. But airing these opinions in a European context is hardly visionary. It is but a reaction to the dissatisfactory performance of the European Parliament, or otherwise the democratic content of the European integration process.[25]

In the light of what we have discussed about scrutiny mechanisms in the national parliaments, the artificiality of the very attempt to upgrade their role by way of powers and privileges, and in the light of the lack of homogeneity, solidarity and a European electoral mandate, there is a certain element of despair in the mobilization of the national parliaments to make a last stand for European purposes. It is the result of a swing back of the pendulum, a default choice, a somewhat uninspired 'Plan B'. The half-hearted involvement of the national parliaments via the early warning system is too meaningless to represent a real 'step back', but there is nothing progressive to it either.

National parliaments are incapable of achieving the results for which they are recruited from an otherwise integrationist European perspective, which should make us critical about the habit of making sweeping and unsubstantiated political statements in favour of stronger national parliaments for one purpose or another. Obviously, that finding leaves the question open as to where exactly the alternatives are. Now it would be inconsistent to reject one sweeping statement as

24 Banchoff/Smith (1999), p. 1.
25 Smismans (1998), p. 49.

unsubstantiated, only to offer yet another sweeping statement instead. The issue of full parliamentarization of the European Union through the European Parliament merits a thorough discussion of its own. In such a discussion, we should for instance seriously question the validity of arguments like the no-*demos* theory, which is put forward to deny the possibility of a transnational identity and democracy. Is it really necessary to define identity via ethnic origin and state sovereignty?[26] Is it really necessary to have a common European language? And while exploring the theoretical foundations of European parliamentarism, we should not lose sight of what is evolving in practice already now. A coherent party structure in the European Parliament is becoming visible, which increasingly allows for political alignment along a left-right scale between conservative and libertarian, free-market and social-democratic orientations.[27] The political colour of the parliamentary majority is starting to have an impact on the political colour of the Commission. Political polarizations are replacing the cross-party family consensus to merely increase the European Parliament's powers.[28]

We might of course wonder whether the European Union's legitimacy is not too fragile, and its area of regulation too complex, to sustain drastic Westminster-type polarizations.[29] We might also wonder whether it is at all wise to allow growing politicization to disrupt the much-tested and efficient neutrality of the Commission.[30] However, it seems that this politicization is on the rise anyway, and it will find its forum. Crushing rejections of treaties in referendums is an obvious valve to let off steam. It will now be the task of the European Parliament to capture this rising politicization, to take advantage of the rising salience and to polarize along political colour lines, rather than national lines.[31]

We may not have all the answers, but it is important to ask the right questions in the first place. If we want genuine parliamentarism to accompany European integration, then the national parliaments are not the destination of choice. The currently fashionable notions of governance and networks, as well as the catchphrases about a greater involvement of the national parliaments, leave us with much the same level of integration, only without any credible means to enforce popular representation at eye-level with the Commission and the Council. The national

26 See Brand (2005), Lord (1998), De Búrca (2004).

27 Cf. Katz (1999b), p. 61 *et seq*. The formation of a European Green party network with a common agenda, for instance, can be a nucleus for an all-European political party platform, and set an example for conservative, social-democratic and liberal counterparts. MPs and MEPs successfully co-operated along political family lines to produce joint party-specific contributions to the Convention, see Brown (2003), p. 4.

28 Thomassen/Schmitt (1999).

29 Blondel *et al*. (1998), p. 253.

30 Smismans (1998), p. 57.

31 Advocating a politicization of the EU: Weber-Panariello (1995), p. 310.

parliaments are too easily put forward as brakes on European integration, whether or not cloaked in rhetoric about subsidiarity and democracy. They are too conveniently entrusted the task of providing democratic legitimacy by holding the Council to account, while the national governments are the first to know that effective accountability in that way is hardly realistic to maintain. Yet where Europe fulfils state functions, it cannot be allowed to falter in bolstering a solid European Parliament, which has one permanent site, an agreeable size, a uniform election system, recognizable political party groups which take responsibility for policies before and after elections, and powers which are worthy of a parliament for the citizens of the European Union. The alternatives are sustained parliamentary gaps, or re-nationalization of decision-making, or post-parliamentary and pluralist multilevel scenarios which may capture reality but offer no political vision. Abandoning the parliamentarization of the EU as a clear normative priority would from the outset deprive the citizens of Europe of a hard-won entitlement to have peace, stability and wealth coupled with the principle of representative democracy. Europe may yet endorse the national parliaments; but if it does, it should do so for the right reasons, know who their supporters are and what motives they have, be aware of the consequences of such endorsement, and remember that national parliaments are not the only option, let alone the best one.

Conclusions

How can the role of the national parliaments in the EU be enhanced? That was essentially one of the four questions raised by the Nice Declaration on the future of the Union. However, this is not the question that we sought to answer in this volume. The purpose of this volume was to see whether that question is valid in the first place, and whether its presumptions are really as self-evident as they may appear. The purpose was to verify whether the national parliaments truly deserve a greater role in the European Union, whether such a role is feasible and desirable, in the light of the different perspectives on the matter that can be identified. So, what have we seen? What we have seen is a series of misconceptions regarding the nature, function and capacities of the national parliaments. One misconception is built upon the other, and together they form a conceptual web which is, not at all surprisingly, inherently flawed.

Instead of embracing the national parliaments unquestioningly, we have identified two perspectives from which stronger national parliaments would actually appear desirable: one is the national constitutional perspective, with a strongly individualized country-based focus, while the other is the European perspective, from which national parliaments may, or may not, yield added value for Europe as a whole.

From a national constitutional perspective, we would assess the impact of European integration on a particular parliament in a Member State setting. A study along these lines could, for instance, be comparative in nature, but would in the end evaluate the situation in one Member State, or a set of Member States. Thus, a British study might analyze the impact of EU membership on the House of Commons, possibly compare it with the situations in, say, Ireland, France, Germany and Denmark, it might identify the weaknesses of the House of Commons, evaluate the practice of document sifting, scrutiny reserves and parliamentary resolutions, it might consider the role of the House of Lords, as well as the role of the Scottish parliament, it might contrast the current position of the UK Parliament with its pre-membership position, and compare the scrutiny of European affairs with the treatment of domestic bills and classical foreign affairs. The study may then go on to advocate a stronger position for the House of Commons, as well as greater interest for European affairs among MPs, and propose measures on how to achieve these goals. The same exercise can be repeated in other case-studies, by legal scholars, political scientists and other disciplines, with respect to the parliaments of Belgium, Austria or Hungary. The crucial point is that the national parliaments are reviewed individually, separately for each Member State, in the light of their respective particularities, such as history, culture, constitutional structure, parliamentarism and devolution, the applicable model of separation of powers, the party landscape, public opinion, the broader national interest which is connected to the size of a Member State, the shape of its economy, its self-perception, its bonds with other nations or its geo-strategic concerns, etc. The result would ideally be twenty-five sets of studies, not counting cross-country comparisons and studies about candidate states, pre-candidate states and non-candidate neighbouring states affected by EU decision-making.

These studies all may, or may not, advocate a stronger national parliament. If there are flaws in the studies' reasoning, they would be a matter for the respective national academic and political discourse to tackle. For instance, a study might overestimate the willingness of MPs to engage in scrutiny, or it might exaggerate the potential cleavages between a parliament and its government. On the other hand, it might be too critical, and unduly ignore a parliament's adaptations to EU membership over time. Political science research of the 1990s has revealed many of the factors that contribute to a parliament's relative strength in EU affairs, and it should be noted that not all observed strengths are feasible or desirable to reproduce elsewhere, that not all weaknesses are unfounded or accidental, and that 'strength' and 'weakness' may not even be the appropriate set of terminology to start with. Yet again, whatever the conclusions for a particular parliament, the debate would take place within the academic or political community that deals with the country involved. Such an approach is valid in itself; frictions only arise where generalizations are made, and broader conclusions drawn, about the value of national parliaments for the EU at large. It is for instance problematic to simply recommend a particular set of parliamentary scrutiny mechanisms for other parliaments to copy. Parliaments may of course prove receptive to constitutional transplants, but simply standardizing scrutiny would fly in the face of the Member States' national constitutional autonomy, and the freedom of parliaments to exercise deliberate self-restraint. It is even more problematic when, based on a particular parliament's experience, the purpose of scrutiny is suddenly defined not just in terms of pressing national ministers, but also in terms of generally legitimizing EU action, in one way or another. Just because we think that one particular parliament is too slow and reactive does not mean that *all* national parliaments can, should, or even want to sharpen their scrutiny. This is in fact where the national constitutional perspective acquires a broader dimension, where it merges with what we have identified as the European perspective, and where the effects of the inherent flaws are aggravated.

From a European perspective, the activity of the national parliaments is understood to have an effect beyond their respective national borders, and beyond the Member States level of government. The central question then is no longer how national parliaments can deal with European integration, but rather what beneficial properties can be extracted from them for an all-European purpose, for instance by recognizing, facilitating and stimulating their domestic activities, and by enhancing cross-border and cross-layer channels of interaction within the European constitutional architecture. The properties of the national parliaments which seem so attractive to the European Union at large have been identified along the lines of two inter-related notions, namely democratic legitimacy and 'bringing Europe closer to the citizens'. Attached to these notions are the notions of accountability, deliberation and communication. Democratic legitimacy of EU decision-making would, following that line of reasoning, be increased by activating the slumbering accountability links that lead from the governments, convening in the Council and the European Council, towards their respective national parliaments. That activation would also bring about an increase in parliamentary debate, which attracts public attention in the Member States, and a greater awareness of the functioning and the very existence of the European Union. Detachment would be bridged, Europe would seem much 'closer', while familiarity with the European institutions and politics is understood as a basic prerequisite not only for putting the EU on a national leash, but also for popular support of the EU and democratic participation therein.

The flaws that are inherent to the European rationale for an enhanced role for the national parliaments start with the identification of the addressees. What is a national parliament? From the national constitutional point of view, such a question is not problematic, since the potential candidates within a given Member State, including upper chambers and sub-national assemblies, are more easily identified and qualified, so that a nuanced view concerning an institution's controlling and law-making powers is possible. From a European perspective, however, a crude standard, a common denominator is required, which is bound to distort the picture. To just pick the unicameral or bicameral institution which comes closest to the concept of a parliament is bound to either overestimate the properties of some candidates thus selected, or to ignore comparable properties of candidates that have not been selected.

To place the unicameral Swedish *Riksdag* and the unicameral Danish *Folketing* into one category of representative institutions may be largely uncontroversial. However to place them in one category together with the German *Bundesrat*, which is a legislator but not a parliament, the federal parliament of Belgium, which is a parliament but not always a legislator, the French *Assemblée Nationale*, to whom the President is not accountable, the Polish Senate, to whom the government itself is not accountable, and the UK House of Lords, which is not even elected, casts serious doubt on the validity of the employed standards. Insufficient regard to the heterogeneity of internal national constitutional arrangements, including the working style of a parliament, its mode of election, its fragmentation, its competences and generally its relation to the government, is therefore the first fundamental flaw in the present context. This flaw is aggravated by the fact that the EU, including the Convention, does not seem to clearly define in what capacity it wishes to address the national parliaments in the first place. Law-making, control and communication are functions that are not fixed to one standard body in each Member State. To be sure, the EU does not always need to clarify whom exactly it means when addressing national institutions, and these institutions can be as heterogeneous as they want: 'national authorities' are assigned the task of implementing

EU legislation and policies, 'national courts' are assigned the task of enforcing EU law in the Member States, and there is no clear statutory definition of what exactly qualifies as an 'authority' or 'court' either. The difference is, however, that the above players are assigned European *tasks*; national parliaments in our context would be assigned European powers and privileges. The most recent European constitution-building exercises seemed to have been addressed at a vaguely defined set of bodies. The Convention did not draw up any exhaustive list of recipients of powers and privileges. However that would have made the selection process a conscious one, it would have made the underlying policy choices visible, and it would also have prevented ambiguities about what powers are given to which assemblies and how free Member States are to implement these powers. The Belgian government felt free to declare that its regional and communal assemblies form part of the national parliament, which would entitle these sub-national assemblies to information facilities as well as veto powers under the early warning system and the passerelle clause. The Constitutional Treaty would prepare the ECJ for hearing annulment actions on subsidiarity grounds that are brought by the governments on behalf of their parliaments or individual chambers, yet the German government felt free to agree with the domestic opposition to bring such annulment actions on behalf of one-third of the *Bundestag*. Of course the German government is free to bring actions as it deems fit, but 'national parliament' is arguably not the same thing as 'national opposition'. The Constitutional Treaty would, to continue, unequivocally award each national parliament the power to veto the application of the passerelle clause, yet the German government felt free to make that veto power subject to internal qualifications, namely by allocating the power to the *Bundestag* in areas of exclusive federal competence, to the *Bundesrat* in areas of exclusive *Länder* competence, and otherwise by providing for the possibility for the *Bundestag* to overrule the *Bundesrat.* And while the Constitutional Treaty would, again, prepare the ECJ for hearing annulment actions on subsidiarity grounds that are brought by the governments on behalf of their parliaments or individual chambers, some upper chambers and even lower chambers have reason to fear that their government will not act on their behalf if it does not suit it. An exhaustive list of recipients of powers would have prevented all these ambiguities, apart from giving an opportunity for reflection and a possible 'bailing out' of the exercise, but all the Convention members apparently could agree on was that whoever they are, the national parliaments deserve a formalized role. Since constitution-building implies distribution of power, it should be taken more seriously than that. Objections that the system might work in practice nonetheless would leave undefined what exactly is meant by 'work', and do not answer the question whether constitutional documents should really be drafted based on spontaneity and gut-feeling, without proper debate and with limited or no foreseeability of effects.

The second flaw in the debate overlaps with the first one, in that the existence of a collective of easily comparable and mutually compatible institutions is assumed. Each national parliament is elected by its own, and for its own citizenry only.

The citizens of Member State A follow the debates in their own parliament, and they demand dismissal of incompetent ministers from their own government. They have little opportunity, nor incentive, to follow parliamentary debates in Member State B, and they have no entitlement whatsoever to demand the dismissal of that Member State's government by its parliament. Conversely, the national parliament of Member State B is itself elected to represent the interests of its own electorate, that is, its own national interest. Its re-election-based incentive structure would not support, and its national constitutional mandate would even prohibit, to take into consideration the interests of Member State A in its will-formation. With national parliaments, therefore, comes national interest: the accountability process would focus on how well the government has followed, and fought for, the pre-determined set of domestic preferences. To assume that a greater number of more active national parliaments would add up to a richer European parliamentary landscape would be to ignore the above points, namely that the citizens of Member State A are not experiencing an elevated level of parliamentarism as a result of the efforts of the national parliament of Member State B. What would they then experience as a result of sharper scrutiny in their own parliament?

The national mandate of a parliament commands activity in the interest of the parliament's own entity, or no activity at all. Sharpened confrontation within parliament, or between parliament and government, over the conduct of European affairs, would put an additional emphasis on the national stakes, and without confrontation and cleavage there is no debate. That way, bringing Europe closer to the citizens would mean to bring closer a bargaining arena of national egoisms, where an individual country first struggles over its national standpoint – what is best for Sweden, what is best for Greece – and then either triumphs over others, or loses out to the interest of other countries, by way of policy concessions or financial contributions. Such an atmosphere does not even reign in the Council itself, which is governed by co-operative repeat games for compromise-finding, and which has thereby become more than the mere sum of its members. Accordingly, twenty-five sets of national parliamentary scrutiny will not add up to a total of European parliamentarism. A national parliament is elected with one national mandate, and not with one-twenty-fifth of a European mandate. And even if bargaining over pre-determined agendas, whether the national parliaments have been involved in their determination or not, is what the Council is really about, then this only constitutes *one* of the aspects in the European Union's bicameral legislature.

The third flaw lies in the depiction of parliaments as unitary institutions, and in the conventional emphasis on adversarial government-parliament relations. In the practice of Western parliamentary democracies, however, the parliamentary majority at least in the lower chamber usually coincides with the party political affiliations within the government. The implication that more adversarial relations between parliament and government, or opposition and government, over Europe will boost support for European integration without bringing to the fore the national stakes is highly misleading. Meanwhile, parliamentary debates in which all parties agree are no debates really, but a balancing act between elite consensus over Europe and the opposition's desire to challenge the government over more salient domestic issues.

A fourth and related misconception concerns the suggestion of enhancing inter-parliamentary co-operation to make a collective stand. Alliances between national parliamentarians of different Member States require more than mutual sympathy and efficient information channels. Instead, they require a sustainable inter-parliamentary solidarity and close co-operation. In the light of the institutional setting in parliamentary democracies, the crucial qualification to make is that such inter-parliamentary solidarity and co-operation would have to bypass the individual governments in order to be meaningful. At the same time, political preferences along the left-right divide have already been expressed in the European Parliament, while bargaining along national lines takes place in the Council, whose members enjoy the support of their own parliaments. Inter-parliamentary alliances therefore denote alliances between principals in parallel to, or even in opposition to, their very own agents who already act on their behalf.

A similar picture arises with vertical co-operation of national parliaments with the European Parliament. While it is convenient to conclude that both levels of parliamentarism fulfil complementary roles in the EU, which seems to solve the controversy, such pictures should not conceal some inherent constitutional tensions. It is questionable to desire that national parliamentary majorities should express a greater solidarity towards MEPs than towards their own government, and it is questionable to assume that parliamentary mandates, national and European, are interchangeable. Where the European Parliament, aware of the structural tensions, embraces national MPs in order to dictate its EU-related agenda and to avoid dangerous outbreaks of rivalry, inter-parliamentary fora deserve a more sober analysis, instead of blue-eyed approval under notions of multi-level governance. The same applies to the enforcement of the principle of subsidiarity, in as far as it seeks to promote a collective European role for the national parliaments. Subsidiarity is in any case a tricky concept that cannot be sharply isolated from substantive criteria, and so far more of a political than legal nature. Even where a parliament – that is, the majority therein – files a complaint, it will more than anything else be an act of support for its own government which is opposed to a Commission proposal itself, or, if a vote is cast or withheld against the government's wishes, it will be an act of domestic opposition. The label of collective inter-parliamentary involvement is therefore very much misplaced. Where a national parliament wishes to include subsidiarity considerations in its regular scrutiny work, our points made on sharpened national parliamentary scrutiny in general apply: any one parliament is free to sharpen its scrutiny, under subsidiarity aspects or otherwise; it just does not mean that *all* parliaments will want that. And if they did, the global effects for the EU as a whole are lower decision-making efficiency and increased salience of national stakes.

Where national MPs are called upon to play a direct role at EU level, instead of the domestic level, for instance in fora together with MEPs or, equipped with a dual mandate, in a new EU institution, a fifth misconception emerges, concerning the democratic credentials of MPs. The presumably undemocratic nature of EU decision-making is not caused by the undemocratic character of the personalities involved, but by the perhaps inherently greater remoteness of the process itself. MPs who engage in the same activities that the European Parliament, the Council or the IGCs engage in today do not guarantee any greater proximity of these activities to the citizens, by virtue of elected parliamentarians' being 'better' in one way or another. Experience with the old dual-mandate European Parliament and the recent Convention shows that educative and integrative effects on national parliaments are limited or absent, that parliaments hardly pick up any corresponding debate of their own, but instead leave these European affairs to the specialists in much the same way as they usually leave European scrutiny to their European Affairs Committees today. MPs themselves do not bring debate to the EU if they leave behind the forum in which they normally operate, and to which their debating functions attach. Instead, they become accomplices of their governments who can pre-empt domestic scrutiny even more, and they possibly enter into institutional competition with the European Parliament. That may not even be the intention of many MPs themselves, if they favour parliamentarization of the EU over interventions from the national level.

All of the above flaws and misconceptions reveal the nature of the exercise of addressing the national parliaments from EU level itself. Whereas in classical international relations the states would be uniformly represented by their governments, the European Union makes the activity of national institutions other than the governments a matter of EU law. While it is not at all contrary to international law to stipulate the roles of trans-government actors in a treaty, including judges or authorities, or regions and municipalities, the artificiality of this top-down exercise imposes inherent constraints. While the EU remains based on treaties signed and ratified by the Member States as represented by their governments, the involvement of the national parliaments collides with the principles of EU neutrality as regards the domestic orders of the Member States and their constitutional autonomy. And while all the Member States may be democratic, the practical content which they give to parliamentarism differs. Depending on the capacity which is sought to be addressed in a national parliament, the exercise brings about national constitutional distortions.

Identifying parliaments as the ratifiers of treaties ignores the weight of a referendum and the powers of sub-national assemblies. Identifying them as actors who elect, control and dismiss the government ignores the position of some directly elected presidents, the position of some of the upper chambers, and generally the different modes of government formation and censure procedures in the lower chambers. Identifying them as law-makers ignores the legislative competences of regional institutions. The European Convention on Human Rights for instance guarantees the right to free elections, but not with respect to 'parliaments' but with respect to the 'legislature', which is a broader term; that allows the Strasbourg Court to qualify the legislative competences of national institutions case by case, and to expand the concept to regional assemblies, parliaments of overseas territories with newly acquired autonomy, theoretically even to heads of state, provided they have sufficient powers to issue decrees or are sufficiently involved in the normal legislative process. Even without any clear set of criteria, the Strasbourg Court can afford to work under the slogan 'I can tell a legislature when I see one'. But then again, the ECHR does not distribute powers and privileges to the national legislatures like the EU seeks to do. To continue, identifying the national parliaments as fora for public debate which can make the EU more accessible, along with alleged scrutinizing and ultimately hand-tying capacities as regards the governments, ignores the side-effects that such EU-level interventions into national parliamentary practice entail.

Courting the national parliaments for European purposes, by way of information and consultation, time-delays for scrutiny and invitations for collective contributions, the subsidiarity enforcement mechanism, the veto under a passerelle clause or other forms of direct involvement means to adopt measures which constitute essentially artificial interventions into a constitutional landscape with the aim of propping up particular beneficiaries who are otherwise perceived to be undesirably weak. These measures however bring about an emphasis on the national interest while, if all parliaments were to adopt Danish hand-tying practice, disrupting the efficiency of Council decision-making. These are hardly the effects that the measures are meant to achieve. The effects which are in fact desired are meanwhile not achieved in a way that is consistent with the presumed intention. A Europe of competing national egoisms, which cannot even be resolved efficiently any longer due to the increased amount of interested parties and the inflated stakes, is arguably, from an integrationist point of view, not the same Europe that should be brought closer to the citizens.

Ultimately, while for the purposes of analysis the suppression of federalist and Eurosceptic ideologies is very useful, the larger constitutional picture cannot be seen without them. Of course, demands for a radical 'step back' from European integration and supranationalism would place great emphasis on the importance of the national parliaments, although regulation by the Member States does not necessarily mean regulation by the respective parliaments. The other extreme would meanwhile emphasize the importance of the European Parliament instead. Radically, the national parliaments would then need to cease their EU-related scrutiny activity altogether or, more realistically, the desired level of scrutiny would be left to the parliaments themselves. While hand-tying practice would still have detrimental effects on the Council, the parliaments could, if the European Parliament were to replace their function at EU level, afford to be more lenient on integration matters.

In between these two extremes, are again the reconciliatory notions awarding both levels of parliamentarism their due place in the European architecture. The national parliaments and the European Parliament complement each other, we are led to believe, as allies instead of rivals, and in a multi-level setting instead of a hierarchical relation. That way, either the European Parliament could increasingly complement the national parliaments at EU level, or the national parliaments could awaken to complement the activity of the European Parliament on the national level. Either way, these notions are appealingly centrist, in that they reflect an equilibrium between, on the one hand, the enthusiasm for the European Parliament of the 1980s, and on the other hand the swing of attention towards the national parliaments of the 1990s. This volume tried to look beyond the reconciliation, to recall the reasons for the pendulum's swing towards the national parliaments in the first place, and the misconceptions and false impressions that it brings. Without purporting to draw an exhaustive blueprint for European parliamentarism, this volume intends to contribute to the debate about the constitutional future of Europe which, just like the integration project itself, remains a dynamic process. In that process, we should not lose sight of what demands for more active national parliaments in the EU reflect. Timid national default options, floated in a time of stalling momentum in European integration, cannot replace what should remain a consistent normative priority of democratization and parliamentarization of the EU level, unless a nationalization of the EU is what we in fact actively pursue.

Should the national parliaments receive a greater role in the EU? Those who are sceptical of the EU, or at least the European Parliament anyway, are free to answer this question in the affirmative, whether they mean their own parliament in particular or, vaguely and therefore less convincingly, the national parliaments in general. Yet those who wish to combine European integration with genuine European parliamentarism should think twice before embracing the national parliaments. The European Parliament will obviously not solve any democratic deficits on its own, and certainly not overnight. Yet nothing will come of nothing, and putting false hopes in the national parliaments would mean to accept far less than what we are entitled to in terms of representative democracy in the European Union. Even if we wish to waive that entitlement and settle for the national parliaments, then at least that choice should be a conscious one, the result of a weighing of pros and cons, and not the result of self-deceit and the internalization of shallow political catch-phrases.

Bibliography

Agh, A. (1998) *The Politics of Central Europe* (Sage, London).

Agostini, M.V. (2001) 'The Role of National Parliaments in the Future EU', *The International Spectator* 36, p. 29-41.

Albæk Jensen, J. (1996) 'Prior Parliamentary Consent to Danish EU Policies', in Smith, E. (ed.) *National Parliaments as Cornerstones of European Integration* (Kluwer Law International, London/The Hague/Boston).

Albi, A. (2003) 'EU Amendments of the Central and Eastern European Candidate Countries', in Ziller, J. (ed.) *The Europeanisation of Constitutional Law in the Light of the Constitution for Europe* (L'Harmattan, Paris).

Albi, A. (2005) *EU Enlargement and the Constitutions of Central and Eastern Europe* (CUP, Cambridge).

Ameller, M. (1966) *Parliaments* (Cassell & Company, London).

Andersen, S.S. and Eliassen, K.A. (eds) (1996) *The European Union: How Democratic Is It?* (Sage, London).

Andriukaitis, V.P. and Kutraite-Giedraitiene, D. (2002) *Strengthening the role of national parliaments* (CONV 220/02, Contribution 75).

Arter, D. (1995) 'The Folketing and Denmark's "European Policy": The Case of an "Authorising Assembly"', in Norton, Ph. (ed.) *National Parliaments and the European Union* (*The Journal of Legislative Studies* 1, special issue 3).

Attinà, F. (2000) *Strategies for democratising multi-state systems and the European Union* (Jean Monnet Working Paper in Comparative and International Politics no. 28).

Banchoff, Th. and Smith, M.P. (eds) (1999) *Legitimacy and the European Union – The Contested Polity* (Routledge, London/New York).

Barrau, A. (2002) *National Parliaments* (CONV 84/02, Contribution 40).

Basabe Lloréns, F. and González Escudero, M.T. (2001) 'The Parliament of Spain: Slowly Moving onto the European Direction?', in Maurer, A. and Wessels, W. (eds): *National Parliaments on their Ways to Europe: Losers or Latecomers?* (Nomos, Baden-Baden).

Basile, F. (2002a) *The Role of National Parliaments* (CONV 239/02, Contribution 85).

Basile, F. (2002b) *The Role of National Parliaments* (CONV 334/02, Contribution 116).

Bengtson, Chr. (2003) *National Parliaments in European decision-making: A real prospect or wishful thinking?* (paper, The Federal Trust for Education and Research, London).

Bergman, T. (1997) 'National parliaments and EU Affairs Committees: notes on empirical variation and competing explanations', *Journal of European Public Policy* 4, p. 373-387.

Bieber, R. (1994) 'The Role of Parliaments in External Relations', in Flinterman, C., A.W. Heringa and L. Waddington (eds), *The Evolving Role of Parliaments in Europe* (Maklu, Antwerpen/Apeldoorn).

Bindi Calussi, F. and Grassi, S.B. (2001) 'The Parliament of Italy: From Benevolent Observer to Active Player', in Maurer, A. and Wessels, W. (eds) *National Parliaments on their Ways to Europe: Losers or Latecomers?* (Nomos, Baden-Baden).

Blondel, J., R. Sinnott and P. Svensson (1998) *People and Parliament in the European Union* (Clarendon Press, Oxford).

Blümel, B. and Neuhold, Chr. (2001) 'The Parliament of Austria: A Large Potential with Little Implications', in Maurer, A. and Wessels, W. (eds) *National Parliaments on their Ways to Europe: Losers or Latecomers?* (Nomos, Baden-Baden).

Boedeker, M. and Uusikylä, P. (2000) 'Interaction between the Government and Parliament in Scrutiny of EU Decision-Making: Finnish Experiences and General Problems', in Finnish Eduskunta (ed.) *National Parliaments and the EU – Stock-Taking for the Post-Amsterdam Era* (October 1999 COSAC seminar, Eduskunnan Kanslian Julkaisu 1/2000).

Bonnamour, M.-Chr. (1995) 'Les Relations Parlement Européen et Parlements Nationaux à la Veille de la Conférence Intergouvernementale de 1996', *Revue du Marché commun et de l'Union européenne* [1995] 393, p. 637-646.

Bossaert, D. (2001) 'The Luxembourg Chamber of Deputies: From a Toothless Tiger to a Critical Watchdog?', in Maurer, A. and Wessels, W. (eds) *National Parliaments on their Ways to Europe: Losers or Latecomers?* (Nomos, Baden-Baden).

Bovend'Eert, P.P.T. and Kummeling, H.R.B.M. (2000) *Van Raalte's Het Nederlandse Parlement* (9th edn, Kluwer, Deventer).

Brown, T. (2003) *National Parliaments in the Convention on the Future of Europe* (Federal Trust online paper 31/03). www.fedtrust.co.uk

Brown, T. (2004a) *Achieving Balance: Institutions and Member States* (Federal Trust online paper 1/04). www.fedtrust.co.uk

Brown, T. (2004b) *Conventional Wisdom – What have we learned from the Convention Experience?* (Federal Trust online paper 11/04). www.fedtrust.co.uk

Carter, C.A. (2001) 'The Parliament of the United Kingdom: From Supportive Scrutiny to Unleashed Control?', in Maurer, A. and Wessels, W. (eds) *National Parliaments on their Ways to Europe: Losers or Latecomers?* (Nomos, Baden-Baden).

Claes, M. (2005) *The National Courts' Mandate in the European Constitution* (Hart, Oxford).

Closa, C. (1995) 'Spain: The Cortes and the EU – A Growing Together', in Norton, Ph. (ed.): *National Parliaments and the European Union* (*The Journal of Legislative Studies* 1, special issue 3).

Conlan, P. (2004) *Parliamentary Scrutiny of European Legislation in Ireland* (Conference presentation, 21-22 May 2004, University of Limerick).

COSAC (2003) *Guidelines for relations between governments and Parliaments on Community issues* (instructive minimum standards) ('Copenhagen Parliamentary Guidelines'), 2003/C 154/01.

COSAC (2004) *Presidency Conclusions* (32nd COSAC, 22-23 November 2004, The Hague).

COSAC Secretariat (2004) *Report on developments in European Union procedures and practices relevant to parliamentary scrutiny* (32nd COSAC, 22-23 November 2004, The Hague).

COSAC Secretariat (2005a) *Third bi-annual Report: Developments in European Union Procedures and Practices Relevant to Parliamentary Scrutiny* (33rd COSAC, 17-18 May 2005, Luxembourg).

COSAC Secretariat (2005b) *Report on the results of COSAC's Pilot project on the 3rd Railway Package to test the 'Subsidiarity early warning mechanism'* (33rd COSAC, 17-18 May 2005, Luxembourg).

Craig, P. and De Búrca, G. (2003) *EU Law – Texts, Cases, and Materials* (OUP, Oxford).

Crombez, Chr. (2003) 'The Democratic Deficit in the European Union – Much Ado about Nothing?', *European Union Politics* 4, p. 101-120.

Cullen, P. (1995) 'Competing Legitimacy at European and National Levels: The Ruling of the Constitutional Court and Parliamentary Scrutiny of European Union Affairs in Germany', in Laursen, F. and Pappas, S.A. (eds) *The Changing Role of Parliaments in the European Union* (European Institute of Public Administration, Maastricht).

Curtin, D. (2002) *Private Interest Representation or Civil Society Deliberation? A Contemporary Dilemma for European Union Governance* (conference paper, Democracy and Legitimacy of the European Union and other International Organizations, EP 11-12 October 2002).

Curtin, D. (2004) *Mind the Gap: the Evolving EU Executive and the Constitution* (Europa Law Publishing, Groningen).

Cygan, A.J. (1998) *The United Kingdom Parliament and European Union Legislation* (Kluwer Law International, The Hague/London/Boston).

Cygan, A.J. (2001) *National Parliaments in an Integrated Europe – An Anglo-German Perspective* (Kluwer Law International, The Hague/London/New York).

Cygan, A.J. (2004a) *Scrutiny of EU Legislation in the UK Parliament – The First Thirty Years... and Beyond?* (Conference Paper, 21-22 May 2004, University of Limerick).

Cygan, A.J. (2004b) 'The Role of National Parliaments in the EU's New Constitutional Order', in Tridimas, T. and Nebbia, P. (eds) *European Union Law for the Twenty-First Century* (Hart, Oxford).

Danish Folketing (2002) *The European Affairs Committee of the Folketing.*

Dann, Ph. (2004) *Parlamente im Exekutivföderalismus – Eine Studie zum Verhältnis von föderaler Ordnung und parlamentarischer Demokratie in der Europäischen Union* (Springer, Berlin/Heidelberg/New York).

Dashwood, A. (1998) 'States in the European Union', *European Law Review* 23, p. 201-216.

Dashwood, A. (2004) 'The Relationship between the Member States and the European Union/European Community', *Common Market Law Review* 41, p. 355-381.

De Búrca, G. (2005) *The EU Constitution: in Search of Europe's International Identity* (Europa Law Publishing, Groningen).

De Gucht, K. (2002) *Another role for the national parliaments in the EU* (CONV 183/02, Contribution 63).

De Winter, L. and Laurent, Th. (1995) 'The Belgian Parliament and European Integration', in Norton, Ph. (ed.): *National Parliaments and the European Union* (*The Journal of Legislative Studies* 1, special issue 3).

Del Grosso, N.Y. (2000) *Parlement en Europese Integratie* (Kluwer, Deventer).

De Witte, B. (ed.) (2003) *Ten Reflections on the Constitutional Treaty for Europe* (EUI/Robert Schuman Centre for Advanced Studies, Florence).

De Witte, B. (2004) *The National Constitutional Dimension of European Treaty Revision – Evolution and Recent Debates* (Europa Law Publishing, Groningen).

Dimitrakopoulos, D.G. (2001) 'Incrementalism and Path Dependence: European Integration and Institutional Change in National Parliaments', *Journal of Common Market Studies* 39, p. 405-422.

Donnelly, B. (2003) *Whither the Council?* (Federal Trust online paper 37/03). www.fedtrust.co.uk

Donnelly, B. and Hoffmann, L. (2004) *The Role of National Parliaments in the European Union* (The Federal Trust for Education and Research European Policy Brief 2004, issue 3).

Döring, H. (ed.) (1995) *Parliaments and Majority Rule in Western Europe* (Campus, Frankfurt/St. Martin's, New York).

Dubouis, L. (1996) 'The European Union: An Opportunity for the French Parliament to Recover Powers?', in Smith, E. (ed.): *National Parliaments as Cornerstones of European Integration* (Kluwer Law International, London/The Hague/Boston).

Duff, A. (1994) 'Building a Parliamentary Europe', *Government and Opposition* 29, p. 147-165.

Duff, A. (2002a) *A Model Constitution for a Federal Union of Europe* (CONV 234/02, Contribution 82).

Duff, A. (2002b) *Code of Conduct on National Parliaments* (CONV 326/02, Contribution 112).

Duff, A. (2002c) *Paper on the role of national parliaments* (European Convention Working Group IV working document no. 4).

Duina, F. and Oliver, M.J. (2005) 'National Parliaments in the European Union: Are There Any Benefits to Integration?', *European Law Journal* 11, p. 173-195.

Dutch Tweede Kamer (2004) *Advies van de Gemengde Commissie Toepassing Subsidiariteit betreffende de parlementaire behandeling van Europese wetsvoorstellen* (12 October 2004, no. GC 64).

European Commission (2001) *European Governance – A White Paper* (COM (2001) 428 final).

European Convention (2002a) *Mandate of the Working Group on National Parliaments* (CONV 74/02).

European Convention (2002b) *The role of national parliaments in the European architecture* (CONV 67/02).

European Convention (2002c) *The Role of National Parliaments in the European architecture* (CONV 68/02).

European Convention (2002d) *Final report of Working Group IV on the role of national parliaments* (CONV 353/02).

European Convention (2003a) *Draft Protocols on: the application of the principles of subsidiarity and proportionality; the role of national parliaments in the European Union* (CONV 579/03).

European Convention (2003b) *Declaration on the role of national parliaments to raise national European awareness* (CONV 834/03).

European Parliament (1990) *Bodies within national parliaments specialising in European Community affairs* (Office for Official Publications of the European Communities, Luxembourg).

European Parliament (1992) *Bodies within national parliaments specialising in European Community affairs* (European Parliament, Luxembourg).

European Parliament (2002) *Report on relations between the European Parliament and the national parliaments in European integration* (2001/2023 INI).

Einem, C. (2002) *National Parliaments* (CONV 81/02, Contribution 37).

Estella, A. (2002) *The EU Principle of Subsidiarity and its Critique* (OUP, Oxford).

Falkner, G. and Nentwich, M. (1995) *European Union: Democratic perspectives after 1996* (Service-Fachverlag, Vienna).

Finnish Eduskunta (2000) *National Parliaments and the EU – Stock-Taking for the Post-Amsterdam Era* (October 1999 COSAC seminar, Eduskunnan Kanslian Julkaisu 1/2000).

Finnish Eduskunta, Swedish Riksdag and Danish Folketing (2002) *The EU and democracy in the Nordic Region.*

Fischer, J. (2000) *From Confederacy to Federation – Thoughts on the finality of European integration* (speech held at Humboldt University in Berlin, 12 May 2000).

Fitzmaurice, J. (1979) 'The Danish system of parliamentary control over European Community policy', in Herman, V. and Van Schendelen, R. (eds) *The European Parliament and the National Parliaments* (Saxon House, Farnborough).

Fitzmaurice, J. (1999) 'National parliamentary control', in Westlake, M. *The Council of the European Union* (revised ed., John Harper, London).

Flinterman, C., A.W. Heringa and L. Waddington (eds) (1994) *The Evolving Role of Parliaments in Europe* (Maklu, Antwerpen/Apeldoorn).

Føllesdal, A. (2004) *Achieving Stability? Forms and Arenas of Institutional and National Balances in the Draft Constitutional Treaty* (Federal Trust online paper 06/04). www.fedtrust.co.uk

Fraga, A. (2000) 'Wanting more power. . . a struggle for what? Comments on the report by Mr Tapio Raunio "Parliamentary Scrutiny of EU Decision-Making: Comparing National Systems"', in Finnish Eduskunta (ed.) *National Parliaments and the EU – Stock-Taking for the Post-Amsterdam Era* (October 1999 COSAC seminar, Eduskunnan Kanslian Julkaisu 1/2000).

Fraga, A. (2001) 'The Parliament of Portugal: Loyal Scrutiny and Informal Influence', in Maurer, A. and Wessels, W. (eds) *National Parliaments on their Ways to Europe: Losers or Latecomers?* (Nomos, Baden-Baden).

French Assemblée Nationale (1997) *La Délégation de l'Assemblée nationale pour l'Union européenne: Compétences et activités*.

French Assemblée Nationale (1998) *L'Assemblée nationale et l'Union européenne* (Connaissance de l'Assemblée series).

Frowein, J. and Peukert, W. (1996) *Europäische Menschenrechtskonvention: Kommentar* (2nd edn, Engel, Kehl).

Fuchs, M. (2000) 'National Parliaments and governments in the EU institutional system after the Amsterdam Treaty: Germany', in Finnish Eduskunta (ed.) *National Parliaments and the EU – Stock-Taking for the Post-Amsterdam Era* (October 1999 COSAC seminar, Eduskunnan Kanslian Julkaisu 1/2000).

Furlong, P. (1995) 'The Italian Parliament and European Integration: Responsibilities, Failures and Successes', in Norton, Ph. (ed.): *National Parliaments and the European Union* (*The Journal of Legislative Studies* 1, special issue 3).

German Bundestag Committee for European Union Affairs (2000) *Die Rechtsgrundlagen des Ausschusses für die Angelegenheiten der Europäischen Union des Deutschen Bundestages* (Texte und Materialien vol. 1).

Götz, V. (2004) 'Kompetenzverteilung und Kompetenzkontrolle in der Europäischen Union', in Schwarze, J. (ed.): *Der Verfassungsentwurf des Europäischen Konvents* (Nomos, Baden-Baden).

Grevi, G. (2004) *Light and Shade of a quasi-Constitution: An Assessment* (Federal Trust online paper 08/04). www.fedtrust.co.uk

Guizzi, V. (1995) 'Italy: A Consideration of the Position of the National Parliaments in the European Union', in Laursen, F. and Pappas, S.A. (eds) *The Changing Role of Parliaments in the European Union* (European Institute of Public Administration, Maastricht).

Gustavsson, S. (1996) 'Preserve or Abolish the Democratic Deficit?', in Smith, E. (ed.): *National Parliaments as Cornerstones of European Integration* (Kluwer Law International, London/The Hague/Boston).

Hansen, I. (2002) *National Parliaments in the European Institutional Framework* (Report for the Conference of Speakers of the National Parliaments of the EU, 7-9 June 2002, Madrid).

Harlow, C. (2002) *Accountability in the European Union* (OUP, Oxford).

Hayes-Renshaw, F. and Wallace, H. (1997) *The Council of Ministers* (Macmillan, London).

Hegeland, H. (2000) 'National Parliaments as Arenas and Actors in Scrutiny of EU Decision-Making – A comment on the report by Mika Boedeker and Petri Uusikylä', in Finnish Eduskunta (ed.) *National Parliaments and the EU – Stock-Taking for the Post-Amsterdam Era* (October 1999 COSAC seminar, Eduskunnan Kanslian Julkaisu 1/2000).

Hegeland, H. (2001) 'The Parliament of Sweden: A Successful Adapter in the European Arena', in Maurer, A. and Wessels, W. (eds) *Parliaments on their Ways to Europe: Losers or Latecomers?* (Nomos, Baden-Baden).

Hegeland, H. and Neuhold, Chr. (2002) *Parliamentary participation in EU affairs in Austria, Finland and Sweden: Newcomers with different approaches* (European Integration online paper 6/10). http://eiop.or.at/eiop/texte/2002-010a.htm

Hegeland, H. (2004) *The European Union in National Parliaments – Domestic or Foreign Policy? A Study of Nordic Parliamentary Systems* (Conference Paper, 21-22 May 2004, University of Limerick).

Heringa, A.W. (1994) 'Democracy in Europe: The Evolving Role of Parliaments – Is there a European Parliamentary Model?', in Flinterman, C., A.W. Heringa and L. Waddington (eds) *The Evolving Role of Parliaments in Europe* (Maklu, Antwerpen/Apeldoorn).

Heringa, A.W. (2002) 'Het Eerste Protocol, Artikel 3: Verkiezingen', in Heringa, A.W., J. Schokkenbroek and J. Van der Velde (eds) *Europees Verdrag voor de Rechten van de Mens – Rechtspraak & Commentaar* (Sdu, The Hague).

Herman, V. and Van Schendelen, R. (eds) (1979) *The European Parliament and the National Parliaments* (Saxon House, Farnborough).

Hilf, M. and Burmeister, F. (1996) 'The German Parliament and European Integration', in Smith, E. (ed.) *National Parliaments as Cornerstones of European Integration* (Kluwer Law International, London/The Hague/Boston).

Hix, S. (2002) *Linking national politics to Europe* (Foreign Policy Centre and British Council, London).

Hoetjes, B. (2001) 'The Parliament of the Netherlands and the European Union: Early Starter, Slow Mover', in Maurer, A. and Wessels, W. (eds) *National Parliaments on their Ways to Europe: Losers or Latecomers?* (Nomos, Baden-Baden).

Hoffmann, L. (2002) *Linking National Politics to Europe: An Opposing Argument* (paper, The Federal Trust for Education and Research, London).

Hoffmann, L. (2003) *Constitutionalism and Federalism in the 'Future of Europe' debate: The German Dimension* (Federal Trust online paper 03/04). www.fedtrust.co.uk

Hofmann, H. (2003) 'Parliamentary Representation in Europe's System of Multi-Layer Constitutions: A Case Study of Germany', *Maastricht Journal of European and Comparative Law* 10, p. 39-65.

Hölscheidt, S. (2001) 'The German Bundestag: From Benevolent "Weakness" Towards Supportive Scrutiny', in Maurer, A. and Wessels, W. (eds) *National Parliaments on their Ways to Europe: Losers or Latecomers?* (Nomos, Baden-Baden).

Holzhacker, R. (2002) 'National Parliamentary Scrutiny over EU Issues', *European Union Politics* 3, p. 459-479.

Holzhacker, R. (2004) *The Power of Opposition Parties in National Parliaments to Scrutinize EU Decision-making in the Member States: Comparing Laws, Institutions, and Party Behaviors* (Conference Paper, 21-22 May 2004, University of Limerick).

Höreth, M. (1999) *Die Europäische Union im Legitimationstrilemma* (Nomos, Baden-Baden).

Hourquebie, F. (1999) *Les organes spécialisés dans les affaires communautaires des parlements nationaux – Les cas français et allemands* (L'Harmattan, Paris).

Hübner, D. (2002) *The role of national Parliaments* (CONV 390/02, Contribution 135).

Jääskinen, N. and Kivisaari, T. (1997) *Parliamentary Scrutiny of European Union Affairs in Finland* (Eduskunta, Helsinki).

Jeffery, Ch. (2004) *Regions and the EU: Letting them in and Leaving them alone* (Federal Trust online paper XX/04). www.fedtrust.co.uk

Judge, D. (1995) 'The Failure of National Parliaments?', *West European Politics* 18, p. 79-100.

Jurgens, E. (1993) *Een onparlementair stelsel – over het toezicht van nationale parlementen op de besluitvorming van de Europese Gemeenschappen* (Kluwer, Deventer).

Jurgens, E. (1994) 'A Federal Option for the European Community or a Permanent Democracy Deficit?', in Flinterman, C., A.W. Heringa and L. Waddington (eds) *The Evolving Role of Parliaments in Europe* (Maklu, Antwerpen/Apeldoorn).

Katz, R.S. (1999a) 'Representation, the Locus of Democratic Legitimation, and the Role of the National Parliaments in the European Union', in Katz, R.S. and Wessels, B. (eds) *The European Parliament, the National Parliaments, and European Integration* (OUP, Oxford).

Katz, R.S. (1999b) 'Role Orientations in Parliaments', in Katz, R.S. and Wessels, B. (eds) *The European Parliament, the National Parliaments, and European Integration* (OUP, Oxford).

Katz, R.S. and Wessels, B. (eds) (1999) *The European Parliament, the National Parliaments, and European Integration* (OUP, Oxford).

Kiiver, Ph. (2004) 'Case-note: ECtHR nr. 36681/97, 1 July 2004, *Santoro* v. *Italy*', *European Human Rights Cases* 5, p. 795-802.

Kiiver, Ph. (2005a) 'Case-note: ECtHR nr. 66289/01, 11 January 2005, *Py* v. *France*', *European Human Rights Cases* 6, p. 257-266.

Kiiver, Ph. (2005b) 'The National Parliaments in an Enlarged Europe and the Constitutional Treaty', in Ott, A. and Inglis, K. (eds) *The Constitution for Europe and an Enlarging Union: Unity in Diversity?* (Europa Law Publishing, Groningen).

Kiljunen, K., M. Vanhanen, E. Helle and R. Korhonen (2002) *Contribution from members of the Convention representing the Finnish Parliament on the role of National Parliaments in the European Union structure* (CONV 82/02, Contribution 38).

Knippenberg, E. (2002) *De Senaat – Rechtsvergelijkend onderzoek naar het House of Lords, de Sénat, de Eerste Kamer en de Bundesrat* (Sdu, The Hague).

Kreitzberg, P. and Kelam, T. (2002) *Role of National Parliaments* (CONV 95/02, Contribution 44).

Kurzmann, G. (2002) *Role of the national parliaments in the EU* (CONV 119/02, Contribution 51).

Laffan, B. (2001) 'The Parliament of Ireland: A Passive Adapter Coming in from the Cold', in Maurer, A. and Wessels, W. (eds) *National Parliaments on their Ways to Europe: Losers or Latecomers?* (Nomos, Baden-Baden).

Laundy, Ph. (1989) *Parliaments in the Modern World* (Dartmouth, Hauts).

Laursen, F. (1995) 'Parliamentary Bodies Specializing in European Affairs: Denmark and the Europe Committee of the Folketing', in Laursen, F. and Pappas, S.A. (eds)

The Changing Role of Parliaments in the European Union (European Institute of Public Administration, Maastricht).

Laursen, F. (2001) 'The Danish Folketing and its European Affairs Committee: Strong Players in the National Policy Cycle', in Maurer, A. and Wessels, W. (eds) *National Parliaments on their Ways to Europe: Losers or Latecomers?* (Nomos, Baden-Baden).

Laursen, F. and Pappas, S.A. (eds) (1995) *The Changing Role of Parliaments in the European Union* (European Institute of Public Administration, Maastricht).

Lawson, R.A. and Schermers, H.G. (1999) *Leading Cases of the European Court of Human Rights* (2nd edn, Ars Aequi Libri, Nijmegen).

Layer, F. (2001) 'Le role collectif des parlements nationaux dans l'Union européenne: une réponse au déficit démocratique?', *Petites Affiches* [2001] 259, p. 4-9.

Lekberg, S. (2002a) *Methods for subsidiarity control by National Parliaments* (European Convention Working Group IV working document no. 3).

Lekberg, S. (2002b) *National Scrutiny Systems: Sweden* (European Convention Working Group IV working document no. 5).

Lodge, J. (1991) 'Democratic Legitimacy and European Union', *Public Policy and Administration* 6, p. 21-29.

Lodge, J. (1996) 'The European Parliament', in Smith, E. (ed.) *National Parliaments as Cornerstones of European Integration* (Kluwer Law International, London/The Hague/Boston).

Lord, Chr. (1998) *Democracy in the European Union* (Sheffield Academic Press, Sheffield).

Lord, Chr. (2003) *Towards a Parliamentary EU* (paper, The Federal Trust for Education and Research, London).

Magone, J.M. (1995) 'The Portuguese Assembleia da República: Discovering Europe', in Norton, Ph. (ed.) *National Parliaments and the European Union* (*The Journal of Legislative Studies* 1, special issue 3).

Mancini, G.F. (2000) *Democracy and Constitutionalism in the European Union* (Hart, Oxford/Portland, Oregon).

Massart-Pierard, F. (2002) 'La Participation des Parlements Nationaux aux Activités de l'Union Européenne: "Problem Solving" ou Nouvelle Zone d'Incertitude? Une Mise en Perspective', *Annales d'Études Européennes de l'Université Catholique de Louvain* 6.

Maurer, A. (2002) *National Parliaments in the European Architecture: Elements for Establishing a Best Practice Mechanism* (European Convention Working Group IV working document no. 8).

Maurer, A. and Wessels, W. (eds) (2001) *National Parliaments on their Ways to Europe: Losers or Latecomers?* (Nomos, Baden-Baden).

Michel, L. and Chevalier, p. (2002) *The role of national parliaments in the European Union* (CONV 308/02, Contribution 103).

Millar, D. (1979) 'Treatment of European Community matters by committees of the national parliaments', in Herman, V. and Van Schendelen, R. (eds) *The European Parliament and the National Parliaments* (Saxon House, Farnborough).

Millar, D. (1995) *The EU and the 1996 IGC, Crisis or Opportunity? Constitutional Issues: The European parliament and the national parliaments* (Centre for European Studies, University of Hull).

Miller, V. and Ware, R. (1996) 'Keeping National Parliaments Informed: The Problem of European Legislation', *The Journal of Legislative Studies* 2, p. 184-197.

Moersch, W. (2001) *Leistungsfähigkeit und Grenzen des Subsidiaritätsprinzips* (Duncker & Humblot, Berlin).

Munneke, S. (2003) 'Controle door de Staten-Generaal op de Europese besluitvorming', in Elzinga, D.J. and Verhey, L.F.M. (eds) *De Nederlandse Grondwet en de Europese Unie* (Kluwer, Deventer).

Munro, C.R. (1996) 'The UK Parliament and EU Institutions – Partners or Rivals?', in Smith, E. (ed.) *National Parliaments as Cornerstones of European Integration* (Kluwer Law International, London/The Hague/Boston).

Neunreither, K. (1994) 'The Democratic Deficit of the European Union: Towards Closer Cooperation between the European Parliament and the National Parliaments', *Government and Opposition* 29, p. 299-314.

Niblock, M. (1971) *The EEC: National Parliaments in Community Decision-Making* (Chatham House, London).

Nicolaïdis, K. (2003) *The New Constitution as European Demoi-cracy?* (Federal Trust online paper 38/03). www.fedtrust.co.uk

Norton, Ph. (1995a) 'National Parliaments and the European Community: How to Strengthen Parliaments?', *Comparative Law Review* 5, p. 5-18.

Norton, Ph. (ed.) (1995b) *National Parliaments and the European Union* (*The Journal of Legislative Studies* 1, special issue 3).

Norton, Ph. (1995c) 'The United Kingdom: Political Conflict, Parliamentary Scrutiny', in Norton, Ph. (ed.) *National Parliaments and the European Union* (*The Journal of Legislative Studies* 1, special issue 3).

Norton, Ph. (ed.) (1998) *Parliaments and Governments in Western Europe* (Frank Cass, London/Portland, Oregon).

Norton, Ph. (ed.) (2002) *Parliaments and Citizens in Western Europe* (Frank Cass, London/Portland, Oregon).

Nuttens, J.-D. (2001) *Le parlement français et l'Europe: L'article 88-4 de la Constitution* (Librairie générale de droit et de jurisprudence, Paris).

Office of the Hungarian National Assembly (2004) 'How Does the Hungarian Parliament Deal with EU Affairs?', *Forum Parliament* 2, p. 6-11.

O'Halpin, E. (1995) 'Irish Parliamentary Culture and the European Union: Formalities to be Observed', in Norton, Ph. (ed.) *National Parliaments and the European Union* (*The Journal of Legislative Studies* 1, special issue 3).

Olson, D. and Norton, Ph. (eds) (1996) *The New Parliaments of Central and Eastern Europe* (Frank Cass, London/Portland, Oregon).

Pahre, R. (1997) 'Endogenous Domestic Institutions in Two-Level Games and Parliamentary Oversight of the European Union', *Journal of Conflict Resolution* 41, p. 147-174.

Pappas, S.A. (ed.) (1995) *National Administrative Procedures for the Preparation and Implementation of Community Decisions* (European Institute of Public Administration, Maastricht).

Pera, M. (2002) *Parliaments and European Construction* (Report of the President of the Senate of the Italian Republic to the Conference of Speakers of the European Union Parliaments and the European Parliament, 7-8 June 2002, Madrid).

Peters, A. (2004) *Citizens' Voices via Referendum?* (34th Asser Colloquium contribution, 13-16 October 2004, The Hague).

Peters, J. (2005) 'National Parliaments and Subsidiarity: Think Twice', *European Constitutional Law Review* 1, p. 68-72.

Pinder, J. (ed.) (1999) *Foundations of Democracy in the European Union – From the Genesis of Parliamentary Democracy to the European Parliament* (Palgrave, Basingstoke/ New York).

Ramstedt, S. (2000) 'Comments on the report by Mr Tapio Raunio "Parliamentary Scrutiny of EU Decision-Making: Comparing National Systems"', in Finnish Eduskunta (ed.) *National Parliaments and the EU – Stock-Taking for the Post-Amsterdam Era* (October 1999 COSAC seminar, Eduskunnan Kanslian Julkaisu 1/2000).

Raunio, T. (1999) 'Always One Step Behind? National Legislatures and the European Union', *Government and Opposition* 34, p. 180-202.

Raunio, T. (2000) 'Parliamentary Scrutiny of EU Decision-Making: Comparing National Systems', in Finnish Eduskunta (ed.) *National Parliaments and the EU – Stock-Taking for the Post-Amsterdam Era* (October 1999 COSAC seminar, Eduskunnan Kanslian Julkaisu 1/2000).

Raunio, T. (2001) 'The Parliament of Finland: A Model Case for Effective Scrutiny?', in Maurer, A. and Wessels, W. (eds) *National Parliaments on their Ways to Europe: Losers or Latecomers?* (Nomos, Baden-Baden).

Raunio, T. (2004) *Two Steps Forward, One Step Behind? National Legislatures in the EU Constitution* (paper, The Federal Trust for Education and Research, London).

Raunio, T. and Hix, S. (2000) 'Backbenchers Learn to Fight Back: European Integration and Parliamentary Government', *West European Politics* 23, p. 142-168.

Raunio, T. and Wiberg, M. (2000) 'Does Support Lead to Ignorance? National Parliaments and the Legitimacy of EU Governance', *Acta Politica* 35. p. 146-168.

Raunio, T. and Wiberg, M. (2001) 'Parliamentarizing Foreign Policy Decision-Making: Finland in the European Union', *Cooperation and Conflict* 36, p. 61-86.

Reich, N. (1999) *Bürgerrechte in der Europäischen Union: Subjektive Rechte von Unionsbürgern und Drittstaatsangehörigen unter besonderer Berücksichtigung der Rechtslage nach der Rechtsprechung des EuGH und dem Vertrag von Amsterdam* (Nomos, Baden-Baden).

Rizutto, F. (1995) 'The French Parliament and the EU: Loosening the Constitutional Straitjacket', in Norton, Ph. (ed.): *National Parliaments and the European Union* (*The Journal of Legislative Studies* 1, special issue 3).

Rizzuto, F. (2003) *The new role of national parliaments in the EU: No longer victims of integration?* (paper, The Federal Trust for Education and Research, London).

Rogers, R. (1995) 'Parliamentary Scrutiny of European Union Affairs: The Case of the United Kingdom House of Commons', in Laursen, F. and Pappas, S.A. (eds) *The Changing Role of Parliaments in the European Union* (European Institute of Public Administration, Maastricht).

Rometsch, D. and Wessels, W. (eds) (1996) *The European Union and member states: towards institutional fusion?* (Manchester University Press, Manchester).

Ronge, F. (1998) *Legitimität durch Subsidiarität* (Nomos, Baden-Baden).

Saalfeld, Th. (1995) 'The German Houses of Parliament and European Integration', in Norton, Ph. (ed.): *National Parliaments and the European Union* (*The Journal of Legislative Studies* 1, special issue 3).

Sasse, Chr. (1975) *Regierungen, Parlamente, Ministerrat – Entscheidungsprozesse in der Europäischen Gemeinschaft* (Europa Union Verlag, Bonn).

Sasse, Chr. (1980) 'The Control of the National Parliaments of the Nine over European Affairs', in Cassese, A. (ed.): *Parliamentary Control over Foreign Policy* (Sijthoff & Noordhoff, Alphen).

Sauron, J.-L. (1999) 'Le controle parlementaire de l'activité gouvernementale en matière communautaire en France', *Revue trimestrielle de droit européen* 35, p. 171-200.

Schoo, J. (2004) 'Das institutionelle System aus der Sicht des Europäischen Parlaments', in Schwarze, J. (ed.): *Der Verfassungsentwurf des Europäischen Konvents* (Nomos, Baden-Baden).

Shephard, M. and Scully, R. (2002) 'The European Parliament: Of Barriers and Removed Citizens', in Norton, Ph. (ed.): *Parliaments and Citizens in Western Europe* (Frank Cass, London/Portland, Oregon).

Sie Dhian Ho, M. (2004) 'Democratisering van de EU: permanente evenwichtskunst', in Scheltema, M. (ed.) *De staat van de democratie. Democratie voorbij de staat* (AUP, Amsterdam).

Smismans, S. (1998) 'The Role of the National Parliaments in the European Decision-Making Process: Addressing the Problem at the European Level?', *ELSA Selected Papers on European Law* 9, p. 49-76.

Smith, E. (ed.) (1996) *National Parliaments as Cornerstones of European Integration* (Kluwer Law International, London/The Hague/Boston).

Straub, P. and Hrbek, R. (eds) (1998) *Die europapolitische Rolle der Landes- und Regionalparlamente in der EU* (Nomos, Baden-Baden).

Swedish Riksdag (2001) *National Parliaments and the European Union* (COSAC Discussion Document, May 2001, Stockholm).

Swedish Riksdag (2002) *The Committee on European Union Affairs*.

Swenden, W. (2004) 'Is the European Union in Need of a Competence Catalogue? Insights from Comparative Federalism', *Journal of Common Market Studies* 42, p. 371-392.

Szukala, A. and Rozenberg, O. (2001) 'The French Parliament and the EU: Progressive Assertion and Strategic Investment', in Maurer, A. and Wessels, W. (eds)

National Parliaments on their Ways to Europe: Losers or Latecomers? (Nomos, Baden-Baden).

Thaa, W. (2002) *Legitimacy in a Context of Internationalized Decision-Making Through International Organizations* (conference paper, Democracy and Legitimacy of the European Union and other International Organizations, EP 11-12 October 2002).

Thomassen, J. and Schmitt, H. (1999) 'Partisan Structures in the European Parliament', in Katz, R.S. and Wessels, B. (eds) *The European Parliament, the National Parliaments, and European Integration* (OUP, Oxford).

Travers, D., H. Coppolecchia and A. Tomlins (2003) *European Affairs Committees – The Influence of National Parliaments on European Policies: An Overview* (European Centre for Parliamentary Research and Documentation, Brussels).

Urbantschitsch, W. (1998) *National Parliaments in the European Union – The Austrian Experience* (Forschungsinstitut für Europarecht, Karl-Franzens-Universität, Graz).

UK House of Commons (2001) *The European Scrutiny System in the House of Commons – A short guide for Members of Parliament by the staff of the European Scrutiny Committee.*

Van der Linden, R. and Van Eekelen, W. (2002) *The role of national parliaments: an example of a good practice* (CONV 182/02, Contribution 62).

Van der Pot, C.W. (1989) *Handboek van het Nederlandse Staatsrecht* (Tjeenk Willink, Zwolle).

Van Schendelen, M.P.C.M. (1995) 'The Netherlands: From Founding Father to Mounding Baby', in Norton, Ph. (ed.): *National Parliaments and the European Union* (*The Journal of Legislative Studies* 1, special issue 3).

Vandevivere, C. (2001) 'The Federal Parliament of Belgium: Between Wishes, Rules and Practice', in Maurer, A. and Wessels, W. (eds) *National Parliaments on their Ways to Europe: Losers or Latecomers?* (Nomos, Baden-Baden).

Vehar, p. (2004) The National Assembly of the Republic of Slovenia and EU Affairs After Accession, *Forum Parlament* 2(1): 16-20.

Verdier, M.-F. (1995) 'La Participation des Parlements Nationaux au Processus de Décision Communautaire', in Roussillon, Henry (ed.) *L'Article 88-4 de la Constitution Française – Le Rôle du Parlement dans l'Élaboration de la Norme Européenne* (Presses de l'Université des Sciences Sociales de Toulouse, Toulouse).

Vergés Bausili, A. (2002) *Rethinking the Methods of Dividing and Exercising Powers in the EU: Reforming Subsidiarity and National Parliaments* (Jean Monnet Working Paper 9/02, NYU School of Law).

Verhoeven, A. (2002) *The European Union in Search of a Democratic and Constitutional Theory* (Kluwer Law International, The Hague).

Van Dijk, p. and Van Hoof, G.J.H. (1998) *Theory and Practice of the European Convention on Human Rights* (Kluwer Law International, The Hague).

Von der Vring, Th. (1996) 'On legitimation of the European Union – National Parliaments and the European Parliament', in Winter, G. (ed.): *Sources and*

Categories of European Union Law – A Comparative and Reform Perspective (Nomos, Baden-Baden).
Walker, N. (2003a) *After the Constitutional Moment* (Federal Trust Online Paper 32/03). www.fedtrust.co.uk
Walker, N. (2003b) 'Postnational constitutionalism and the problem of translation', in Weiler, J.H.H. and Wind, M. (eds) *European Constitutionalism Beyond the State* (CUP, Cambridge).
Weatherill, S. (2003a) 'Competence', in De Witte, B. (ed.) *Ten Reflections on the Constituutional Treaty of Europe* (EUI/Robert Schuman Centre for Advanced Studies, Florence).
Weatherill, S. (2003b) 'Using national parliaments to improve scrutiny of the limits of EU action', *European Law Review* 28, p. 909-912.
Weber-Panariello, Ph. (1995) *Nationale Parlamente in der Europäischen Union* (Nomos, Baden-Baden).
Weiler, J.H.H. (2003) 'In Defence of the status quo: Europe's constitutional Sonderweg', in Weiler, J.H.H. and Wind, M. (eds) *European Constitutionalism Beyond the State* (CUP, Cambridge).
Weiler, J.H.H. and Wind, M. (2003) (eds) *European Constitutionalism Beyond the State* (CUP, Cambridge).
Wessels, B. (1999) 'Decision-Making and Institutional Change', in Katz, R.S. and Wessels, B. (eds) *The European Parliament, the National Parliaments, and European Integration* (OUP, Oxford).
White, S. (2004) *European Constitution: what is new in the area of judicial co-operation in criminal matters and police co-operation* (Federal Trust online paper 07/04). www.fedtrust.co.uk
Zervakis, P. and Yannis, N. (2001) 'The Parliament of Greece: Slow but Constant Moves Towards European Integration?', in Maurer, A. and Wessels, W. (eds) *National Parliaments on their Ways to Europe: Losers or Latecomers?* (Nomos, Baden-Baden).
Zweifel, Th.D. (2002) *Democratic Deficit?: Institutions and Regulation in the European Union, Switzerland, and the United States* (Lexington, Lanham).

Index

EUROPEAN MONOGRAPHS

1. Lammy Betten (ed.), *The Future of European Social Policy* (second and revised edition, 1991).
2. J.M.E. Loman, K.J.M. Mortelmans, H.H.G. Post, J.S. Watson, *Culture and Community Law: Before and after Maastricht* (1992).
3. Prof. Dr. J.A.E. Vervaele, *Fraud Against the Community: The Need for European Fraud Legislation* (1992).
4. P. Rawortli, *The Legislative Process in the European Community* (1993).
5. J. Stuyck, *Financial and Monetary Integration in the European Economic Community* (1993).
6. J.H.V. Stuyck, A.J. Vossestein (eds.), *State Entrepreneurship, National Monopolies and European Community Law* (1993).
7. J. Stuyck, A. Looijestijn-Clearie (eds.), *The European Area EC-EFTA* (1994).
8. R.B. Bouterse, *Competition and Integration – What Goals Count?* (1994).
9. R. Barents, *The Agricultural Law of the EC* (1994).
10. Nicholas Emiliou, *The Principle of Proportionality in European Law: A Comparative Study* (1996).
11. Eivind Smith, *National Parliaments as Cornerstones of European Integration* (1996).
12. Jan H. Jans, *European Environmental Law* (1996).
13. Siofra O'Leary, *The Evolving Concept of Community Citizenship: From the Free Movement of Persons to Union Citizenship* (1996).
14. Laurence Gormley (ed.), *Current and Future Perspectives on EC Competition Law* (1997).
15. Simone White, *Protection of the Financial Interests of the European Communities: The Fight against Fraud and Corruption* (1998).
16. Morten P. Broberg, *The European Commission's Jurisdiction to Scrutinise Mergers*, Second Edition (2003).
17. Doris Hildebrand, *The Role of Economic Analysis in the EC Competition Rules: The European School*, Second Edition (2002).
18. Christof R.A. Swaak, *European Community Law and the Automobile Industry* (1999).
19. Dorthe Dahlgaard Dingel, *Public Procurement. A Harmonization of the National Judicial Review of the Application of European Community Law* (1999).
20. J.A.E. Vervaele (ed.), *Compliance and Enforcement of European Community Law* (1999).
21. Martin Trybus, *European Defence Procurement Law: International and National Procurement Systems as Models for a Liberalised Defence Procurement Market in Europe* (1999).

KLUWER LAW INTERNATIONAL – THE HAGUE/LONDON

EUROPEAN MONOGRAPHS

22. Helen Staples, *The Legal Status of Third Country Nationals Resident in the European Union* (1999).
23. Damien Geradin (ed.), *The Liberalization of State Monopolies in the European Union and Beyond* (2000).
24. Katja Heede, *European Ombudsman: Redress and Control at Union Level* (2000).
25. Ulf Bernitz, Joakim Nergelius (eds.), *General Principles of European Community Law* (2000).
26. Michaela Drahos, *Convergence of Competition Laws and Policies in the European Community* (2001).
27. Damien Geradin (ed.), *The Liberalization of Electricity and Natural Gas in the European Union* (2001).
28. Gisella Gori, *Towards an EU Right to Education* (2001).
29. Brendan Smith, *Constitution Building in the European Union* (2001).
30. Freidl Weiss and Frank Wooldridge, *Free Movement of Persons within the European Community* (2002).
31. Ingrid Boccardi, *Europe and Refugees: Towards an EU Asylum Policy* (2002)
32. John A.E. Vervaele, André Klip (eds.), *European Cooperation Between Tax, Customs and Judicial Authorities* (2001).
33. Wouter P.J. Wils, *The Optimal Enforcement of EC Antitrust Law: Essays in Law and Economics* (2002).
34. Damien Geradin (ed.), *The Liberalization of Postal Services in the European Union* (2002).
35. Nick Bernard, *Multilevel Governance in the European Union* (2002).
36. Jill Wakefield, *Judicial Protection through the Use of Article 288(2)EC* (2002).
37. Sebastiaan Princen, *EU Regulation and Transatlantic Trade* (2002).
38. Amaryllis Verhoeven, *The European Union in Search of a Democratic and Constitutional Theory* (2002).
39. Paul Torremans, *Cross Border Insolvencies in EU English and Belgian Law* (2002).
40. Malcolm Anderson, Joanna Apap (eds.), *Police and Justice Co-operation and the New European Borders* (2002).
41. Christine M. Forstinger, *Takeover Law in the EU and the USA: A Comparative Analysis* (2002).
42. Antonio Bavasso, *Communications in EU Antitrust Law: Market Power and Public Interest* (2003).
43. Fiona Wishlade, *Regional State Aid and Competition Policy* (2003).
44. Gareth Davies, *Nationality Discrimination in the European Internal Market* (2003).

KLUWER LAW INTERNATIONAL – THE HAGUE/LONDON

EUROPEAN MONOGRAPHS

45. René Barents, *The Autonomy of Community Law* (2004).
46. Gerhard Dannecker, Oswald Jansen (eds.), *Competition Law Sanctioning in the European Union. The EU-Law Influence on the National System of Sanctions in the European Area* (2004).
47. NautaDutilh (ed.), *Dealing with Dominance. The Experience of National Competition Authorities* (2004).
48. Stefaan Van den Bogaert, *Practical Regulation of the Mobility of Sportsmen in the EU Post Bosman* (2005).
49. Katalin Judit Cseres, *Competition Law and Consumer Protection* (2005).
50. Philipp Kiiver, *The National Parliaments in the European Union: A Critical View on EU Constitution-Building* (2006).

KLUWER LAW INTERNATIONAL – THE HAGUE/LONDON